The
Spirit
and the
Bride

The Spirit and the Bride

Meditations on the Work of the Holy Spirit

BY CLARENCE STAM

PREMIER PUBLISHING
WINNIPEG

Stam, Clarence, 1948-
   The Spirit and the bride: meditations on the work of the Holy Spirit /
by Clarence Stam

Includes bibliographical references and index.
ISBN 0-88756-083-0

   1. Holy Spirit – Meditations. I. Title

BT122.S68 2004   231'.3   C2004-901405-6

1st Printing — 2004
2nd Printing — 2005

PREMIER PUBLISHING
One Beghin Avenue, Winnipeg, Manitoba, Canada R2J 3X5

Table of Contents

The
Spirit
and the
Bride

For my bride.

To our grandchildren:

Jordan, Austin, Logan, and Liana.

Preface

Over the past thirty years of service in the ministry of the Gospel, I have gathered and compiled many notes about the work the Holy Spirit. My intention always was to prepare these notes for publication in book form.

During the last five years I developed medical problems causing lack of mobility. In 2003 I was given a partial medical leave of absence so that the cause of this malady could be found and treated. This leave of absence took place from July-December 2003.

Unfortunately I was diagnosed in May 2003 as having progressive MS. The medical leave now focused on what could be done in this respect. I started a process of injections.

In the meantime, I could still conduct one service on Sunday mornings, give some catechism classes, and attend some (important) meetings. Also I was to prepare various manuscripts for publication. One of these is, then, the work on the Holy Spirit.

A word of thanks is again due to the council and congregation of the Hamilton Cornerstone Canadian Reformed Church for their kindness and support in times of health and sickness. Without their cooperation and patience, this would never have been published.

In the course of 2004 it will be decided whether I can continue with a full-time workload or whether some other arrangement must be sought. I hope that by that time, this book will be published.

The purpose of this book is simple: to show the great riches that we have in Christ. The Holy Spirit completes and perfects the counsel of the Triune God by bringing to perfection and glory the work of the only true Savior, our Lord Jesus Christ.

Writing this book in a time when sickness became apparent was rather challenging. Yet it also provided an opportunity to look away from one's own condition to the larger scheme of things, the promises we have in Christ.

At the publication of this book, I am again indebted to many people who have supported the project. Most of all I wish to thank my bride and wife for her constant support through the years and now in a time when I am faced with disability. I am deeply sorry for all the hurt she bears, and stand amazed at her strength and faith. The Spirit has always been with my bride.

Hamilton, 2004
Clarence Stam

Introduction

...no one can say, 'Jesus is Lord,' except by the Holy Spirit.

(I CORINTHIANS 12:3)

One might wonder whether another book on the Person and work of the Holy Spirit is necessary. Many scholarly volumes have already been written on this topic. This book, however, is not a systematic treatise on the doctrine of the Holy Spirit, but it focuses primarily on key Scripture passages from Old and New Testament that speak to us about the Holy Spirit.

It is always necessary to go back to the source, to the Scriptures. This is especially important when in our post-modern world we see the emphasis coming to fall again on human experience and feelings. It is said that the rationalistic orthodoxy of the past centuries has stifled human emotion and that a correction is required to restore proper Biblical balance. We hear that the emphasis must now come to lie on the fact that we must be spiritual people, guided, governed, and filled with the Holy Spirit. While this may in itself be true, we must be careful not to fall into an extreme reaction.

Many see the new millennium as the age of the Holy Spirit in which the final events of history are about to take place. We are certainly drawing ever closer to the glorious return of our Lord Jesus Christ, but we do not know the date itself. While many signs will point to the end of days, the coming of the Lord will be unexpected like that of a thief by night (Matthew 24:36-51). A sign is not a date.

When we speak about the person and work of the Holy Spirit, we must keep in mind that we speak about one of the persons of the Holy Trinity. The Holy Spirit may never be separated from the Father and the Son, although the three persons are distinct. This truth will emerge constantly throughout this book. Similarly, we must remember that the Holy Spirit has worked from the beginning with the Father and the Son, and that his work in the last ages is in complete harmony with what he has always done from the beginning of time. He perfects and completes the counsel of God.

The Holy Spirit did not on Pentecost, when he was poured out, begin something new. He came to finish the work he started many centuries before together with the Father and the Son. His outpouring meant an intensification of his work in harmony with the work of the Father and the Son. The Father sent the Son, and the Spirit proceeds from the Father and the Son to complete the gathering and perfection of the holy, catholic church.

Meanwhile we have progressed in the ages after Pentecost. Pentecost does mean a great step forward[1]. Therefore it is good now to consider how the relationship between the LORD and his people has intensified through this outpouring. We will discuss important passages of Scripture that cast further light on this relationship.

One matter must be emphasized from the very start. The involvement of the Holy Spirit is required for salvation. The Apostle Paul makes this quite clear when he writes to the Corinthians, "...no one can say 'Jesus is Lord', except by the Holy Spirit" (1 Cor 12:3).

The statement "Jesus is Lord" is probably the first form of a Christian profession of faith. The Greek version has the word Kurios, translated by Lord, and the Septuagint (the official Greek translation of the Old Testament) uses the same word for Yahweh, the LORD. To profess Jesus as Lord means to receive him as the God of salvation. This cannot be done by human impulse; it can only happen by the Holy Spirit. This profession of faith must be worked in us by God the Spirit through the Word. Paul wrote the same to the Romans, "...faith comes from hearing the message, and the message is heard through the Word of Christ." (Rom 10:17).

Paul wrote to the Corinthians about the key work of the Holy Spirit because in the church at Corinth there were various factions, each claiming the greatest gifts of the Holy Spirit and disqualifying others who did not have these gifts (1 Cor 12:31). But Paul makes clear that no one can truly profess the Lord Jesus except by the Holy Spirit. The same Spirit gives gifts to individual members as he sees fit for the benefit of the whole body. The gifts may vary, but the source of faith lies in the one Spirit.

We need to receive the Holy Spirit because only by his personal involvement in our lives can we become spiritual people, professing Christians directed towards Jesus Christ and the service of God. Without the Holy Spirit we cannot function as Christians. Instead of claiming among each other the gifts of the Holy Spirit, the Corinthians ought to focus on the one Giver, the Spirit himself. No one who truly confesses Christ and shows this in his life, ought to be disqualified for not having certain spiritual gifts

---

[1] I have written about this in an earlier publication, *Celebrating Salvation* (Premier Publishing, Winnipeg, 1998.

The Bride of Christ, the holy catholic church, is a work of the Holy Spirit to the glory of God the Father. The Spirit seeks the Bride; the Bride cannot be without the Spirit. The Holy Spirit binds the Bride to the Bridegroom, the Lord Jesus Christ.

Glory be to God the Father
Glory be to God the Son,
Glory be to God the Spirit,
God Almighty, Three in One!

(*Book of Praise*, Hymn 5:1)

The Holy Spirit and Creation

...and the Spirit of God was hovering over the waters.

(GENESIS 1:2)

Every year on the day of Pentecost we remember the outpouring of the Holy Spirit and speak about his work of sanctification and renewal. This is good and necessary. We must be careful, however, not to restrict our focus to the inward work of the Spirit in our hearts. There are those who say that we must become spiritual people, who live as sojourners on this earth, and look only for the new heaven and the new earth. The created earth is of little meaning, except maybe as a collector lane for the elect.

This line of thinking contains important truths. The Bible indeed warns us against world-conformity. We are called to live as aliens and exiles (cf. 1 Pet 2:11) and to look for an enduring city (Heb 13:14). Although in the world, we not part of it. Rather than setting our mind on earthly things our attention is to be directed to the glory that is to come. Our citizenship is in heaven, from where we eagerly await a Savior, the Lord Jesus Christ (cf. Phil 3:20).

All this does not mean, however, that we are to ignore the world or deny the gifts that God gave us in creation. The Bible makes clear that God himself cares for the world he made. It also tells us that the Spirit guides us in the use of created things. Sin does not lie in things but lives in persons. The Lord Jesus warned the Pharisees to use proper discretion: "...out of the heart come evil thoughts, murder, adultery, sexual immorality, theft, false testimony, slander." (Mat 15:19).

Creation, then, is the work of God, and we may not take a negative attitude toward it. For it, too, is the domain of the Holy Spirit. Creation is the domain of the Holy Spirit himself. It always has been his realm and will continue to be so. The Holy Spirit does not manifest himself first at Pentecost, or at the end of time, in the latter days. He reveals himself already at the beginning of time, precisely in connection with the creation of this world, where he works and we may live.

To begin our study of the person and work of the Holy Spirit, we will take a close look at the very first passage in Scripture where the Spirit is mentioned. We read in Genesis 1:2 that "the Spirit of God was hovering over the waters." In what follows we will note that his glory is revealed already in the divine work of creation; that this work is deeply pastoral and that it is also powerful and promising, setting the tone for all the work that the Spirit will do in the development and history of this world.

In the beginning: the Holy Trinity

In the first verses of the Bible we meet God, Genesis 1:1, "In the beginning God created the heavens and the earth." From this passage we draw some important conclusions. God, who lives from eternity to eternity, is the supreme, intelligent Being who has called all things into existence. The Bible does not explain God's existence, but simply states that he lives and acts, revealing himself first of all in his work of creation.

Later (in John 1) we learn that everything was created through the Word who is the only-begotten Son of God. The expression, "God said", which later in Genesis 1:26 is shown to be a plural ("Let us...") may be understood as the Father creating through the Son.[2] God the Father and God the Son were both actively involved in the mighty work of creation.

In Genesis 1, we read about the Spirit of God being present as well. One might say, then, that in the first two verses of Scripture we already have

---

[2] Article 8 of *The Belgic Confession* speaks of the Son being the Word, the wisdom and the image of the Father, the Word capitalized. The expression "God said" may be taken then to refer to the creating through the Word, the Logos. H. Bavink writes, "Even though creation is a work of the whole Trinity, it can not be denied that in the Bible it has a special relation with the Son...." "The Old Testament says in many places that God created all things through the word. Word and wisdom are presented personally as counselor and master of creation." Therefore we read in the New Testament "not only that God has created all things through the Son, but Christ is also called the first-born of all creation, the beginning (source) of the creation of God..." (Colossians 1: 15-17). See H. Bavinck, *Gereformeerde Dogmatiek* 2, Kok, Kampen, 1967, page 386 ff.)

the contours of the doctrine of the Holy Trinity: Father, Son, and Spirit, co-operating in the same work, the work of creation.

The question is: what exactly was the Spirit doing at this point? It appears that the earth, though created, was still "formless and empty" (Gen 1:2). It was a great, undefined mass of water, which did not sustain any life. It was cloaked in darkness that lay as a thick blanket over the waters of the deep.

Storm or Spirit?

What is the Spirit doing with these dark, inhospitable, even fearsome waters of the measureless depth? There are explainers who suggest that no reference is made here to the Holy Spirit. They translate the words, "the Spirit of God" differently. The word for Spirit is the same word as that used for breath or wind. Remember how the Lord Jesus uses a play on words in his conversation with Nicodemus about the Holy Spirit, recorded in John 3:8: the wind blows where it wills... so also with the Holy Spirit you cannot tell where he comes from or where he is going.

What about the additional words "of God"? These explainers suggest that the word God was in ancient times added to something when it was very great and powerful, almost divine. Then it would read as follows: a god-like wind, that is, a mighty storm was (not hovering but) beating upon (or against) the waters. The passage then does not refer to the Holy Spirit, but to a great force being exerted on the waters to bring them under control. As supporting evidence, pagan myths about the origin of this world which speak about a wild chaos, are quoted. There was a heavy battle of God against nature, according to these legends, a battle in which God ultimately prevailed. The so-called Gnostics in the early Christian church still spoke in these terms.

But all this is nonsense. When elsewhere in the Bible the same expression, Spirit of God, is used, and it always denotes the Holy Spirit. Why should it have a different sense in this passage? The context neither requires it nor allows it.

Hovering?

We must also seek to ascertain what it means that the Spirit of God was hovering over the waters. The word suggests the hovering of a bird, as it floats in the sky on the currents of air, turning gracefully, going up and down over the same spot. The idea is that the Spirit of God in his hovering keeps a watchful eye on the surging waters. The Spirit is watching intensely over the creation of God.

The same verb is used in Deuteronomy 32:11, "...like an eagle that stirs up its nest and hovers over its young, that spreads his wings to catch them, and carries them on his pinions." We find these words in Hymn 8 (*Book of Praise*), *Lo, as an eagle, hov'ring o'er its young....* This hovering of the Holy Spirit over the waters means that the Holy Spirit is not just governing creation, but also caring for it with tender love.

Pastoral work

For that reason I wrote that the work of the Holy Spirit is *pastoral*. He cares about this world, about all who live in it, and he has done so from the very moment it came into being. The word hovering indicates a constant influencing, searching, and correcting of any situation, wherever this might be needed.

Was this work of the Holy Spirit necessary? Was there any remote possibility that the waters would go beyond their boundaries and break free? I do not believe this to be the case. This is not a passage about the waters, it is a statement about the Spirit. It tells us something very important about the person and the work of the Holy Spirit, something that became abundantly clear later on Pentecost, but that finds its root in the personality of the Holy Spirit. He is deeply involved in this creation because it is God's world, and he exercises over it his pastoral care, in order that all things go as they should, that everything will function properly, and that nothing is left to itself. All creation is under the power of God through the Holy Spirit.

Through the Spirit, God manifests his pastoral care over the world that he has created and is still shaping and forming according to his pleasure and plan. Why through the Spirit? The Father and the Son also show this care. But the Spirit is the One who searches and examines all things, and leads them where God wants them to be. All the world is from the beginning the domain of the Holy Spirit.

The Holy Spirit and the covenant of love

We know from Scripture that God entered into a special relationship with Adam and Eve, a covenant of love,[3] and that the entire creation benefited from this love. With this knowledge, we can the more easily understand

---

[3] See my publication, *The Covenant of Love*, Premier Publishing, Winnipeg 1999.

Psalm 104:30, where we read how the LORD by the Spirit creates and renews the face of the earth. This, too, is pastoral care from above. We understand what it means in Psalm 139 that David asks God to search him, to know his heart and thoughts. This is a psalm that sings of the pastoral care of God by the Holy Spirit: (verse 7) "Where can I go from your Spirit? Where can I flee from your presence?" If this care is true for God's creation, how much more will it be true for God's children. We are assured as Christians about spiritual, pastoral care from above, wherever we go. In subsequent sections we will pay more attention to these important passages.

There are, as we have always recognized, various dispensations in the covenant (see chapter XV in this book). The Bible makes clear that as time progresses, God gives or dispenses his grace in different, that is, in more beautiful and richer ways. But the Holy Spirit was always present and active in caring for God's creation. At this point, nothing yet exists, except the heavens above and the waters below, shrouded in darkness. But the Spirit is hovering, moving, watching, and caring. This is his character. In this way he leads all things to God.

When it then comes to the new covenant, to the time when God will dwell in Jesus Christ with his people, and when the Gospel will go out into the world, the Holy Spirit is the One who is poured out over the disciples, over the church. To whom better to entrust this mighty pastoral work among the nations, calling God's children, watching over them, and leading them home to the Father's house, like an eagle hov'ring o'er its young, than to the Holy Spirit? Who shall be sent for the great re-creation, the making of a new humanity, other than the Holy Spirit proceeding from the Father and the Son?

It is true that the event at Pentecost, the outpouring of the Holy Spirit, is new, for the Holy Spirit has not lived in this way in the church before. But the fact that the Holy Spirit is poured out, made abundantly available, and presents himself for the work of recreation should not surprise us. For the world that God made was never without the Holy Spirit, and he worked in it from the first day, governing, shaping, guiding, and leading. When man fell into sin the Holy Spirit intensified his efforts so that the Son of man would be revealed, the King of glory!

A perfect pastor

The Holy Spirit is a true and perfect pastor. That is why he is called by the Lord Jesus our Counselor or Comforter (cf. John 14:24; 15:26; 16:7; see also chapter VII of this book). The Holy Spirit does not receive

from Christ a new name or task, for he always was a counselor and comforter to God's people. This pastoral work may intensify, but it is not a new
characteristic or strange dimension. The eternal Spirit has always done the
pastoral work required among and in the people of God.

The word pastoral is very important here. We speak of the love of
God and the grace of the Lord Jesus. But there is also the fellowship of the
Holy Spirit. What is more pastoral than fellowship? He is always beside you,
all around you, even within you, and has laid his hand upon you. He has
observed you from your conception on. David expresses in Psalm 139 in
moving words what this fellowship means.

In the Heidelberg Catechism, Lord's Day 20, we may therefore profess
this wonderful work as follows: [the Holy Spirit] "is also given me to make
me by true faith share in Christ and all his benefits, to comfort me, and remain with me forever." The fellowship never ends. The bond has now become through Christ's sacrifice even closer: he dwells *in us* making us par-
takers of what we have in Christ.

Powerful

This same passage in Genesis 1 reveals that the work of the Holy
Spirit is powerful. This hovering of the Holy Spirit is not some detached
floating over the waters. It means exercising powerful control. We might
say that these waters would have been under God's control, even if the
Spirit had not hovered over them. That may be true, but it is irrelevant. We
are to know that the Spirit of God did hover over the face of the deep, as
he will later watch over the face of all the earth. We learn that the Holy Spirit is exercising the power of the God over all of creation from its earliest beginnings to its very end. He is mentioned in the first verses of the Bible as
well as in the last (Genesis 1:2; Revelation 22:17).

The Old Testament also teaches that the Holy Spirit is powerful and
sovereign over all flesh, over the entire world. Moses and Aaron call upon
God as the "God of the spirits of all mankind" (Numbers 16:22). No spirit
stands above God's Spirit. His dominion was never restricted to Israel,
even if he for a time limited his saving work to Israel. There was always
with the Holy Spirit an open eye to the whole world, and God's house would
be called a house of prayer for *all* nations! Who could ever bring this about
except the Spirit of God? As Nehemiah confesses, the Spirit of the LORD
was given especially to Israel to instruct them (9:20), but that same Spirit
controlled world powers, moved kings and princes to act favorably towards
God's people (cf. Daniel 2:36-45).

18

This Spirit was powerfully involved in creation. Consider Isaiah 40:12ff., "...who has measured the waters in the hollow of his hand or with the breadth of his hand marked off the heavens...?" God took all the waters of the great deep, and put them in the hollow of his hand, casting them up (sky) and down (seas). What a powerful work. Imagine all the water of the sea in your palm. Then we find in verse 13: "...who has understood the Spirit of the LORD or instructed him as his counselor"? The NIV translates with the "mind" of the LORD, but the original has here indeed the *Spirit* of the LORD.

Did anyone tell God what to do? Did anyone give advice at creation to the Holy Spirit as he hovered over the waters? Consider his powerful work. Isaiah 40:15: "...surely the nations are like a drop in a bucket." See also the verses 21 and 22, "Do you not know? Have you not heard? Has it not been told you from the beginning?" (Genesis 1) "Have you not understood since the earth was founded? He sits enthroned above the circle of the earth, and its people are like grasshoppers. He stretches out the heavens like a canopy, and spreads them out like a tent to live in." As great as creation, so powerful and more is the Spirit of God. It is important to note that Isaiah speaks in the same breath about God and the Holy Spirit.

In Isaiah 40 the work of creation is mentioned. The context of all this in Isaiah is to show forth the certainty of God's great work of redemption and renewal. Let no one doubt it. For the Spirit of God is all-powerful. That Spirit is upon the Son, "The Spirit of the LORD is upon me," the Lord Jesus said in Nazareth, quoting from Isaiah 61:1, and he added, "Today this word is fulfilled in your hearing" (Luke 4:21).

Promising

On Pentecost the Holy Spirit came to complete his work of the ages, to put that work into its final phase, and to have the Gospel of Christ – once revealed in Paradise – preached in its full riches now to all nations. Therefore we may see this hovering of the Spirit over the waters as being promising indeed. Why would the Spirit hover and why would he linger, if all that water was of no consequence? But as he hovers over it and looks into it, does the Spirit, who from eternity knows the mind of God, not see the great promise that lies in it, which God has attached to it?

God's world will come out of this water. In this world God's children will be placed. Out of this world God's people will be gathered. And the Holy Spirit from the very beginning takes an integral part in all this, as do the Father and the Son. Even when there is the fall into sin, the Spirit will not leave the earth. He will work through the generations to bring forth the seed of the promise, the great Savior, conceived by the Holy Spirit, born of the virgin Mary.

There will be some dangerous times. When you read about the Spirit here hovering over the waters, you think of the great waters of the *flood*. The waters came back, up from below and down from above. But as the ark rode the crest of the soaring waves, the Holy Spirit watched carefully over those eight people, for to them God had given the promise of his covenant. That's why we can sing from Hymn 36:3, "Praise the Spirit who will never/ leave the church by blood once bought. Would he not securely keep/ those whom Christ bought as his sheep?" (*Book of Praise*).

The presence of the Holy Spirit is promising. As he then hovered over the waters, so he now regards the sea of nations. We never need to doubt whether he will bring the work of God to completion. He did this at creation. He did this in the conception and birth of Christ. He will do it in the gathering of the holy, catholic, church. He will do it in our lives. The Holy Spirit will impart unfailingly to believers and their seed whatever promises the Father has given in Christ to them. He will watch until the great day dawns and the Morning Star rises. He makes us faithful, for *the Spirit* and the bride say: come, Lord Jesus! (Revelation 22:17). We could never say this on our own, but through the Spirit we learn to long for the coming of the Son and the dwelling with the Father.

Why do we not make this the basis of our lives? He searched the waters of the deep. Now he seeks the earth's remotest end. He also wants to search your heart, and lead you in the way everlasting. Open your life and heart to him The Spirit's vision is far and wide, but also near and deep. He brings from the Father and through the Son immense comfort in all the trials and pains of life. He watches over God's work of creation, redemption, and perfection so that the great day may come when God is everything to everyone.

The Spirit and the Earth

When you send your Spirit, they are created, and you renew the face of the earth.

(PSALM 104:30)

Most churches have an annual prayer service in which the Lord's blessing is asked over the summer season of growth and labor. We draw near to the throne of God in prayer with a sincere faith. He alone is able to provide in all our needs, and he has also promised to do so. "Open wide your mouth and I will fill it." And God's people are told that they "… would be fed with the finest of wheat; with honey from the rock I would satisfy you" (Psalm 81:16, 10). God loves to give.

The same teaching is found in the New Testament. God is generous and giving, even more than earthly fathers, as Christ said, "If you, then, who are evil, know how to give good gifts to your children, how much more will your Father in heaven give good gifts to those who ask him?" (Mat 7:11).

Our Lord specifies that the recipients are those who ask. The Lord God wishes to be petitioned, for therein he is recognized and glorified. God wishes to be acknowledged as the Creator and Giver of all. There are many psalms which lead us clearly in this direction. Perhaps no psalm is as powerful and elaborate in this respect as Psalm 104, sometimes called a hymn to the Creator.

The Spirit as Creator?

What is remarkable in this psalm is the confession that God creates and re-creates by the Holy Spirit, verse 30, "When you send your Spirit, they are created.…" The Holy Spirit is named here the agent of creation, the One by whom God creates. This is said more often of the Son. For example, we read in Colossians 1:15, 16, "He (Jesus) is the image of the invisible God, the firstborn of all creation. For by him all things were created, things in heaven and things on the earth, visible and invisible, whether thrones or powers or rulers or authorities; all things were created by him and for him." We can think also of John 1:3, "Through him (the Word, Christ) all things were made, without him nothing was made that has been made."

So the Lord Jesus is the One through whom the Father made all things. The work of the Holy Spirit is often imagined by us as being more a matter of the inner space than of the outer space. When you consider what the Holy Spirit does, you tend to think of regeneration, sanctification, or renewal, the spiritual transformation that takes place and must take place within us. You look for the Spirit's work within you, and not so much outside of you or around you.

The Bible, however, does not restrict the Spirit's work in this manner. One can argue that this passage from Psalm 104 does not speak about creation in a strict sense, as does Genesis 1 and that it refers more to ongoing creation in the sense of maintaining, preserving, and restoring what once was created. This is indeed true. But the Spirit restores and renews what he himself also has created. This is done in full unity with the Father and the Son. It is not without reason that the verb to create is ascribed also to the Holy Spirit. We want to look closer at this important work of the Holy Spirit. We will see in this passage the power of the Holy Spirit in maintaining creation to the glory of God, in giving new life, and in sustaining all life.

Ode to the Creator

This psalm is definitely an ode to the Creator. When we look at the way the psalm is organized, we see that the days of creation, as described in Genesis 1, determine the unfolding of the psalm. Obviously the writer is fascinated by all that he sees around him in this vast, glorious creation of God. "I say to myself: what a wonderful world," as Louis Armstrong sang. From beginning to end, the LORD, the Creator, is praised as being very great. Verse 1, "Praise the LORD, O my soul. O LORD my God, you are very great; you are clothed with splendor and majesty." This praise is carried through to the end, verse 35, "Praise the LORD, O my soul. Praise the LORD." "How great Thou art," states the well-known hymn.

What is further striking about this psalm is that it describes the ongoing involvement of God in this creation, in this world. The LORD did not create everything to let it run by itself, but he governs and guides all things. His creation is followed by his government and providence. This is a very important aspect. You may have heard of the teaching of *Deism*, the idea that God created everything to run perfectly like clockwork through natural laws or ordinances without his direct, daily involvement. Just wind it up, set it down, and let it go on its own. If this is true, God is not involved in his creation. In fact, then he is irrelevant. We are on our own. If things really turn sour, God might perhaps act to reset the clock, but that's about it. We have to trust the laws of nature and where possible assume control ourselves.

Human reason failed

This kind of approach led to the modern glorifying of human reason. As enlightened and highly-developed beings, we ourselves will keep everything under control. Just as God is not interested in us, we do not really need him. All we have to do is stay cool, calm, and collected, think things over carefully, develop our scientific skills, and everything will be fine.

The last century has shown how far we came with our reasoning and our skills. World wars, atomic explosions, genocide, ethnic cleansing, and many other unspeakable horrors have happened. As we came to the end of another century, a millennium even, there was much searching for meaning and purpose. Was there a seeking after God? Should the Creator not be more involved in his struggling and crumbling creation?

This psalm tells us that he is involved, has always been involved, and wants to be heard and obeyed. Rejection of God leads to the judgments that we have seen in the world wars and in other calamities. If people would break with their idolatry, they would see the only living God at work in his world.

How the world turns

The psalm paints a very vivid picture of how the world turns in the hand of God. There is a remarkable fascination in this psalm with water, thunder, clouds, wind, and springs. You can understand this emphasis, for the psalm was written in a dry land where the people prayed to Baal, the god of rain and thunder, where fertility was given by Baal and Astarte, and where heavenly bodies like sun and moon were worshiped, because they determined ebb and flow, rain and drought, warmth and cold. There was great temptation for the people of Israel to fall prey to this pagan cult of materialism.

Therefore the psalm places great emphasis on the fact that that the LORD is the living God, who interacts constantly with his creation, who fills it with all good things, so that all creatures are cared for properly. The same

God is also revealed as awesome, the God who can terrify creatures by hiding his face (verse 29). He can simply look at the earth and it trembles (verse 32). It becomes evident that from the hands of this God, the LORD, come life and death.

In wisdom you made them all

We may not take life for granted, because it is a sovereign gift of God. We should not become accustomed to death, for it is the righteous curse of God. Even more, we must recognize that all life depends fully upon God's providence and government, and that only those who seek him are blessed.

Verse 24 of this psalm is perhaps the best-known, "How many are your works, O LORD! In wisdom you made them all; the earth is full of your creatures." There is an endless variety of life, a constant movement and shifting of tides, and everything has its place, function, and time, but all depends on God. In the verses 27-30 this truth is applied to food and sustenance, and to life and death. Put in the simplest terms: when God opens his hand, we live, but when he hides his face, we die. "When you take away their breath, they die and return to the dust" (verse 29b).

Notice the word breath here, for it is the same word that is also used for spirit and for wind. As he writes about the breath of living creatures being taken away, and their bodies returning to the dust, the psalmist is led to speak of the Holy Spirit. Verse 30: "When you send your Spirit, they are created, and you renew the face of the earth." Life can be given, received, and experienced only through the power of the Holy Spirit.

Focus on man

The writer of this psalm is talking here about all creatures (see verse 27, "these all"). But the description of death as a taking away of breath and a returning to dust reminds us of Genesis 1 and 3, the creation and fall of mankind. Of all creatures, humans are the most concerned with the ultimate question of life and death, and with the intermittent struggle for survival. We caused this awful reality by our willful sins, and only the LORD can undo it by his power and grace.

It pertains to all the living, but especially to mankind: when you send your Spirit, they are created. It is important to note at this point that, aside from the writer referring to himself, man was mentioned twice before in this psalm. In the verses 14 and 15 he writes about the grass that grows for the cattle, but then elaborates on the gifts God gives to man: food-bearing plants to cultivate (vegetables), wine that gladdens the heart, oil to make his face shine, and bread that sustains his heart. Here the main essentials which we need are mentioned in their richest measure. We receive not just water to drink or wash, but also wine and oil.

In the verses 21-23 a distinction is made between the night and its creatures, especially the lion, and the day and its creatures, especially man. As the lion rules by night, so man rules by day, and can go out to do his work. The king of beasts is subjected to the king of creation who is called man. Yet like all creatures, man is dependent upon God.

The sending of the Spirit

In the text the focus is general: when you send your Spirit, they (all creatures) are created. What requires our attention now is the verb "to send," that is, the Holy Spirit being sent. The Lord Jesus later also spoke about the Spirit being sent. See John 14:26, "But the Counselor, the Holy Spirit, whom the Father will send in my name, will teach you all things." This sending of the Holy Spirit does not mean that he has an inferior position to the other persons in the Trinity, even though the sender is usually more than the one being sent. But it means coming with the authority of the Sender to complete his work. The Spirit does not just come on his own, but he comes from the Father and the Son to complete and perfect legitimately and authoritatively the one work of God. The use of the verb "to send" here means having an official mission.

We learn that only when the Holy Spirit comes from the Father and in the name of the Son, can life be created. The breath of all living creatures, and especially that of mankind in whom God specifically breathed life, is a wonderful gift of the Holy Spirit who comes from the Father and the Son. Life is a gift of the Triune God. God's people of old have known that life, also new life, is a direct work of the Spirit.

Ongoing creative work

I ask your attention now for the next verb that is used here: they are *created*. To the Spirit of God is ascribed the work of creation. The same verb is used as in Genesis 1:1, "In the beginning God created the heavens and the earth." What does this mean? Generally we assume that the work of creation was finished on the sixth day, and that God then rested on the seventh. And this is true indeed. The initial and official work of creation was done on the sixth day.

Yet here we find that the creative work of God continues. Every living creature is a new creation of God, a work of the Holy Spirit. Its life is directly linked to the design, purpose, and will of God. There is no life outside the one true God. It is therefore totally absurd when people tell themselves that they are a product of circumstances, or that they can control the origin of life. Scientists work in clinical laboratories, use all kinds of fancy techniques and expensive paraphernalia, but only when God speaks his powerful word in the midst of this world and sends his Spirit is life created. Life exists because God wants it to exist, and it exists exactly as he wants it to exist.

We should have an keen eye for the ongoing creative work of God in this world, for only then we can really see and enjoy the beauty of all things. If you are oriented to God and his word, and orient yourself in this way to the world around you, creation also becomes to you an open book, where every creature great or small is like a letter spelling out the majesty of God (Belgic Confession, Article 2; Psalm 19:1-4). Many people see little of the beauty of creation because they do not see it as a result of God's power and majesty. Every creature and each life is a work of the Holy Spirit's influencing, working, determining, and leading. You can see this work everywhere, but you notice it especially when you work closely with the soil, under the sun, and in the fields.

The origin of life

In this light we can also better understand Psalm 139, which speaks of the origin of life. We read in the verses 13 and 14, "For you created my inmost being; you knit me together in my mother's womb. I praise you, because I am fearfully and wonderfully made; your works are wonderful, I know that full well." When it comes to our origin, there should be no doubt whatsoever that God created each one of us.

We will focus in a next chapter on Psalm 139. I refer to it here only to note who is specifically mentioned in this same Psalm 139 in connection with creation: the Spirit of God, his power, his leading, and his guidance. Psalm 139:7: "Where can I go from your Spirit? Where can I flee from your presence?" Then we read in verse 13 about this Spirit, "For you created my inmost being, you knit me together in my mother's womb." Here the Holy Spirit is mentioned in connection with conception.

God who regarded me when I was still in my mother's womb, also throughout my life brings about what he has ordained. Therefore, since nothing is hidden from the LORD, we are called to open our life to him.

"Search me, O God, and know my heart; test me and know my anxious thoughts. See if there is any offensive way in me, and lead me in the way everlasting." (Psalm 139:23, 24)

We may believe that every person is a creation of the Holy Spirit. The Lord uses us as his instruments, and we must be responsible parents, but each life, each baby born is a creation of the Spirit of God. And when born of believers, this child belongs to God's covenant, for so God has decreed his involvement with mankind. Let us receive our children in this way, treat them from this perspective, and as we work with them, pray for them that they may come to love the LORD.

Sustaining all life

As the Spirit creates new life, so he also sustains it. Psalm 104:30: "...and you renew the face of the earth." In the previous lines, the psalmist has spoken about the cycle of death and life. All creatures die, and new creatures take in their place. One generation goes, another comes. There is in this respect a constant process of change. Everything has its place and time under the sun (cf. Ecclesiastes 3); all things are here temporarily.

The important thing, according to many people, is that we should "live and let live, never take more that we give." That line is from Walt Disney's *The Lion King*. We all appear on the circle of life: we come in on the circle, and we all go off that circle. Meanwhile we go round and round. It's like being on a wheel of fortune. Some are lucky, others are not. In the eyes of many, life is a circle, sometimes a vicious circle.

The movie urges us to make the best of it. We should take life as it comes, not get too worried, and show a stiff upper lip. That's the warthog's song: "Hakuna Matata: it means no worries for the rest of your days. It's our problem-free philosophy, Hakuna Matata!" Life comes and goes like a "twisting kaleidoscope," but the spirit of man is triumphant.

However, it says here that the LORD by his Spirit renews the face of the earth. He sustains life, and keeps this world inhabitable. We are not caught up in the circle of life, but we are on an open road that leads us to the new world, where we shall live forever with our great King, the Lord Jesus Christ. Circles are endless; roads lead somewhere.

Spring is here again

What does the expression "renewing of the face of the earth" mean? Are we to think in terms of a superficial face-lift? We understand that more is meant. When the LORD sends the Holy Spirit, a powerful work happens; something occurs that goes very deep and has amazing consequences. It says: you renew the face of the earth.

The verb used here is a rather interesting one. It means to make new by giving a new spirit, especially in this sense: a completely fresh look. It means that whatever hinders and holds back growth is removed. The time of stress or restraint is past; the time of growth has come. Explainers who think here especially of spring are correct. After the fall season, winter comes. In Palestine winter is the dry season, when everything withers and dies. In Canada, we are faced with the great deep freeze. For months snow can cover the frozen ground. Animals go into deep hibernation, all plants are dormant, and the cold wind ruffles the snow banks. Sometimes we wonder how the earth can ever recover from such a devastating process. Will the new growing season ever come?

People say: in due time, it will be spring. One day the rain will fall, warmth will return. The seasons follow a natural course. To a certain extent this is true. But sometimes there is a long and widespread drought in areas that are already dry. Sometimes a number of poor growing seasons follow one another. There are storms that can inflict much damage. Who has not read about the dust bowls of the thirties and the forties, when nothing grew, farms were abandoned, and people looked in vain for jobs. It happened in North America where otherwise prosperity reigns. We may not take anything for granted.

Same old world: fresh new look

God renews the face of the earth. This means that everything starts to grow again. Seed, perhaps sown in the fall, germinates. The sap of trees begins to run, and buds and blossoms appear. How accurate and beautiful is the expression "the face of the earth." Everything looks different, fresh, new, and vibrant. The cold winds are driven away; the rays of the sun are warm. We rediscover the great outdoors. It's the same old world, but with a fresh, new look.

Is it any wonder that spring is welcomed by all people? Especially at the end of the winter we look forward to it with great longing, and it cannot come soon enough. In many languages, the word for spring literally means the beginning of the year, the first time, and it is often compared with youth. Everything is young again and looks fresh: he renews the face of the earth. It is the Spirit's work. He brings back the life that seemed to be gone and causes growth to commence once more. The Holy Spirit watches over the fields, the orchards, the meadows, the valleys, and the streams. He causes the weather to change and the earth to be renewed.

Produce and sustain

The renewal of the face of the earth is not meant only to make things look nice; its purpose is to make the earth produce what its inhabitants need for life. The Spirit sustains life. Creatures are given what they need in order to function properly. The earth is made to support those who live on it, and the Spirit time and again each year sets things in motion for this purpose. People enjoy the bounteous gifts of God. The Lord nurtures the life he has given.

This is also true in a spiritual sense. The Holy Spirit works in us to renew us, to bring forth new life. That is one of the promises of God, signified in holy baptism, with which we must work. It is also true in a physical sense: the Spirit brings forth the bounty of this earth to sustain life.

Does this not sound too optimistic? Not all baptized children come to faith. Not all people have a good meal every day. There is the third world, being destroyed by terrible poverty and extreme hunger. There are countless refugees who line the streets of inhospitable cities and stand before closed borders. The psalm paints a rosy picture, but what about all the problems of food shortages on this earth?

The eternal Spring

Indeed, there is one great difficulty. The destructive power of sin and its curse permeate everything. It leads to the situations I just mentioned. Psalm 104 is not an idyllic psalm that ignores reality. The psalmist writes in verse 35, "But may sinners vanish from the earth and the wicked be no more". Do not overlook that petition. Sinners and wicked people are not just to be kept in check, but must vanish and disappear. The psalm teaches us to anticipate a new world where there will be no exploitation and upheaval, no hunger and sickness, no strife and tears.

There is a longing for a greater renewal than only spring. The great regeneration is coming when all things will be made new by the Spirit. But first the Lord Jesus Christ must come to redeem his people from their sins.

He will come, for the ultimate renewal depends on his work of deliverance. This psalm, too, as do many other psalms, looks forward to the new heaven and earth.

The same longing is expressed at a child's baptism, as it enters this world and embarks on its journey through this life. We pray that the child may stand "without terror before God in the assembly of the elect in life eternal" (Form for the Baptism of Infants, *Book of Praise*, page 584). There lies the focus of our labor under the sun. We look for the final renewal, the eternal spring, to live with the Lord Jesus forever in the life that never ends. "Praise the LORD, O my soul" (Psalm 104:3).

The Omni-present Spirit

Where can I go from your Spirit? Where can I flee from your presence?

(PSALM 139:7)

This psalm, ascribed to David, is remarkable because it describes the ultimate relationship between God and his covenant children, between the LORD and us. It is striking that the Lord is fully acknowledged in his glory and power, which are evident in his omnipresence, and at the same he is embraced in his love and grace, and experienced in his constant nearness. This almighty God is our Father.

There is another element here to which we must pay attention. In the text the Holy Spirit is mentioned specifically: where can I go from your Spirit? As we annually consider the meaning of Christ's ascension and the subsequent outpouring of the Spirit on Pentecost, we must remember that the Holy Spirit always functioned on earth, dwelt and worked among God's people, and was recognized as God.

Pentecost does not mean that the Holy Spirit comes to earth for the first time, but that he comes in a special manner because of the redeeming work of Christ. Yet the Spirit has from the very beginning of time cared for this earth and also dwelt among God's people. Pentecost does not come falling out of the blue sky, but builds on the presence of the Spirit under the Old Testament. The work of the Spirit becomes richer all the time, but new work always flows forth from work done since the beginning of time. This is the order which the Bible emphasizes.

Omnipresence and Omniscience

In this Psalm we are taught to praise the LORD our God who knows our lives and guides them. David first tells us that the LORD is with him every step of each day. The LORD can do this because he is omnipresent

31

and omniscient (is everywhere and knows all things). Hence there is no escape from God. Instead there is an acknowledgement that the LORD knew his child even from the time he was still in the womb of his mother. God sets the day of our birth and our death: (verse 16): all the days ordained for me were written in your book.

Because all this is so, David ends the psalm by *inviting* the LORD to come and know his heart, to search his (anxious) thoughts, to see if there is an offensive way in him, and to lead him in the way everlasting. Do not shut God out; invite him in. Search me O God! You can say: he is already in, but nevertheless we are called to open our heart and mind to the LORD. God wants to be a part of our lives with our love, cooperation, and recognition.

In that light we can better understand the passage about going from the Spirit and fleeing from God's presence. It is impossible to escape and foolish even to try. It is unnecessary for obedient children of the LORD to try to escape. The presence of the Holy Spirit should be to us not a matter of fear but a matter of great of joy.

This psalm teaches us that the loving care of the LORD is expressed in the powerful presence of the Holy Spirit. We focus on two aspects: the Spirit's infinite omnipresence and his intimate omniscience.

Written for everyone

It says above this psalm: for the director of music. When we read about a director, we think of a choir. When we hear about a choir in the Old Testament, we think of the Levites. They were taught by the director, and in turn they taught the people to sing. This is a psalm, therefore, not just for personal use or family devotion, but one written for all God's people.

I mention this because of the very personal character of this psalm. Sometimes people see a big gap between personal worship and corporate (or congregational) worship, but the gap should not be there. The one flows into the other. What we may sing about ourselves, we may sing also about the LORD's covenant people.

This means also that the passage about going from God's Spirit or fleeing God's presence is true for all Israelites. At this point Pentecost has not yet occurred and the indwelling of the Spirit in each heart is not yet a reality, but David recognizes that the Spirit does function and work in Israel.

Please notice also one other important aspect. In the first line of this text, David speaks about the Spirit. Then he adds in the same

breath: your (i.e. Yahweh's) presence. Omnipresence is ascribed both to the Spirit and to the LORD. The LORD is the Spirit. We see here again clear proof that also under the Old Testament the Holy Spirit was considered to be God.

Two questions in one

Now David is actually asking two questions here, or possibly, we can say, one question. Let us examine the first one, "Where can I go from your Spirit?" The second question has the element of "fleeing" from God, which is probably, in the line of parallelism, the sense also of the first question. Where can I go from your Spirit, namely, to get away?

We wonder why an Israelite, or any one of us, would ever want to get away from the Spirit or flee from God. Is life with the LORD not much more pleasant than without him? Why run away? What reason could there possibly be?

There may sometimes be important though invalid reasons to run, but where can we go to hide from the LORD? The question is, of course, rhetorical. The answer is nowhere. We cannot get away from the Holy Spirit. David is not speaking about the desirability of getting away, but about the comforting impossibility. No matter where he goes or whatever overcomes him, the Holy Spirit is right there, all around him, protecting, guiding, and leading. Therefore I wrote about the infinite omnipresence of the Spirit.

Now one might say: that is saying the same with two words. We call that a pleonasm or a redundancy. Does omnipresence (being everywhere) not mean also infinite (without boundaries)? This is true. But David wants to stress very strongly that no matter where we go we cannot hide from the Holy Spirit. He mentions places which we might not immediately think of to stress that this omnipresence is indeed infinite, without any limit whatsoever.

Sometimes we confess the Spirit's omnipresence, but then in our mind immediately restrict it. The Spirit is everywhere, but....we haven't noticed it lately. We do not see him. There were times and places when we did not feel the presence of the Spirit. Or we think that we somehow can do something that will escape the Holy Spirit's attention, something which he will not see. After all, he is too busy with the grander scheme of things than to worry about us.

The heart of the psalm?

Perhaps here we come to the heart of this very Psalm. David expresses his wonder that God through his Holy Spirit pays personal attention to each detail of his life. This is part of the omnipresence: God oversees his entire people in one glance, but he also notices each person in the specific details of his life.

Where can I go from your Spirit? Notice how David speaks about height (heaven) and depth (Sheol), and the most faraway places ("the far side of the sea"). That means all the way at the other end of the Mediterranean in uncharted waters where no one has gone before. David also mentions the *darkness*, the cover of the night, when people cannot see and many crimes are committed. Sometimes in a situation of warfare, when an enemy attack is expected at night, defending troops send up flairs to light up the surrounding area. But all you can see is shadows moving. Nowadays there are night vision binoculars, special infrared scopes that pick up the advancing enemy. We have found ways to break through the dark, at least partially. But of the Spirit it is said: the night will shine like the day, for darkness is as light to you. The Spirit does not need flares or scopes. There is no barrier for him, not even pitch black darkness.

Everywhere in full measure

There is no place of escape. We can take that even in a more positive sense: there is no need ever to fear that the Holy Spirit is not present with us, because for the Holy Spirit there are no obstacles, no borders, no situations, and no created entities that can hinder him from being with us. There is truly here infinite omnipresence, the presence of the Holy Spirit everywhere in full measure, a presence that knows of no bounds.

Go up to heaven, there is the Spirit. Go to the realm of the dead, to Sheol, from which there is no return, but the Spirit can enter and leave there freely at will. Do you think that when you die, you are beyond the reach and power of the Holy Spirit? You cannot go so far away that the Spirit even momentarily loses track of you. God never has to say: where is so-and-so? I don't see him at the moment.

Why the Spirit?

Why is the Spirit mentioned specifically in this connection? David could have written simply: where can I go *from you*, Yahweh, where can I flee from your presence? The Spirit is specified here, because he is the one

who lives among God's people, watches over them, cares for them, keeps them together, brings back those who stray, and causes Israel to be a spiritual people. This was so already under the old dispensation, and it became only richer in the new dispensation.

Here we see already the contours of what happens through and after Pentecost. The disciples, enabled by the Spirit, go everywhere in the whole world, and there are no boundaries for the Holy Spirit. Distance means nothing to him. All obstacles are overcome by the Holy Spirit. While we work in faith, the Spirit manifests his infinite omnipresence.

There was a time when the Spirit withdrew from a place or person. That was at the cross of Golgotha, and he removed himself from our Lord Jesus Christ. David may confess: You have laid your hand on me, in a protecting and a guiding sense, but Jesus Christ must say: You have taken your hand from me and instead of protecting me, You have crushed me, This is stated in Psalm 22 which contains the complaint: my God, my God, why have you forsaken me? That is the price for our sins. The Spirit is holy, and where he now goes he purifies and sanctifies with the blood of the cross shed by our Lord. Jesus Christ.

Remember Jonah?

We must understand that we now speak about the Spirit sent by our Lord Jesus Christ. We have received the Spirit of son ship, by which we cry Abba, Father! He is the same Spirit as from eternity, but one who now hands out to us what Christ has earned for us on the cross. For the Lord Jesus said: he will take from me, and give it to you.

You cannot get away from the Spirit. Remember how the prophet Jonah tried to do so. He boarded a boat that was going to Spain or beyond, farther than civilization itself. But he ran into the wall of God's omnipresence. We ask sometimes how Jonah could ever survive for three days and nights in the belly of a fish, but the real question is: how did he ever think he could hide from the LORD? There are people today on the run, some literally trying to block out the Spirit by breaking with the church, but they find no rest, even if they plunge themselves into this world to hide there.

No secret places

I want to look yet at the expression, "Where can I flee from your presence?" The answer to this question is, of course, clear: nowhere. In Jeremiah 23:23, 24 we read, "Am I only a God nearby, declares the LORD, and not a God far away? Can anyone hide in secret places, so that I cannot see him? declares the LORD. Do I not fill heaven and earth? declares the LORD?" Even the great exile will not pose a problem for the LORD to find and to bring back his people whom he has chosen.

There are no secret places before God. No secrets can be kept from the LORD. We should remember this constantly. Instead, it says, where can I flee from your presence? Please note carefully the word presence. God is present, not far away, but near. Literally it says: where can I flee from your face.

We live and work before the face of the LORD. He is present wherever we are, whatever we do, and he looks upon us. If the first part of the verse indicated infinite omnipresence, the second part is not a mere repetition, but deepens the original thought: your Spirit...your presence... is everywhere.

The Spirit: God's Presence

I find it remarkable that often when the Spirit is mentioned in the Old Testament the word "presence" is used, as in this passage and also elsewhere. I think of Psalm 51:11, "Do not cast me from your presence, or take your Holy Spirit from me." Or consider Ezekiel 39:29, "I will no longer hide my face (presence) from them, for I will pour out my Spirit on the house of Israel, declares the Sovereign LORD."

God's face or God's presence are experienced in the nearness of the Holy Spirit. The Holy Spirit is the presence of God among his people. When God turns his face toward us, his Holy Spirit comes among us, and we live in his presence. The outpouring of the Spirit on Pentecost deepened this presence. The Holy Spirit then came to dwell within our hearts. The new dispensation is richer and deeper, because it is based on one perfect sacrifice of Christ, made once for all.

Sometimes, when we were children and we learned something new, like being able to swim with our head under water, we'd say: look dad, look, mom, and then we wait till they actually look at us, and under we go. As we rub the water from our eyes, we first look in the direction of mom and dad to determine if they have indeed watched us. When they have seen, and acknowledged our achievement, we feel so happy. Mom and dad do love me, for they have watched me, and turned their face towards me. I am important to them, and I live in their presence, before their face. So it is in a much deeper sense with the Holy Spirit and God's children.

From infinite to intimate

What is infinite has now become intimate. When you are in the presence of others, you are very close to them. They can speak with you and you can respond. There is an exchange of love. God's eyes rest on us and our eyes look to him. We pray and we know he is listening. We cry and we know he hears. We laugh and we know he shares our joy.

God's presence has always been experienced in the nearness of the Holy Spirit. He was set among Israel. Look at Isaiah 63:11b, "Where is he who set his Holy Spirit among them?" We will look closer at this passage in a next chapter. The Spirit then restricted his close presence to certain office bearers, for example, to Moses and the seventy elders. But God did live among Israel, and they were all in his presence.

He knew all things about each one of them. This is what omniscience means. No matter what they did, when or where, he knew of it. He knew it in its depth: intimate omniscience. Israel had to recognize this time and again. This was brought home very clearly and strongly to the Israelites when they entered the promised land in the example with Achan who took from the spoils of Jericho. He did it in the presence of God, before the face of God, who watched him all the time and knew of his deepest motive (cf. Joshua 7). We find a similar example in the New Testament in the case of Ananias and Sapphira (Acts 5).

Greater intimacy now

Now the Spirit has been poured out, and dwells in our hearts. There is today even a greater reality of intimate omniscience. Let us say that David can speak about himself still as an exception. Most Israelites did not have such a close bond with the Holy Spirit as we do. He now dwells within our hearts. Intimate omniscience means that he knows the deepest secrets of our heart. Our life is to him an open book.

When someone looks at you all the time, knows all about you, and sees deep into your heart, there is one of two things you can do. One reaction is that you can become quite nervous and try to live a life of constant, futile cover-up and denial. We often try to cover up and deny what we did. We try to get the focus on the sins of others by pointing to their errors. It is senseless, because God sees anyway, also how we try to hide and run, bob and weave. Do you live in denial and excuses? Then how does the Spirit, the presence of God, function in your life?

When someone looks at us all the time, is constantly watching us, we can become very uneasy. We say: stop staring at me. Quit looking at me all the time. We try to get out of the line of vision. As a matter of fact, we say: staring is rude.

But God does not stare with accusing eyes. He looks at us in love. Sometimes he looks in anger and grief, when we do not obey his will. It is not without reason that the Bible tells us already in the Old Testament that Israel rebelled "and grieved his Holy Spirit" (Isaiah 63:10). This matter resurfaces in the New Testament, but it happened also before Pentecost. The great sin of Israel was grieving the Spirit of God, rejecting his word, and breaking his covenant.

Invite God in

There is the other way shown by David in this Psalm. If my life is open to God from my conception on, from birth to death and beyond, what else shall I do but open it also myself? I will not try to keep God out, but I will invite him in. Look at the last verses of the psalm, 23 and 24. "Search me O God and know my heart, test me and know my anxious thoughts. See if there is any offensive way in me, and lead me in the way everlasting."

The psalm started with the words: O LORD, you have searched me. We cannot keep God out. David sees this as a great comfort. God is with him all the way, every step of the way, by the omnipresence and omniscience of the Holy Spirit. There is no running away nor is there any need to run. We do not play hide and seek games with the LORD. Come in. Continue to search me, O God, and know my heart. Keep me on the right path, the one that is everlasting.

Difficult decisions

This does mean that we must sometimes make very difficult decisions. There's also in this Psalm the section about the wicked (verses 19-21). It sounds like a sudden, angry outburst that does not really fit. But it fits perfectly. "Do I not hate those who hate you?" In the presence of God, before his face, with his Spirit in your heart, you cannot love God's enemies. His enemies are my enemies. I hate those who hate him. All they try to do is ruin the relationship with the LORD and one another.

What this means very simply is that we have to be consistent. We do not associate with those who hate God. How could we? We live in God's presence, do we not? But then it is also true for us: we love those who love God and we exercise with them the communion of saints.

The apostle Paul wrote in this vein to the Corinthians (1 Cor 5:9 ff). We cannot altogether avoid going about with unbelievers. Then we'd best leave the world completely. There are business dealings and social obligations, whatever, that we must be involved in. But we do this only as far as we must. We do not engage in fellowship or communion with the ungodly, for we have no common basis with them. Either we live together as God's children, or we do not live together.

God is watching us closely

Do we have a very keen awareness of the fact that we are always living in the presence of God, not just in church on Sundays but every day, every night, and all week long? The Holy Spirit watches us, not as an uninterested spectator, but as an intimate counselor. Our life is his concern, at home or at work, at school or at play.

God is watching us in the love that he manifested in Jesus Christ on the cross like a Father watches his children, or a mother, to keep them from danger and harm.

The Spirit regards us with intimate omniscience. This is true even more now since Pentecost. We were bought by the blood of Christ and our life is now a workplace of the Holy Spirit. God's eyes are upon us in Christ. He misses nothing. He sees our good works and our transgressions.

We thank him for the good works because he worked them in us. We confess our sins believing that he takes them away. He renews my life. He knows me through and through. From the day I was conceived, he watched over me, and now he dwells in me. I open my life to him, seek him in the beauty of the Holy Scriptures and in the intimacy of prayer. In the love of Jesus Christ, I find the Father and the Spirit, the one True eternal God, who has laid his hand upon me and leads me in the way everlasting.

All this is too wonderful for me, I cannot comprehend it. But I believe it and seek to live it every day again.

IV The Holy Spirit and Israel

Where is he who set his Holy Spirit among them... they were given rest by the Spirit of the LORD.

(ISAIAH 63:11, 14)

In the previous chapter I referred to this passage from Isaiah 63. We noted the use of the verb to set. This indicates a permanent position. Also under the old dispensation, the bride (Israel in this case) was never to be without the Spirit. Spirit and Bride belong together in close-knit unity.

This passage, however, struggles with the very opposite. The question is asked: where is he? This is undoubtedly a reference to God's abandoning of his permanent dwelling among his people. This would indicate that also the Holy Spirit has removed himself and is no longer among the people of Israel. To use the language that some of the prophets employ: the bride that has become a harlot, no longer has the LORD or the Spirit of the LORD. We may think here especially of the prophet Hosea who was to take an adulterous wife "because the land is guilty of the vilest adultery." (1:2) Israel's apostasy is called adultery, a breaking of the holy covenant of the LORD.

The Holy Spirit in Israel

In Isaiah 63 the Holy Spirit is mentioned three times. In verse 10 we read about the grieving of God's Holy Spirit. The same expression is used in the New Testament, as we will see later. In verse 11 the question is asked, "Where is he who set his Holy Spirit among them?" Finally, in verse 13 we read that the Israelites were "given rest by the Spirit of the LORD."

In each of these verses the Holy Spirit is presented as a Person. If we may see in the expression "the angel of his presence" a reference to the pre-incarnate Lord Jesus Christ, and note that in verse 16 the Father is specifically mentioned, we have here in Isaiah 63 a clear revelation of the work of the Triune God, Father, Son, and Holy Spirit[4] .

Isaiah 63 is important in this respect because in no other chapter in the Old Testament is the relation and cooperation between Father, Son and Holy Spirit so explicitly made clear. The expression *Holy* Spirit is found in the Old Testament only in one other place, Psalm 51:11, "Do not cast me from your presence, or take your Holy Spirit from me." But from Isaiah we learn that the Holy Spirit was actively present in Israel from the time of their formation as a people throughout their entire history, leading them from bondage, through the Red Sea (verse 12) to the promised land (verse 14).

It would therefore be wrong to conclude that in Israel the emphasis was on the physical and the natural, while in the New Testament this emphasis has become spiritual and celestial. Also from the Old Testament we learn that the Holy Spirit is always present in and among God's people. The Spirit and the bride are together in every dispensation.

The Holy Spirit set among them

Isaiah speaks about the fact that the Holy Spirit was *set* among Israel. Apparently the text can be translated differently to state that the Holy Spirit was given to Israel within Moses. Then the emphasis is not on Israel's receiving of the Holy Spirit, but it lies on Moses' special ordination and qualification as leader of God's people. In this passage the prophet twice mentions Moses by name, and therefore our attention is indeed focused on the work of the Holy Spirit through Moses and other office bearers.

While the emphasis in the Old Testament falls on the presence of the Spirit through chosen office bearers, this does not do away with the fact that all the Israelites were aware of the presence of the Holy Spirit. The Holy Spirit may have manifested himself in certain persons, but by their authority he worked among all Israel.

Isaiah's prophecy does not cover only the time of Moses. In chapter 63 Isaiah speaks of the longing that the Israelites will have in their exile for

---

[4] See J. Ridderbos, *Het Godswoord der Profeten*, Tweede Deel, Jesaja, Kok, Kampen, 1932, page 434 and 435.

the time when they lived close to the LORD, when he worked miracles of deliverance, and led them to the promised land where they enjoyed rest and peace. The days of old are all the days from the time of Abraham (verse 16) up to the present exile, and these days are characterized by the dwelling of the Holy Spirit among Israel.

While we do not speak here of an indwelling of the Spirit in each and every Israelite, it is clear that the history of Israel is unthinkable without the presence and work of the Holy Spirit. No one can on his own serve God; the power of the Holy Spirit is needed for faith and obedience. The verb to set has the strong implication of constancy and permanence. Israel is the covenant nation of the LORD in whose midst the Spirit lives and works. The manner of the Spirit's presence may differ from that in the new dispensation, especially in degree and effect, but the reality of his work under the old dispensation is undisputable.

The tabernacle and temple, built under the strict supervision of the Holy Spirit, with their special liturgy were a constant reminder that God lived in Israel's midst in the presence of the Holy Spirit.

Herman Bavinck has written that "the doctrine concerning the Holy Spirit is the same in all the Scriptures of the Old and New Testament. Although this doctrine is more clearly revealed in the New Testament, it is present in principle in the Old Testament. The same Spirit who spoke by the prophets, testified in Noah's days, was resisted by Israel, and worked faith, would descend upon the Messiah, and lives in the congregation." [5]

The Shepherd of his flock

It is true, as is evident from this passage in Isaiah 63, that the Holy Spirit worked mightily in Israel through specially appointed and anointed office bearers. In the case of various office-bearers, this is specifically mentioned. Moses is mentioned here by Isaiah, and we may think also of the seventy elders upon whom the Holy Spirit rested and they prophesied (Numbers 11:25). It is reported by Moses of Bezalel, who is appointed as the chief designer of the tabernacle, that God has "filled him with the Spirit of God..." (Exodus 35:30).

When Moses is about to die, he asks the LORD to appoint a man who might properly guide Israel, so that they will not be like sheep without a shepherd, and the LORD replies, "Take Joshua, the son of Nun, a man in

---

[5] *Gereformeerde Dogmatiek* 2, Kok, Kampen, 1967 ed., pages 217 and 218).

whom is the spirit and lay your hand on him (Numbers 27:28)." (Numbers 27:18) In Deuteronomy 34:9 it is reported that "Joshua son of Nun was filled with the spirit of wisdom because Moses had laid his hands upon him." In both passages most Bible versions translate with spirit, and it is not made clear why the rendering Spirit is not followed. Is there any other spirit meant here than the Holy Spirit?

It is reported of Gideon, Jephthah, Samson, Saul, and David, to mention some examples that the Spirit of the LORD came upon them in power. In the case of Saul it is specified, "Now the Spirit of the LORD had departed from Saul, and an evil spirit from the LORD tormented him." (I Sam 16:14). From these accounts we receive the impression that the Holy Spirit did not always remain on these persons with the same power and intensity, but took hold of them from time to time whenever this was needed for their work. Of Samson it is mentioned at least four times that the Spirit came over him with power (Judges 13:25, 14:6, 14:19, and 15:14). Samson's strength was not physical; it was spiritual.

While the failures and sins of these men are not left unmentioned in Scripture, the mighty works of these men are consistently ascribed to the power of the Holy Spirit. The Holy Spirit protected Israel in times of danger and peril.

The temporal and restricted working of the Holy Spirit in these imperfect office bearers directs us to the great Shepherd of the flock, our Lord Jesus Christ. He is the good Shepherd, the true office bearer. Elsewhere we will take a closer look at the relation between the Holy Spirit and the Lord Jesus Christ, but it is evident that what was spiritually powerful in the lives of these men from time to time for certain tasks finds its glorious fulfillment in the perfect ministry of the Lord Jesus Christ, of whom Isaiah may prophesy, "The Spirit of the Sovereign LORD is on me because the LORD has anointed me...." The ministry of the Lord Jesus will never end, as he is "a priest forever, in the order of Melchizedek." (Psalm 110:4; see also Hebrews 7)

They were given rest

Isaiah mentions the fact that the people of Israel were given rest by the Spirit of the LORD. This occurred through the service of Moses and others, although we note that Moses did not accompany Israel into the promised land where the rest was enjoyed.

What is the meaning of the verb *to give rest*? We find this verb also in Exodus 33:14 where the LORD assures Moses, "My Presence will go with

you and I will give you rest." Rest means here that there is safety from enemies. In the context of Exodus it means that the LORD will accompany
his people and be with them until the time they come to the promised land
and receive this land as their inheritance.

In Joshua 11:23 we read, "So Joshua took the entire land, just as the
LORD had directed Moses, and he gave it as an inheritance to Israel according to their tribal divisions. Then the land had rest from war." Here the
promise of Exodus 33 is fulfilled. The rest is rest from war and is a living in
security and peace in the place which the LORD had given them. This rest
would be lost in the exile and restored only in the safe return of the remnant of Israel.

I find no rest

The word rest, however, does have further meaning and significance.
Just as the word peace (shalom) means more than the absence of war, so the
word rest also means more than physical security and safety. There is a
spiritual dimension to the idea of rest which explains why in this connection
the prophet Isaiah specifically mentions the Holy Spirit, "They were given
rest by the Spirit of the LORD."

We may think here of what is written in Psalm 22:2, "O my God, I cry
out by day, but you do not answer, by night and am not silent." The RSV
has a different translation, "...and by night, *but find no rest.*" The two trans-
lations are similar: David continues to cry out and even at night he does
not cease to call upon God, because he receives no response which will remove his fear and give him rest.

Is this rest not the inner peace of the soul, the knowledge that the
LORD is present and is near? Is it not in this light that we understand
David's petition in Psalm 51:11, "Do not cast me from your presence or
take your Holy Spirit from me." David knows that this rest is crucial, for he
has first prayed, "Create in me a pure heart, O God, and renew a steadfast
spirit within me."

The spiritual aspect of rest is indicated also in Jeremiah 6:16, where
the LORD says, "Stand at the crossroads and look; ask for the ancient paths,
ask where the good way is, and walk in it, and you will find rest for your
souls." The true rest is given to the people that live by the Word of God in
his covenant of love. They may know that sin is forgiven and that life is secure in the grace of God in Jesus Christ.

It is no wonder that our Lord Jesus Christ, when dealing with the
harsh and hard doctrine of the Jewish scribes, quoted from this passage of

Jeremiah 6, "Come to me, all you who are weary and burdened, and I will give you rest. Take my yoke upon you and learn from me, for I am gentle and humble in heart, and you will find rest for your souls. For my yoke is easy and my burden is light" (Matthew 11:28-30).

Our Lord himself would have to pay for our rest by his fathomless agony on the cross and his utter loneliness in the darkness of hell.

Where is he?

The question in Isaiah 63 about the presence of God has to do with the Person and character of the Holy Spirit. When God set his Spirit among his people, Israel had to understand that this Spirit is *holy*. The Father and the Spirit cannot live where sin is practiced and condoned. After constant grieving of the Spirit and the people's stubborn refusal to repent, the Holy Spirit withdraws.

Then, also, God has withdrawn himself. Where is he? Israel discovers that the LORD has left his people in righteous anger. Therefore the land is no longer safe. There is no rest from enemy attacks. The LORD is no longer a refuge for his people, where they can safely hide.

If the demand, "Be holy because I am holy," which underscores the spiritual nature of Israel's relationship with God, is not met, the LORD departs and in the process also his Holy Spirit is removed from the midst of Israel. Recognizing the holiness of God, evident in the presence of the Holy Spirit, is of fundamental significance in Israel's service of the LORD (Lev 19:1; I Pet 2:13).

When the Spirit withdraws, prophecy ceases and uncertainty sets in. The people become more and more victimized by false prophecy. Humanism replaces true spirituality.

The fact that the Holy Spirit does withdraw from God's disobedient people who refuse to repent, is a warning to the church of all ages. The working of the Holy Spirit under the Old Testament in Israel may have been more corporate and less personal than in the New Testament, but the bottom line is the same. Where there is no Spirit, there is no rest.

The word rest comes close to the word peace in Isaiah 48:22, "'There is no peace', says the LORD, 'for the wicked.'" The same expression is found in Isaiah 57:2, preceded by these words, "But the wicked are like the tossing of the sea, which cannot rest, whose waves cast up mire and mud." (Isaiah 57:20).

The Spirit and the Remnant

The active presence and the governing power of the Holy Spirit are decisive for the being and well-being of God's people in both the old and new dispensation. The Spirit is never separated from the Bride, except when God himself departs from his people. Even in this extreme measure the LORD still seeks and preserves a remnant to whom he gives his Holy Spirit. "Once more a remnant from the house of Judah will take root below and bear fruit above. For out of Jerusalem will come a remnant and out of Mount Zion a band of survivors." (2 Kings 19:30, 31)

The notion of a remnant in the Old Testament is significant because it is messianic. God will preserve a remnant, not because the people are worthy, but for the sake of his name and covenant, so that out of this remnant the Messiah may come forth. God's work of redemption in Christ must come to its fulfillment

When Isaiah may prophesy of this remnant, about the shoot from the stump of Jesse and the Branch that will bear fruit, the work of the Holy Spirit is specifically mentioned, "The Spirit of the LORD will rest upon him – the Spirit of wisdom and of understanding, the Spirit of counsel and of power, the Spirit of knowledge and of the fear of the LORD – and he will delight in the fear of the LORD" (Isaiah 11:2, 3). The Bridegroom who seeks the Bride shall do so in the love of the Father and by the power of the Holy Spirit.

In the formation and the reformation of Israel, the Holy Spirit is one with the Father and the Son.

The valley of dry bones

The element of spiritual restoration comes very clearly and strongly to the fore in the well-known prophecy concerning the vision about the valley of dry bones, recorded in Ezekiel 37. The prophet is taken into a valley filled with bones that were very dry. There were many bones, but all were bleached by the sun, so dry that one would never expect any life to enter these bones again.

The Lord then asks Ezekiel, "Son of man, can these bones live?" (verse 3). Ezekiel does not want to answer positively or negatively, and simply answers, "O Sovereign LORD, you know." God is able to bring the driest bones to life, but the prophet does not know yet what will happen and how things will unfold.

The LORD tells Ezekiel that the bones will receive muscles, tendons, and flesh, and be covered with skin. Physically the bodies were reassembled. But "there was no breath in them." They are still lifeless bodies. (verse 8). Ezekiel must then prophesy to the breath, the four winds, so that these bodies come to life. This happens, "So I prophesied as he commanded me, and breath entered them; and they came to life and stood up on their feet – a vast army." (verse 10)

Breath and wind which are common expressions for the Holy Spirit are also identified in this manner, "I will put my Spirit in you and you will live, and I will settle you in your own land" (verse 14). The people will be brought to life by the Holy Spirit and they will again enter the rest that God gives them in the land of promise.

This vision shows us that only the Holy Spirit can give the restoration that is needed, and that he must dwell in Israel to assure that they will live and function as God's covenant people. The expression, "...and I will put my Spirit *in* you..." may refer to what happens later at Pentecost, where the indwelling becomes a reality, but already in the days of the exile, Israel knows what it takes to be fully the people of the LORD. Having the Holy Spirit, the breath of the LORD, is indispensable for life.

V

The Spirit and the Lord Jesus

"As soon as Jesus was baptized, he went up out of the water. At that moment heaven was opened, and he saw the Spirit of God descending like a dove and lighting on him. And a voice from heaven said: This is my Son, whom I love; with him I am well-pleased."

(MATTHEW 3:16, 17)

There is an important question which inevitably comes up when looking at the passage of Scripture which tells us about the baptism of our Lord Jesus Christ. I do not mean the question which John the Baptist himself asked Jesus. He said, "I need to be baptized by you, and do you come to me?" (Mat 3:14) It was difficult for John to accept that the Lord Jesus, who is without sin, needed to be baptized, that is, to be cleansed of sin. How can one be cleansed of what one does not have?

Our Lord's answer is simple and straightforward, "Let it be so now; it is proper for us to fulfill all righteousness." (Mat 3:15). Though Christ is without sin, and does not require the ceremony of baptism for himself, yet as our Mediator, he was "made...to be sin for us, so that in him we might become the righteousness of God." (2 Cor 5:21). He was sent with a mission, for "the LORD has laid upon him the iniquity of us all." (Is 53:6). For this reason, he had to be baptized.

The question that concerns us now is why the Lord Jesus, who is God of God, needs to receive the Holy Spirit, descending and lighting on him. Was the Lord Jesus not "conceived by the Holy Spirit" (cf. Mat 1:20). Did he not already before the occasion of his baptism have the Holy Spirit? Is this having of the Spirit not also a consequence of the doctrine of the Holy Trinity? Was the Son ever without the Holy Spirit?

49

Is the Lord Jesus divine?

This passage appears to give ammunition to those who like to shoot holes in the doctrine of the Holy Trinity. Some say that Jesus is not divine, for he needs the special help of the Holy Spirit descending upon him, as happened later at Pentecost with the disciples (Acts 2). Without the support of the Spirit, Jesus is merely human, just as we are.

Why did our Lord, who is true God, require the Holy Spirit to descend upon him and empower him to fulfill his task? Could he not do his messianic work on his own steam? Or is the descending of the Spirit, as described here, to be regarded as a symbolic gesture, like the voice of the Father expressing love for his Son? In that case, this passage would tell us no more than that the Father, Son, and Spirit are on-line with one another, fully cooperating in the venture of our salvation. It is no wonder that this passage has become a classic proof-text for the doctrine of the Holy Trinity.

In dealing with this important matter, we learn to understand better the relation between Jesus and the Holy Spirit. This understanding, in turn, may help us better to see the relation between the Holy Spirit and *us* through our Lord Jesus Christ. We see here how the Holy Spirit visibly descends upon our Lord Jesus Christ to anoint him for the work of his public ministry. It is important to consider the moment of this anointing and the manner of this anointing.

Heaven opened

The exact moment of the descending of the Holy Spirit on our Lord is emphasized in this passage. In verse 16 we read, "As soon as Jesus was baptized, he went up out of the water." We might even translate: when Jesus was baptized, he *immediately* went up out of the water. Some explainers connect the word "immediately" with the next passage: immediately at that moment, heaven was opened. Whatever the exact translation may be, the idea is that Christ right after his baptism went out of the water and that right away, immediately, at that moment, heaven was opened.

The two events, the baptism and the opening of heaven, with all that follows, are therefore inseparably connected. The Lord God has waited for this precise moment to reveal the anointing of Christ with the Holy Spirit. Also, we understand, just as the baptism with water was a one-time event, so also the visible descending of the Spirit on Christ did not occur again.

I mention this because we do read in other places that the voice of the Father was heard again. When the Lord Jesus was on the mount of transfiguration, a voice from the cloud said, "This is my Son, whom I love; with him I am well-pleased. Listen to him!" (Mat 17:5). However, only Peter, James, and John were present to hear this voice.

Later, after Christ's triumphal entry into Jerusalem, when he is troubled and prays, "Father, glorify your name," there is again a voice from heaven, "I have glorified it and I will glorify it again." (John 12:28). Those who are standing around knew that something special had occurred, but they could not understand what was said. They thought it was either thunder or the voice of an angel.

A visible descending?

In both these instances the understanding of what the voice says, is limited. The text here in Matthew 3 does not tell us how many people were present at the baptism of Jesus. So we are not sure whether, besides John the Baptist any, few, or many saw that "heaven was opened." We also do not know how many people actually saw the appearing of a figure as a dove over Jesus, and heard a voice from heaven.

We know from verse 5 that people out of the whole region flocked to John the Baptist at the river Jordan. John also had a number of disciples who were involved in his work. They were with John constantly and possibly assisted him in baptizing the multitudes who came. It stands to reason, then, that some of these people saw and heard what John did see and hear: heaven opened, a dove descending, and a voice speaking.

Matthew twice even uses a word that has for some unclear reason been left out in the NIV translation, even without footnotes. It is the word "see" or "behold." The RSV properly has, "And when Jesus was baptized, he went up immediately from the water, and *behold*, the heavens were opened and he saw the Spirit of God descending like a dove and alighting upon him; and *lo*, a voice came from heaven saying, 'This is my beloved Son, with whom I am well pleased.'" This implies clearly that there is something to be seen and heard. There was a visible manifestation and an audible declaration.

Official presentation

Now basically it is not of decisive importance for the truth of what is recorded whether only John the Baptist (and Jesus) or also others saw and heard these things. John the Baptist later testifies about what he *himself* clearly saw and heard, and does not mention others (John 1:32-34). But it is important for us to note that what was seen and heard functioned as a visible and audible *sign from above* that Jesus of Nazareth is truly the Christ of God, a sign that was clearly observed by John the Baptist, the one, trustworthy witness who really counts. It was a sign from above precisely at that specific moment.

For the baptism of our Lord Jesus is his official and legitimate presentation to Israel as the Messiah of God. Coming forward to be baptized is a public act of commitment to God to place himself under the law of righteousness. Jesus will be "cleansed" and set aside for service to the very same kingdom which he embodies and secures. The great King comes as a humble servant to be baptized. But his identification and authentification are not made lesser by it: *immediately* thereafter heaven is opened, a dove descends, and a voice is heard from above, and Matthew presents this clearly as a divine token, a very important sign, and undisputable proof: behold, look!

When the Lord Jesus comes out of the water and proceeds to the shore, it says, heaven was *opened*. The verb is a very intensive verb, and some translate: heaven was rent asunder or torn open, not for a long vision, but for a brief interlude. When the great Son of God thus presents himself for his public ministry on earth, heaven cannot remain uninvolved and aloof. When the Son comes to his point of appearing to Israel, the Father and the Spirit cannot remain hidden, for they, too, are fully *involved* in the one work of salvation. It is the work of the Father, the Son, and the Holy Spirit by which we are saved.

We may speak (e.g. in the Heidelberg Catechism, Lord's Day 8) about God the Son and our *redemption*, and he is indeed our one Redeemer, but his work is not loose from the love of Father and without the fellowship of the Holy Spirit. Heaven, as it were, breaks open, and the glory of the Triune God is manifest, Father, Son, and Spirit.

We should not here isolate the Spirit from the Father, but see the application of the Spirit as connected to the proclamation of the Father and the dedication of the Son. The descending of the Spirit upon Jesus at this precise moment means that he who was ordained by the Father to be our only Savior, now is anointed by the Holy Spirit to function fully as our perfect Savior. Ordination – official appointment – and anointing – or complete equipping – always go together, for God equips whomever he appoints. This is how it has always been, and so it is especially now.

Did the Lord need this sign?

Did Jesus, then, *need* to be equipped? Did he miss something before this anointing? Was he unsure of himself? This cannot be the case. There was nothing lacking that needed to be given. There were no uncertainties that needed to be taken away. Such conclusions are offensive to God. But do remember that the Lord came into the weakness of human flesh, in the form of a servant, one who came to humble and even empty himself. This public presentation means: in Jesus the Triune God officially manifests himself for our salvation. The sign of this is baptism. Baptism points to the anointing with the Spirit. For in this work, the Lord indeed will be guided by the Spirit of God, just as he will be surrounded by the love of the Father, so that *we* may surely know that our entire salvation rests in him alone.

We must clearly understand that it was not first for Christ's sake that these things happened. That's often the direction explainers take. The Lord's humanity is stressed. At this point, they say, Jesus needs reassurance and he also gets it in these signs. Indeed, he will have been greatly encouraged by them. As our Mediator, come into the flesh, he will require encouragement and support from above. He knew this himself, for he relentlessly searched out the Father in prayer. But the dove and the voice, the signs, are first meant for John the Baptist, for *us*, for the holy, Catholic Church, so that we may all know how Jesus was called, ordained and anointed to perform his task as the great Shepherd and Lord of the flock.

The point is not whether Jesus ever doubted himself, for he knew exactly who he was and what he had to do; the point is that we will never doubt him or disbelieve what he did and still does for us. At the very moment he presented himself to enter into his public ministry, these signs happened to confirm that he is indeed the Anointed One, and may we then doubt him, now that he has been glorified and is seated at the Father's right hand?

Fatherly Pride

The Father only spoke, but this was a wonderful and emphatic endorsement of Jesus as our Lord and Savior. It is the official presentation of Jesus as the Son of God. It is as if the pride of Fatherhood shines through: this is my Son! About the Son, then, two things are said. The first is, "whom I love." It is no light matter for the Father to give his only-begotten Son into the flesh of man, so that in the flesh sin might be judged. The love between Father and Son is an eternal, always proceeding, and perfect love.

The Father also says: with him I am well pleased. It can happen that a father has reasons to be displeased with his children, with his son. Sometimes a father can be deeply disappointed with the views and actions of his son. In how many parental hearts is there not a constant, nagging pain over the disobedience of a son or daughter? Sometimes the situation is so extreme that a father needs to disown his son to preserve his own name and sanity. You wonder how we ever come that far sometimes in our families. But it happens: this is my son, with whom I am deeply displeased.

It could even be that some of the people who later see Jesus in his misery on the cross think: surely this man is accursed by God. How can God ever be well pleased in such a man who hangs naked on the cross as a criminal? What great crime did this son commit that he is thus left to die by his own Father? Some say mockingly: he trusted in God, let us see if God will save him (cf. Luke 23:35).

But there is no reason whatsoever for the Father in heaven ever to be displeased with this Son. That needs to be said at his baptism. I find no wrong in him. I am pleased with him. This Son has always done exactly what the Father has required, not out of mere duty, but in true love. Who would not deeply love such a Son?

Many explainers see this verse not so much as a personal endorsement of Jesus as the beloved Son, but as a fulfillment of Psalm 2: he said to me, you are my Son, today I have become your Father! The Son is then the One who shall in the Father's Name destroy all the enemies of the kingdom of heaven. Through this Son the glory of God will forever be established. In Psalm 2 the Son is presented almost in militant terms: kiss the Son, lest he be angry, and you are destroyed in your way, for his wrath can flare up in a moment. This element of Psalm 2 is certainly present, but it really comes to the fore later. I think of Acts 4, where the congregation at Jerusalem appeals to Psalm 2 when persecution begins against the church of the risen and ascended Christ.

In the form of a dove

What we focus on now is that John saw the Holy Spirit "descending like a dove upon and lighting on him." Descending *like* a dove indicates that there was not really a dove, but only the form or shape of a dove. The verb lighting simply means that this form came down over the Lord and disappeared into him, or was taken up by him. I'll come back to that in a moment.

It is clear from the text that this form of a dove is, in truth, as John sees and Matthew writes, the Spirit of God. The question is: why does the Spirit of God manifest himself in this form? When the Holy Spirit was first mentioned in Genesis 1, it was said: the Spirit of God was "hovering" over the waters. This manner of speaking reminds us of a bird, but why, then, a dove? Are not other birds (e.g. eagles) more impressive or suitable?

The dove functions as a symbol of hope and peace. This becomes clear, for example, when Noah lets out a dove from the ark to determine how far the waters of the flood have receded (Gen 8:8). The dove is also a bird that comes "home" again. It may fly out far and wide, but always returns from where it came. Yet a dove is a very fragile bird; in various places in Scripture we read how a dove moans and mourns.

Here the element of peace is also important. Jesus later said: be as shrewd as snakes and as innocent as doves (Mat 10:16). Innocence is meant here as being without any guile or deceit. So a dove also still today is a fragile but enduring symbol of hope, life, freedom, innocence, and of peace.

Why does the Holy Spirit use this form to light upon the Lord? This has something to do with the different characters of Christ's and John's ministry. Remember that John was the Elijah, who came to announce *judgment*. John proclaimed that the axe was already at the root of the tree (Mat 3:10). John functions more as a hawk, not a dove. John spoke about the winnowing fork and the threshing floor, where the wheat is gathered into the barn, but the chaff is burned with unquenchable fire (Mat 3:12). And that is an element which we will also see on the great day of judgment. John's words will never go away, but will all be fulfilled. In the ministry of Jesus Christ on earth, however, there is emphasis on peace, life, hope, and grace.

Ministry of love

The manner of this anointing by the Spirit, "in the form of a dove," tells us that the ministry of our Lord will be one of great love that seeks peace. In this way the Spirit will guide him, and he will fulfill the prophets: the people living in darkness have seen a great light. Jesus will say, quoting from the prophet Isaiah, now is the time of "the year of the Lord's favor." (Luke 4:19; cf. Is 42).

Therefore we may say that the manner of Christ's anointing also indicates the style of his earthly ministry. He came to show forth God's love, to make peace by the shedding of his blood, and to grant us hope for the future. The Lord Jesus went about preaching the love of God for sinners, healing the sick, and driving out demons. It was in sharp contrast with what John actually expected from him, and it is not without reason that John later , when he is in prison, asks Jesus, "Are you the one who was to come, or should we expect someone else?" (Mat 11:2, 3) Then John has to learn not to be offended at Christ, for the Lord works according to the Scriptures. John the Baptist has to go back to the Bible.

The form of a dove qualifies what kind of a ministry Christ will publicly serve in the midst of Israel. He still does so today: showing forth God's love and working love for God, calling us to peace and hope in him, and bringing us to new life that reflects peace and hope also for our neighbor.

We sometimes speak about doves and hawks as peacemakers and warriors. The warrior image is very strong in our society. The peacemaker image has been much distorted. But Jesus said, "Blessed are the peacemakers, for they will be called "sons of God" (Mat 5:9).

The measure of Christ's anointing

We noted earlier that this form of a dove comes down and then *lights* on Jesus. How are we to understand this? Lighting upon someone means gently setting down on him. The Holy Spirit did not come with a loud crash or a heavy thud. There was no sound as of a rushing wind, and no tongues of fire were seen, as later at Pentecost (cf. Acts 2). There was just a form as of a dove descending and lighting upon him, gently, carefully.

This lighting means that the Holy Spirit did not actually land on Jesus' head, or hover above his head, but came over him. The figure of the dove comes over Jesus and completely disappears into him, and that means then that the Spirit fills him fully from top to bottom. Therefore we may speak here about the *measure* of this anointing.

It is a full measure. In this connection we may look at an intriguing passage in John 3:34, where specifically John the Baptist, testifying about Jesus, makes an important point about the relation between Jesus and the Holy Spirit, "For the one whom God has sent speaks the words of God, for God gives the Spirit *without limit.*" I emphasize here the words without limit.

The Spirit came over Christ in a full and complete measure, so that Christ was filled with the Holy Spirit. For the great work of redemption, Christ needed and received as our Savior and Mediator the full measure of the Spirit.

Once Elisha asked from Elijah a *double portion* of Elijah's Spirit. Elijah answered: this is difficult thing, I cannot guarantee it (2 Kgs 2:9, 10). But here Jesus Christ receives the full measure of the Spirit, without limit so that he might also in every way be our complete Redeemer.

When the Spirit comes upon our Lord Jesus Christ after his baptism, it is then without limit so that Christ may draw up out of the Holy Spirit whatever is needed for the great work of redemption. Ever wonder how he could do what he did? Why demons shuddered before him? Because he received the anointing that was without limit to do all that was required for our salvation.

Utterly forsaken

God always gives in full measure. The opposite is that when God withdraws his Spirit, he does so also completely: my God, my God, why have you *forsaken* me? (Mat 27:46) Here lies the heart of Christ's redemptive work. He did it all by the power and will of the Spirit. But when the Spirit departed from him, he stood firm because of his perfect love and divine nature.

It is then no wonder that the risen Lord Jesus Christ can say: I will *send* the Spirit (John 15:26). I will give you the anointing with the Holy Spirit. He who has the fullness of the Spirit, can also fill us with his Spirit and does fill us with the rich blessing of his Spirit. He comes, like the wind blows, in sovereign power and pleasure. He anoints one and all with holy fire. It has been Pentecost. What the Father gives to Christ, Christ now gives to us. From his fullness we have all received grace upon grace, and the Holy Spirit in great measure (cf. John 1:16).

What a strong bond exists between the Father and the Son. What a deep and intense relationship exists between Jesus and the Spirit. All this is now applied to us by the Gospel, and to this we must respond. We may by faith and through prayer in Christ tap into this great love and this rich fellowship every day again.

Here I am

This passage about Christ's anointing with the Spirit, by which he commences his public ministry, leads us today to understand our calling as children of God in a wicked world. Can the Father say of us: behold, my children, in whom I am well-pleased? Would God have any reason to be displeased with us? Do we pray to God for his grace and Spirit every day that we might make progress in the battle against sin?

Christ stepped forward, and said: here I am, let us begin. Now God asks us: where are you? If we are in Christ, we, too, will step forward and say: here I am, to do your will, O God, living from your grace, and walking by your Spirit in accordance with your word.

Here I am.

VI

Born of the Spirit

"In reply Jesus declared, 'I tell you the truth, no one can see the kingdom of God unless he is born again.' 'How can a man be born again when he is old?' Nicodemus asked. 'Surely he cannot enter a second time into his mother's womb to be born!' Jesus answered, 'I tell you the truth, no one can enter the kingdom of God unless he is born of water and the Spirit'."

(JOHN 3:3-5)

A book of meditations about the Person and work of the Holy Spirit would be incomplete if attention was not given to what is related in John 3 about the matter of rebirth, as it came up in a conversation between the Lord and Nicodemus. The Lord Jesus had a rather remarkable talk with the Pharisee Nicodemus. Through this conversation we receive deeper insight into the key matter of rebirth and, more importantly, the work of the Holy Spirit in this respect.

The passage in verse 7, "you must be born again," is perhaps one of the most-used and most-quoted texts of Scripture. A passage of such fame generally starts to lead a life of its own, and becomes almost like a slogan for a single cause. Some movements have based their whole theology on this single aspect of being reborn. We will not deny the importance of this aspect, but must seek to understand it properly.

The identity of Jesus of Nazareth

In order for us to determine what this passage means, it is important that we look at this passage in its *context*. We learn that the purpose of this meeting was not to engage in a theoretical, theological discussion about regeneration. The discussion was (and still is) very concretely about the true identity of Jesus of Nazareth.

For Nicodemus comes with a question (verse 2). It is a veiled question. Like a true member of the Jewish ruling council, Nicodemus is a careful and diplomatic man. But nevertheless it is a very obvious question.

The fact that Nicodemus comes at night is often interpreted as resulting from fear of his fellow-Pharisees, but this need not be the case. Sometimes the best time for a deeper and longer discussion is at night, when there is peace and quiet. Nicodemus really wants to get to the bottom of things here, and needs the time and privacy with the Lord Jesus to do so.

The real question

What exactly is his question? We find in verse 2, "Rabbi, we know you are a teacher who has come from God. For no one could perform the miraculous signs you are doing if God were not with him." By "we" (plural) Nicodemus must mean himself and many of his fellow Pharisees. Not everyone might perhaps be open about it like Nicodemus is here, but everyone, including the Jewish rulers, knew that Jesus was special. His signs and wonders were too convincing to dismiss him lightly. The Lord Jesus indeed takes the "we" to mean the Pharisees and the other members of the ruling council. See verse 11, where we find: you, people (plural), do not accept our testimony.

Nicodemus is asking: who are you really? Surely Jesus is someone who came from God, a miracle worker, a prophet of sorts, but is he the one whom the Jews ardently expect, the great Messiah? By leaving the question unspoken, Nicodemus actually emphasizes it. Note that the Lord does not directly answer the unspoken question either. He does not say: I am, or am not, the Messiah. Instead he indicates that the matter goes much deeper: no one can see the kingdom of God unless he is born again (verse 3).

Rebirth: a divine working

To come to the right conclusion about Jesus Christ, much more is needed than any human reasoning or conclusion. What is needed is nothing less than rebirth, and this is what a person cannot do on his own. It is remarkable that many have taken this passage to demonstrate the need for a personal human decision and commitment. But that is what this very passage actually denies. We learn that rebirth is nothing less than a mighty work of God through the Holy Spirit, which is needed by everyone who will enter the kingdom of heaven.

We will look at three aspects here. This passage emphasizes the necessity of rebirth. It acknowledges the mystery of rebirth. And it rejoices in the simplicity of rebirth. The prevailing line is that rebirth is not a human achievement, but it is the working of the Holy Spirit in us. Without the Spirit, the bride cannot be reborn and adorned for the Lord.

Rebirth: a very serious matter

Nicodemus comes with an unspoken question. At this point in his ministry our Lord's emphasis in his teaching is on the coming of the kingdom of heaven. See, for example,. Matthew 4:17, "From that time on Jesus began to preach: repent for the kingdom of heaven is near." He therefore responds to Nicodemus in this vein as well (verse 3), "I tell you the truth, no one can see the kingdom of heaven unless he is born again."

The words "I tell you the truth" are the translation of "Amen, amen." Whenever the Lord uses these words, he indicates that what follows is not only true, but is of the *utmost importance*. The Lord Jesus repeats the double amen (verse 5) to counter Nicodemus' rather silly response: how can a man be born when he is old? Surely he cannot enter a second time into his mother's womb to be born? The Lord then strongly indicates that this rebirth is a very serious matter.

The double amen even has the quality of emphasizing what precedes it. Nicodemus can say that the Jewish leaders know that Jesus has come from God, but little do they know how true it is. And they will never begin to see how true it is, and so enter the kingdom of God, unless they are born again.

Notice that the Lord uses two different verbs here. In verse 3 we read: no one can *see* the kingdom of God, unless he is born again. Seeing is here meant in the sense of "discerning." In verse 5, after Nicodemus' light-hearted retort, the Lord tightens up the matter: no one can *enter* the kingdom of God unless he is born of water and the Spirit. To see the kingdom, even more, to enter that kingdom and be saved, one definitely needs to be born again. There is here not a mere repetition but a progress of thought. Rebirth is vital; do not make light of it.

Supernatural

At first the Lord Jesus used only the expression: if someone is not born anew, he cannot see the kingdom of heaven. However, the verb can also be translated as born *from above* (as the NIV text note indicates). The idea of being born from *above* is apparently not close at all to what Nicodemus understands, for he takes it in a natural and earthly manner. Therefore the Lord Jesus has to explain further that being born anew means being born of "water and the Spirit." Rebirth is not a natural matter, but something that is *supernatural*.

This is precisely one of the words used by the *Canons of Dort* to describe regeneration, " (III/IV, Article 12), "This conversion is the regeneration, the new creation, the raising from the dead, the making alive, so highly spoken of in the Scriptures, which God works in us without us. But this regeneration is by no means brought about only by outward teaching, by moral persuasion, or by such a mode of operation that, after God has done his part, it remains in the power of man to be regenerated or not regenerated, converted or not converted. It is, however, clearly a *supernatural*, most powerful, and at the same time most delightful, marvelous, mysterious and inexplicable work."

Is Nicodemus serious?

How are we to regard the response of Nicodemus to Christ's first statement about rebirth? Nicodemus talks about literally entering again into the mother's womb to be born. Surely the Lord Jesus cannot mean that! Is Nicodemus trying to be funny, or is he serious? Or is he, perhaps, just plain ignorant? In verse 10 we read that the Lord says: you are Israel's teacher, and do you not *understand* these things? Is it a lack of understanding? There is a sense of reproach in the Lord's question.

All this prompts us to ask in general: did the Jewish leaders really not understand anything about rebirth, regeneration, or renewal? Did they know of its necessity? I think it is safe to say that they did know. They knew about the necessity of a new heart (Psalm 51). They knew about the coming new covenant when the law would be written on the hearts of God's people (Jeremiah 31). The Jews referred to a proselyte (a convert to Judaism) as a child newly-born. If you wanted to be a part of the covenant people, you had to be like a new-born child. A whole new beginning must be made. If Nicodemus knew all this, why did he respond in such a flippant manner?

At bottom the matter is not so difficult to understand. Birth is the beginning of physical life outside the womb. Rebirth is the beginning of spiritual life. As we are born to live in this world, we must be reborn to enter God's kingdom and to function in this world as God's children. Did Nicodemus not know of this basic truth?

A tactical move?

Various answers are given to these questions. Maybe Nicodemus was deliberately trying to feign ignorance because he did not like the direction of the conversation. This is a common tactic: pretend you do not understand. Perhaps as a Pharisee he did not like to be addressed as someone who has to make a whole new start like a proselyte. Or maybe he was trying to say that an entirely new start is impossible in life. After all, we carry with us all kinds of baggage, from our upbringing, our past, and our life's flow, and it is impossible to start over. It's nice to talk about rebirth, but it is really an impossible matter, like coming again out of your mother's womb. Anyway, it is clear that Nicodemus cannot really work with this concept of rebirth.

What about you? Can you work with it? Do you become uncomfortable or uncertain when it is said that you have to be born again, and when the necessity of rebirth is stressed? Does this bring us suddenly into uncharted waters, into the open ocean of which we do not know where our vessel will go? Rebirth is taught in the Scriptures, confessed in our creeds, but does it also function in our lives?

Born of water and the Spirit

The Lord Jesus does not retreat one inch because of Nicodemus' reaction. Typically, he makes his previous statement even clearer and stronger. No one can enter the kingdom of God unless he is born of water and the Spirit! Nicodemus may not evade the issue. Do not use any debating tactics here to get away from the real point. It is not a physical matter, as Nicodemus can well know. If it must be said more plainly and clearly, let it be so: unless one is born of water and the Spirit, he cannot enter the kingdom of God.

What does it mean to be born of water and the Spirit? Again we must consider the context. John the Baptist was at that very time baptizing with water. What did this baptism with water mean? It was symbolic of the washing away of sins. It meant also that one entered a new life, a life that is dedicated to the service of God. The Jews knew all about water baptism. They knew of washings and cleansings in the law. They had a special proselyte baptism which was required (besides circumcision) for any heathen to become like a Jew and have access to the temple of the LORD.

An entirely new life

Nicodemus knew that baptism with water meant beginning a whole new life, not in a physical sense, but in a deeply spiritual manner. To make sure that Nicodemus did fully understand, the Lord added born of water *and the Spirit*. John the Baptist was the one who first very clearly spoke to the Jews about the fact that baptism with the Spirit was necessary. The water is an outward sign of what must take place internally. And then John the Baptist (see John 1:29-36) clearly and unmistakably identified Jesus of Nazareth as the one who would do this great work: bring about the forgiveness of sins and grant renewal of life.

Nicodemus asked: who are you really? Jesus answered: John the Baptist identified very clearly who I am, but you need rebirth to grasp it in faith. You need a whole new beginning, a new way of looking at things, and a totally unobstructed openness to my words and works by the working of the Holy Spirit so that you may confess me and embrace me as the Messiah of God.

The Lord Jesus adds a simple but important sentence: flesh gives birth to flesh, but the Spirit gives birth to spirit. We are not talking about our natural birth into the flesh, but we are talking about spiritual birth in the kingdom. This birth can only be brought about by the Holy Spirit.

Rebirth is mysterious

Perhaps the Lord saw that Nicodemus was surprised at what he was saying. In any case he adds: you should not be surprised at my saying: you must be born again! It is not as if Nicodemus is now being confronted with something never spoken of before. But there is an element which is not easily understood: this rebirth by the Spirit is mysterious.

The Lord Jesus uses the example of the wind. This is possible, as we saw earlier, because in the original the word for Spirit and wind are the same. The Spirit is in a certain sense like the wind: you hear it, but cannot see it. You feel it, but you do not know its origin. It goes by, and you do not know exactly where it is headed. Above all, the Spirit is sovereign: the wind blows where it pleases. No one can govern it, guide it, direct it, claim it, capture it, govern it, or limit it. The wind brings the water that brings the crops to grow. The Spirit of God causes the new life to start and sprout so that we may bring forth fruit unto God.

What is of interest here is that the working of the Spirit is experienced, just like you can feel the wind, but this working remains *mysterious*,

beyond our vision and control. Rebirth is completely from beginning to end a work of the Holy Spirit alone, and since it is mysterious, we cannot comprehend it or customize it. Therefore we must be careful when speaking about rebirth. We should not try to make it into something that we can bring about through some extra sensory perception devices. Mysterious means that we know this work exists, takes place, and can be experienced, but it can never be fully explained or comprehended.

The Canons of Dort, as we saw in the quote given earlier, use the same word mysterious to describe regeneration or rebirth (III/IV, Article 12). The church has believed and confessed these things for centuries.

In us, without us

God himself by his Holy Spirit must change us, renew us, and grant us in his mercy and love a new beginning, a spiritual birth. Otherwise we will never see, much less ever enter, the kingdom of God. I think that one point then stands out very clearly. The Spirit of God alone initiates spiritual life. We cannot by any attempt or act from our side bring about this regeneration. It is the work of God in us, without us (i.e. without our effort), and for us, and it is done because of God's sovereign grace.

It becomes clear that this is an important element when you compare this teaching of the Lord Jesus with the official Judaist line of the Pharisees of whom Nicodemus was a member. The Judaists taught that good works are meritorious. They earn salvation. Keep the law and live. Salvation is at bottom a matter of the human will and effort. But Jesus says: forget it; there is no way that you can bring this new life about, not even by any well-intentioned effort. It is a mystery which points to one source: God's sovereign and omnipotent grace.

So it is with everyone born of the Spirit. Those born anew will not stress their effort, but confess God's grace. This is not a matter of arguing about words or of finding the right formulation. This is the essence of our Christian faith. This is also the experience of the Christian faith: you hear the wind, but cannot tell from where it comes and where it does. Why me, Lord? What have I ever done to deserve even one of the blessings you give? I have certainly not deserved the great blessing of redemption, salvation from sin and death.

Straightforward

Let rebirth be mysterious, there is one thing about it that is very simple and straightforward: it leads us to Christ. Sometimes we unnecessarily make things very complicated or complex. About regeneration and its effects there has been much debate and strife, also in the Reformed churches. It touches a personal level: how do I know that I am born again? The emphasis then comes to lie sometimes on the fruits of faith, or on the good works that must follow from faith.

It can be a proper and healthy emphasis. By its fruits true faith is known (Hymn 24, *Book of Praise*). But it can also be lethal or deadly, if not properly understood. Paul warns us in Galatians 3 about the danger we face. He exclaims: O foolish Galatians! After beginning with the Spirit, are you now trying to attain your goal by human effort? (verse 3) When we start with the sure faith that we are saved by grace alone, we would still derail if we suggested in any way that our works have a bearing on being saved.

Discussions about rebirth can sometimes be endlessly complicated. Let us understand the true simplicity of it all. Where did the whole nightly discussion with Nicodemus lead to? It led to the wondrous declaration of John 3:16: for God so loved the world that he gave his one and only (only-begotten) Son that *whoever believes in him shall not perish but have everlasting life*. This is the simplicity of rebirth. It leads to faith in Christ and him crucified. Do you believe that Jesus Christ is your one and only Savior?

A key question

The discussion on rebirth leads to a key question: do you believe that Jesus Christ died for your sins and that in him you are forgiven and have received the gift of eternal life? If you do, the floodgates of thankfulness will go open. The simplicity of rebirth, of living faith in Jesus Christ and him crucified, will lead to the activity of rebirth: a life of thankfulness and good works to the glory of God.

Rebirth must be given to us, or we cannot be saved. Rebirth is given in a clear and yet a mysterious manner. Rebirth leads to one hope. This hope is in Jesus Christ, our crucified and risen Lord. This is called the hope of faith. This faith activates us to a life of service.

Let it be so.

VII

The Holy Spirit given as the other Counselor

"And I will ask the Father, and he will give you another Counselor to be with you forever – the Spirit of truth."

(JOHN 14:16, 17A)

"What do you believe concerning the Holy Spirit?
First, he is together with the Father and the Son, true and eternal God.
Second, he is also given to me, to make me by true faith share in Christ and all his benefits, to comfort me, and to remain with me forever".

(HEIDELBERG CATECHISM, LORD'S DAY 20, BOOK OF PRAISE)

When we speak about the Person and work of the Holy Spirit we can do so in a very theoretical manner by merely expounding the doctrine. This approach, however, will not really help or satisfy. The danger is that we run the risk of knowing a lot about the Holy Spirit, but not knowing him ourselves.

How can we be sure that we really have the Holy Spirit? There is in our time again a renewed emphasis on "experiential" faith, and thus also on experiential preaching.

What is meant here by the word experiential?[6] It means that we have to experience somehow that we are truly children of God. It must be an experience to be a Christian. Faith is a life-changing power, and herein especially we may see the work of the Holy Spirit.

The Reformed churches have always stressed this aspect of faith. In the *Heidelberg Catechism* there is a section on God the Holy Spirit and our sanctification (Lord's Day 20). Sanctification means that our life is being made holy and is renewed. When we speak about the Holy Spirit, we acknowledge that the Spirit brings about change or new life. This change is something that we must and do experience. Can you change without knowing it?

The promises of God

A new life is something that we may joyfully experience for it is one of the great promises given to us already at our baptism: the Holy Spirit promises that he will dwell in us, imparting to us what we have in Christ (Form for the Baptism of Infants, *Book of Praise*, page 584 ff.). This promise is real, and we may build on it, work with it, and plead on it. In that sense we should speak about the Holy Spirit in a very child-like and confident manner, as the Heidelberg Catechism also does.

For the tone of the catechism is very striking. It asks: what do you believe concerning the Holy Spirit? The intent is not to discover what we believe on the basis of our experiences, for human experience is sometimes untrustworthy, but on the basis of God's Word, his given promises.

What do you believe concerning the Holy Spirit? The answer is very straightforward: He is true God; He is also given me, to comfort me, and to remain with me forever. I just picked out some elements of the answer which show us the calm confidence of faith.

Yet it may be asked whether this manner of speaking about the Holy Spirit is not presumptive. May I simply say that he is also given me? Is he not given only to true believers? How can I be sure that I am among these true believers?

---

[6] The word "experiential" is a poor translation of the Dutch word "bevindelijk." Actually the word experiential does not really function in Anglo-Saxon/American theology. It denotes a conscious undergoing of some concrete and strong, spiritual experience which authenticates a person as a true believer.

Notice that the catechism also mentions the element of faith: to make me by true faith share in Christ and all His benefits. But first comes the Spirit, and then comes faith. The Holy Spirit is given to make us by faith share in Christ. Otherwise we never would become believers. The very existence of faith is already evidence of the work of the Holy Spirit. Without the Spirit of Christ there would be no church, no faith, no sanctification, and no spiritual life.

Three are One

The catechism, therefore, teaches us to rejoice in the presence of God the Holy Spirit. In the presence of the Holy Spirit we also receive the Father and the Son. Note how the catechism stresses that the Holy Spirit is together with the Father and the Son true and eternal God. This means that we cannot have the One without the others. The Three are one. The work of the Holy Spirit may therefore never be made loose from the work of the Father and the Son.

This may seem pretty straightforward, but it is very important. In John 14:16 the Lord Jesus speaks about the coming of the Holy Spirit. We find there these words, "And I will pray the Father, and he will give you another Counselor, to be with you forever...." This text lies at the bottom of Lord's Day 20: the Spirit is given, and he stays forever. It is almost as if this text is quoted literally in the catechism.

Jesus says: I (the Son) will pray the Father, and he will send the Spirit. Father, Son, and Holy Spirit are together. They belong together, come together, and work together, as we saw also when discussing the baptism of Jesus. In that sense there is no separate experiencing of the Holy Spirit: you receive either the full blessing of the Triune God or you receive nothing. The Spirit may be distinguished from the Father and the Son, but not separated. I mention this again to show the Biblical foundation and importance of the first sentence of this answer: [the Spirit] is together with the Father and the Son true and eternal God. The doctrine of the Holy Trinity is crucial for our understanding of the Person and work of the Holy Spirit.

Pending Departure

When the Lord Jesus said, "I will pray the Father and he will give you another Counselor to be with you forever," he was talking about his pending departure, his ascension. He would die, be raised from the dead, and then go to the Father. That is the context in John 14 which must be appreciated.

69

Christ spoke about these monumental events in such a simple and open way. He said: I am going to the Father's house, and I am going to prepare a place for you there. When that is done, I will come and take you so that we may be always together.

He concluded simply (verses 3 and 4): so you know where I am and how to get there. But Thomas said to him: but, Lord, we don't know where you are going, let alone how to get there ourselves. Then follow Jesus' well-known words: you do know; I am the way, and the truth, and the life. You can go to the Father by me.

The Lord then speaks about the work that the disciples must do in the meantime and how they must live through prayer. In the interim it is our calling to pray and to work. But Christ adds: I will not leave you on your own, by yourselves, "I will pray the Father, and he will give you another Counselor, to be with you forever." The disciples will not be left alone, for another Counselor, the Holy Spirit, will come and he will stay forever.

Pentecost: the Spirit given

We know that this promise of Christ was fulfilled on the day of Pentecost. Then the Spirit came to stay in the church. It is in this light that we understand what the Heidelberg Catechism means, when it says: he is also given to me. The Spirit is *given*. No one can claim the Spirit. No one can take the Spirit. No one controls the Spirit. No one deserves the Spirit. He is simply given by the Father and through the Son. We do not climb up to the Spirit, but he comes down to us.

It says in the catechism: he is given *also* to me. There is a sense of awe and amazement in that little word *also*, for we do not receive the Holy Spirit on our own or just by ourselves. We receive the Spirit together with others. The expression, also to me, means that others, too, have been given the Spirit.

Who are these others? It can be no otherwise than that these others are the fellow members of the church of Christ. For the Spirit is not poured out over single individuals – that's not the essence of Pentecost – but over all the believers gathered that day. The whole body shares in the anointing of its Head, Jesus Christ. It says in Acts 2:7: they were *all* filled with the Holy Spirit.

The Holy Spirit was poured out over the church of Christ. In that sense, since I belong to the church, he is given also to me. That is what the catechism means. This is our joy: together we may share in the presence and gifts of the Holy Spirit.

Given to the church of Christ

Now we have to keep this simple. Someone might ask: does this mean that every single member of the church has the Holy Spirit simply because he is a member? What about unbelievers in the church? Are there not hypocrites in the church? It is dangerous to say that everyone in the church has the Spirit. It is also rather presumptuous, for only true believers have the Spirit of God. So I should say: *if* you are a true believer, then you have the Spirit, and otherwise you do not have the Spirit. And you'd better start doing something about it.

That's not how the Bible speaks. What we read in Scripture is this: the Holy Spirit is given to the church of Christ. This is a tremendous and joyful reality. As members of the church we may and we must stand and grow in that reality. We should not doubt this reality and spurn this grace. We must be careful that we do not grieve or quench this Spirit, for, indeed, unbelievers and hypocrites will not last in the realm of the Holy Spirit.

That's also the sense of Paul's statements about the Holy Spirit in Romans 8:9, "You, however, are controlled not by the sinful nature, but by the Spirit, if the Spirit of God lives in you." Paul does not make this controlling indwelling of the Spirit questionable, but he appeals to the Roman believers' own experience: if the Spirit of God lives in you. Is it not so that he does? Is that not a fact, a joyous reality?

He is also given to me. Now, of course, the calling that comes with this promise is that I then place myself where the Spirit works, namely in the church of Christ. I will go to church, hear the Word, believe the Word, and strive to live the Word. I will be found in the fellowship of the saints. Psalm 16: I love thy saints, with them I am united, and in their midst my soul will be delighted (*Book of Praise*). The Spirit dwells and works in the midst of the saints.

If you want to receive something, you have to go where it is given. It is true that the wind blows where it wills, and the Spirit of God is almighty and sovereign, but we have to go where the Spirit has been poured out, where the Word of life is proclaimed, and there we must begin to set ourselves under the power of the Holy Spirit. In the fellowship of the saints we find also the fellowship of the Holy Spirit. When we seek the Spirit in faith and in truth where he can be found, he will be found. He will find us. That is the promise of the Lord Jesus Christ.

VII · *The Holy Spirit given as the other Counselor*

Corporate or Personal?

Someone might ask if it is not dangerous to speak of the Holy Spirit in a corporate sense that he is given to the church, for is it not the work of the Spirit to dwell in persons and in person's hearts, and not, as such, in a larger, perhaps undefined, body? Should we not speak about the Spirit in a personal sense, as the catechism also does, given to me, rather than in a corporate sense, given to the church?

We should not make any false dilemma's here, as if everything can be pressed into a certain scheme. The church is not an undefined body, but a visible gathering of saints. When we seek the Holy Spirit, where he is given in the fellowship of the saints, it becomes very personal.

The Holy Spirit is very active, and indeed he works in our hearts. Our Lord said it this way in John 14:17: for he lives with you and will be in you. The Lord Jesus here uses the word you in the plural (meaning all the disciples) Therefore we can speak of the indwelling of the Holy Spirit in the church. In this way he dwells within us, in our hearts. This indwelling makes the work of the Spirit for everyone a very personal matter. Emphasis on the corporate aspect of the Spirit's work does not deny his work in persons. United to Christ, we are also united with his body (cf. I Cor 12:12-27,"…Now you are the body of Christ, and each one of you is a part of it…") These things belong together.

The Spirit makes us share in Christ

The catechism shows us something of this when it says about the work of the Holy Spirit that he is given me "to make me by a true faith share in Christ and all His benefits." The Holy Spirit makes us share in Christ. That is here the central element. The Holy Spirit binds us to Christ and through Christ to the Father.

The Holy Spirit does not tell us how great and good we are, but he leads us to Christ. In John 16:14 we find this stated very strongly, "He (the Spirit) will bring glory to me (Christ), by taking from what is mine and making it known to you." Notice the next verse 15, "All that belongs to the Father is mine. That is why I said the Spirit will take from what is mine and make it known to you." So the Holy Spirit takes from Christ, who has received from the Father, and he then gives to us. See again the unity in the Trinity.

We must realize that the great work of the Holy Spirit is to make us share in Christ and all his benefits. The Spirit is Christ-directed and so

oriented to the Father also. What the Holy Spirit does, is take us and lead us to the Lord Jesus, and says: receive all the blessings of your Savior.

The Holy Spirit is then the living Person who unites us with the Son and through the Son with the Father. How does he do this? It says: we share in Christ by true faith. Faith is the only possible linkage. The Holy Spirit brings about this immense miracle that he works faith in us, and by that faith we start to reach out to Christ and receive him and all his benefits. The Spirit took my hand and put my hand in the hand of the man from Galilee, as the song goes. The Spirit has one message: look away from yourself; look only to Jesus.

Faith is the Connection

Faith is the connection. The catechism reminds us that this must be true faith. That is not meant to make us doubt the quality of our faith, but to remind us of the genuine character of faith. For what is true faith? That is explained in Lord's Day 7 of the Heidelberg Catechism. True faith is unconditional acceptance of all that is promised in the Gospel and (at the same time) a complete trust that these promises are true for me. True faith is simply that I know deep within my heart that the Gospel is true for me. Jesus loves me, this I know, because the Bible tells me so.

And so the work of the Holy Spirit goes deep into the heart. He works in us faith, and feeds and nurtures that faith. To this end he is constantly with us and in us. He lives in us, and we have become temples of that Spirit. He makes alive what is dead, restores what is lost, and strengthens what is weak. We confess joyfully that the Spirit never ceases in this work. If he did, we'd be lost. We build on him alone. We accept the promise of his permanent indwelling. And then it truly becomes a wonderful experience.

The other Counselor

For this work of the Holy Spirit is known and experienced by us. How could this great miracle of faith be happening in our lives, and we do not know of it? The catechism speaks of this when it says that the Holy Spirit is given to *comfort* me and to remain with me forever.

The Spirit is given to comfort me. The Lord Jesus called him *the Counselor*. Actually it says in John 14:16: another Counselor. So we already had one, namely, Jesus himself. But since the Lord Jesus is going to the Father, he will give us another Counselor who will never depart from us. That again is the context. Jesus is saying: I have to leave you (ascension) but the

Holy Spirit will come (Pentecost) and he will always stay with the church, with you.

This does not mean that Jesus is not with us anymore. We also believe that with respect to his divinity, majesty, grace and Spirit, Christ is never absent from us (*Heidelberg Catechism*, Lord's Day 18, Matthew 28:19). It means that Christ is with us in the Holy Spirit, and the Holy Spirit never leaves. After his outpouring, he stays. Pentecost can never be reversed.

The name Counselor

The name *Counselor* is beautiful. Sometimes it is rendered as in the original, which has the word *Paraclete*. Literally it means: someone who is called in to give help in an official capacity. Christ has the right to ask the Father to send the Spirit; he has earned that privilege on the cross. So the Spirit comes officially to stay. He does not do free-lance work, but is commissioned to stay forever with God's people.

He has come to help and to comfort us. The word comfort basically means: to give strength. We certainly do need help and strength, for our faith is weak and the enemy is strong. There are so many adverse conditions that might lead us to doubt and draw us away from Christ and from the church. Satan likes to take us by the hand and lead us down a path of desperation and doom.

How is the Spirit then known? He will not permit Satan to succeed. He hangs on to us. As much as we may feel the magnetic pull of this world, the call of the Gospel is stronger. As often as we feel the world trying to swallow us, the embrace of Christ is more powerful. Whenever we wonder if we will persevere, we are reminded of the fact that the Spirit will stay with us forever.

Jesus said: I go to the Father, and I will come back to get you. In the meantime I will ask the Father to send you another Counselor, a real helper, and he will stay with you always. I know that you need this Counselor. This Counselor will connect you to me and to the Father, and you will be fine.

Let us look now at John 14:17. Jesus speaks there about the Spirit of truth, and says, "The world cannot accept him, because it neither sees him nor knows him. But you know him, for he lives with you and will be in you."

There are immense ramifications here. You know him. The world does not see or know him. That's why they cannot receive him. The world wants nothing to do with the Son, Jesus Christ. The church, not the world,

is the object of the Spirit's attention. The world cannot recognize the Holy Spirit. They do not understand whom or what Christians are talking about.

You know him

But, says the Lord, you know him. Why do we know him? We know him because he is living in us. How could we have this Spirit and not know it? How could we have this Spirit and not show it? How could all the gifts of Christ flow to us through the Spirit and not become evident in our lives?

You know him. It means to have intimate knowledge of and personal fellowship with the Holy Spirit. When the Spirit comes to you, said the Lord, you'll know him. Is this because you are so good or because you have better eyes than the world? Is it because you are smarter? We don't read that anywhere in Scripture. We know him because the Spirit of God is given to the church of Christ, and as living members of this church, we experience the comfort and strength of the Spirit.

The Holy Spirit can be known and is known in the Christian life. His presence is a great comfort. This does not mean that our relationship with the Spirit is always so good. We often give the Spirit – to use a blunt expression – a very rough time. The Bible warns us for that. We are warned not to grieve or quench the Spirit. We should not make things difficult for the Holy Spirit within us. We will only increase our own pain and sorrow. We will look at these passages more closely later.

The presence of the Holy Spirit is also shown in the Christian life in works of faith, in a service of love, in humility, and in hope. But all these works are only the fruits of faith and fruit of the Spirit. They are simply evidence of a living faith.

We can not climb over the wall of the sheepfold through our faith and its works. There is only one way into the sheepfold. Jesus said: I am the door (John 10:7). The Spirit leads us to and through this door.

The presence of the Spirit is known. You know him, Jesus said. The power of the Spirit is shown. You crucify the flesh with its demands, said Paul (Galatians 5:24). Paul actually states that those who belong to Christ *have* crucified the sinful nature with its passions and desires. We have this reality only in Christ. This is not yet perfect in us. But it has begun. One day the Spirit's work in this respect will be finished. Then Christ will present us to the Father as a Bride without spot or blemish.

 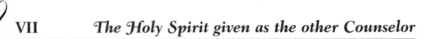

VIII

The Holy Spirit and the World

When he comes, he will convict the world of guilt in regard to sin and righteousness and judgment; in regard to sin, because men do not believe in me; in regard to righteousness, because I am going to the Father, where you can see me no longer; and in regard to judgment because the prince of this world now stands condemned.

(JOHN 16:8-11)

Often passages which tell us about the work of the Holy Spirit speak of the work which the Holy Spirit does *within* us. The Holy Spirit opens our minds and hearts for God's Word, by which he works in us faith, and so we come to serve God. All this activity of the Spirit is internal; it has to do with inward renewal, personal piety and heart-felt holiness. Our focus is often: what does the Spirit do for me and within me? It is a legitimate and important focus, but it should not be the only one.

In a next chapter we will look at a text which tells us about the inward working of the Spirit. The present passage speaks about the work of the Holy Spirit in the *world*. This is a fascinating angle and important aspect of the Spirit's work which we should not neglect. The Holy Spirit's radius of operation is wider than the scope of the pious Christian or the introverted church. He will convict the *world*, it says. The word *kosmos* is used, that means, the world as a vast, created entity and organic unity, that has become hostile to God through the fall into sin. This world has its own prince or ruler, namely, the devil, as the Lord Jesus has repeatedly

noted (John 12:31; 14:30). Something is happening in this world by the power of the Holy Spirit.

Common Grace?

It says that the Holy Spirit will convict the world. It is important to note that this passage is sometimes used to defend what is known as common grace or prevenient grace, the idea being that the Holy Spirit has given to *all* people a sense of sin and guilt, a longing for truth, a yearning for God, and that everyone is therefore, in principle, ready for the Gospel. All they really need is to be addressed. All entry ports are open; only the right connections must be made.

By this prevenient grace all people are still by nature favorably disposed towards God. It is suggested that some people can even know him and be righteous *without* the preaching of the Gospel. This is the classic Arminian position. Some people simply are nobler than others.

We also should note that this passage is unique in Scripture. No where else is spoken about "convicting the world." To build a grand system of prevenient or common grace on one text is rather weak. The consistent testimony of Scripture is rather the complete opposite: people are *not* by nature inclined to hear the Gospel but are prone to reject it immediately. The word convicting already suggests that its takes a lot of work to bring someone to accept the Lord Jesus Christ.

Eye for the context

As usual, we must have an eye for the context in which the passage stands. It is during the last Passover, in the night he was betrayed and in a moving "fare-well" that Christ a number of times speaks about the work of the Holy Spirit, the Counselor or Comforter. He promises the coming of this Comforter (15:16) who will stay forever, and will live in the disciples, as we saw in the previous chapter. The Counselor will also equip the disciples for their work, "[He] will teach you all things and will remind you of everything I said to you." In this connection (John 15) the Lord speaks about his disciples bearing much fruit. They are to be diligent in the work of furthering the Gospel. All this will lead to persecution, but the Comforter will testify about Christ and enable also the disciples to do the same (John 15:27).

Until now the emphasis has been on the Holy Spirit equipping the disciples for their great work of apostolic ministry. That's why he came and

that's how Christ will continue to be in their midst. The Spirit abides with the Bride. Although all this is still an internal matter, it already has an outward perspective: the ministry will take place in and to the *world*. This is the emphasis in the passage presently before us.

The power of the Gospel

The question could arise: who will ever listen to us, men of Galilee? The Jews will reject the apostles and the world will laugh, but Christ assures his disciples ahead of time: when the Holy Spirit comes, he will convict the world. Not: *you* will convict the world, but *he* will convict the world. The power of the Spirit will become evident in the faithful ministry of the church, the preaching of the Gospel to all. This text, then, does not speak about some preparatory or prevenient grace, but it speaks of the saving power of the Gospel because by it the Holy Spirit works faith in the hearts of men who are dead in sin and transgression.

By the power of the Gospel proclaimed by the apostolic church, the Holy Spirit will convict the world. This is far-reaching and effective. He will convict the world of sin, the one source of all misery, of righteousness, the only way of full redemption, and of judgment, the certain day of final reckoning.

Convict the world

He will convict the world. The word convict is stronger than the word convince, which is sometimes used as translation. The idea is then that as the Gospel is preached, the Spirit convinces the hearers that it is true. This is fine and even true in itself, but that is not really the point of this text. The word *convict* has the connotation of a judicial hearing, a trial and a legal battle. The Comforter or Counselor has the task of conducting such a trial, and therefore he is called in as an "advocate." To convict means to come with solid proof or undisputable evidence, so that everyone, even the accused, must admit: yes, it is true. Conviction then leads to a righteous verdict, and that is followed by judgment. These elements are also specifically found in the text, so we are going here in the right direction.

It says: convict the *world*. This does not mean that all people or all persons will be convicted, but that the Gospel will go world-wide, to the ends of the earth, and *in this process* indeed the entire world will be approached and convicted. The Holy Spirit will use the Catholic Church with the apostolic doctrine to convict the entire world.

We note in passing that John has a particular interest in the theme "world." This is true throughout his Gospel and also his letters later. In John 1 we already read: the *world* did not recognize him. Jesus is called the Lamb of God who takes away the sins of the *world*. God so loved the *world* that he gave his only-begotten Son...etc. The world which was created by God himself, and which fell under the power of the prince of darkness, will be restored to God through his only-begotten Son, and out of this world shall then come forth the new humanity, raised up by the power of the Word.

The great sin: apostasy or unbelief

He will convict the world of *guilt*, it says. That word is added by the translators, but is probably implied in the convicting. I'll just leave it out to show the lines a little more clearly.

He will convict the world of *sin*. What is the sin that is meant here? Of course, it is the original sin of mankind, which is the rebellion against God already in Paradise, by which all mankind became corrupt. Out of that sin flow forth all the actual sins which people commit.

What does this mean? Will the Holy Spirit give to all people some kind of knowledge of sin, even a sense of guilt? It means that when people are convicted, they do know and must admit that their sin is great. Notice how the Lord Jesus in the next verse (9) zeroes in exactly on *the sin* that he really means: of sin, *because men do not believe in me*. This is the real issue, the underlying issue, in the work of the Spirit through the apostolic preaching. This sin – rejecting the Lord Jesus Christ as the Savior of God – is the one that will lead to condemnation. The great sin of the last days is *apostasy* or *unbelief*. The sin is rejecting the truth once embraced (apostasy) or rejecting the truth now proclaimed (unbelief).

The Holy Spirit has come to glorify Christ. He will bring glory to me by taking what is mine and making it known to you (16:14). Jesus Christ will be proclaimed everywhere as the God-given Savior and the only Mediator. He alone delivers from all sin. The Gospel tells us about the one source of all misery, namely sin. This is the clear confession of the church. I think of Lord's Day 2 of the *Heidelberg Catechism*: from where do you know your misery? The world must come to know its real situation, the sin in which it lays, and the curse under which it lies. Through the preaching (for Christ is here preparing his disciples for preaching) the one cause of all human misery will be exposed, which is sin, the conscious, willful transgression of the law of God.

People will have to come to confess their sins. But what is then immediately important is that they must accept Jesus Christ as their Savior. They must believe in him, as the one given by God for redemption. The sin of the world will from then on be the sin of *unbelief*. The Jews will in that night already reject the Lord Jesus and consign him to the cross. The prince of darkness will appear to triumph. But he will not triumph at all. Now the claim that Jesus Christ is the God-given Savior must go worldwide, and what is the most serious and prevalent sin which the world will commit in the last days? It's the sin of unbelief, of the rejection of Jesus Christ. Whoever does so, will not be saved, but will be convicted by the Spirit of God himself.

We belonged to that world. It is out of that world that Christ has called us by the Gospel. Have we truly come to confess our sins? Do we also see that the greatest sin of all would be the rejection of Christ, and do we therefore embrace him with a believing heart and a joyous spirit? Are we deeply convicted of sin?

The lesson of life

I read somewhere that this convicting is the most difficult with long-standing members of the church, with people who are noted as believers for many years. Recent converts tend to admit to sin readily; but established members become set in their ways and have learned to live with certain sins. As a grown man in a special relation with the LORD, David still had to learn the greatest lesson of his life: be convicted of sin with Bathsheba. That took some doing. So do not see this convicting as something that applies only to recent converts. Even the most holy and the most pious of believers must experience this convicting powerfully from time to time, whenever sin has crept in or set in.

We constantly need to be brought back to Christ to see our sins, repent from them, and ardently seek our Savior. We need to watch and pray that we may live in accordance with the Gospel, as it has come to us. Only then does Christ by the Holy Spirit take proper shape in our lives.

The big question of the last days is not one about all kinds of spiritual phenomena, charismatic revivals, and millennial hoopla. The big question is: do you believe in Jesus Christ as the Savior from sin? At this point in Jesus' ministry, the world had not yet been confronted with this question. Only the Jewish people were forced to make a decision. The world did not know of Jesus Christ as yet. But through the Gospel they will be told exactly who he is. They will have to admit that the testimony concerning Jesus is

clear and true. They will be shown their sin and misery, and also asked: do you now believe in the Lord Jesus Christ?

Focus on Christ

We see here again a very important matter about the Holy Spirit that is central to this book: he is always focused on the Son, Jesus Christ. He lights up the work of our Lord, and so directs all men through him to the Father. The spotlight of the Spirit is on the Son, and that light flashes up to the throne of heaven. We must be aware of this and not wrongly internalize the Spirit by thinking that he can be locked up inside of us. The Spirit seeks the world with the Word so that all may know the Son, and through him be reconciled to God.

The question will be asked all over the world: how do we know that Jesus is the true Savior of the world? There are so many world-religions, and Christianity does not have sole rights here in this world. World religions like Islam are growing, while Christianity is faltering and fading. What *right* does the church have to come with the apostolic testimony that Jesus alone is the Savior?

It says: the Spirit will convict the world of *righteousness*. Righteousness means that everything was done and is done in complete agreement with and conformity to the law of God. In righteousness, by justice, we are legitimized as God's children.

In this world the idea of self-righteousness prevails. World religions and false Christianity all teach that we can be righteous or become righteous through our will and effort. Hence these religions show the path of self-righteousness that people should follow in order to become one with God and to escape death or condemnation in whatever form.

But the Spirit will convict of a righteousness that does not lie in people but only in Christ. How is this righteousness of Christ manifest? The Lord in this text speaks about it in very clear terms (verse 10) the Spirit will convict the world of righteousness "because I am going to the Father, and you will see me no longer." Christ will be condemned and executed. He will be treated as an unrighteous man, as the greatest of sinners, and as the most blasphemous of criminals. But, says Jesus, I am going to the Father, and you will see me no longer. This speaks of his *glorification*. He will die but he will rise from the dead, and ascend into heaven. He will be seated at God's right hand. In all this he will be justified and vindicated as the righteous one.

Apostolic Preaching

The apostolic preaching sums it up in simple yet deep terms. Jesus Christ is crucified for our sins, is raised for our justification, and has ascended for our benefit. The Holy Spirit will convict the world of the fact that where this righteousness in Christ by faith is rejected, there is no more righteousness to be received anywhere else. This also implies that whoever is righteous in Christ is one hundred percent righteous, because Christ is fully righteous.

The Spirit will uncover the basic misery of man, namely, sin and also show the only way of true redemption: finding righteousness by faith in Christ. His righteousness, demonstrated in his resurrection and further glorification, will come upon us. The world did not yet know all this in the night Jesus was betrayed, for the Counselor had not yet come, but *today* we know it, and millions of others know it. The question is still the same: do we seek and find all righteousness outside of ourselves in Jesus Christ, our risen and glorified King? This is always a key question for the church and for every member: do you seek your righteousness in Christ alone through the personal bond of faith, in the way of the means he has provided? This is the central issue of our lives.

Convicting of judgment

It is a very serious and urgent question. For, says the Lord, the Spirit will also convict the world of *judgment*. Many people live by a no-fault, no judgment policy. If they admit to sin, they certainly do not seek to be justified by faith; neither do they worry about judgment. They live carelessly, as if there is no day of judgment coming (cf. 2 Pet 3:4).

It is also on this point that the Spirit will convict the world. The world that does not recognize God's justice in Christ will undergo the same fate as the prince of this world. It says: the Spirit will convict the world of judgment, because the prince of this world now stands condemned.

Notice the word *now*. When Jesus goes into this night and to the cross, the prince of this world will undertake a final attempt to make the Son of God fall, but he will be unsuccessful. Therefore, now he stands condemned. He has played out all his cards, so to speak, has exerted all his energy, and has not been able to overcome the Son of God. Now he stands condemned. He can never escape his final undoing. He has no hope left whatsoever.

The prince of this world

Notice the expression the prince of this world. The Lord Jesus does not say: Satan or the devil stands condemned, but *the prince of this world* stands condemned. The world is still at that point Satan's territory. He rules over it as prince of darkness. The world is in his grip, and he will not let go. But Jesus says: now he stands condemned. When Christ rises from the dead, Satan is cast into the bottomless pit, so that he can deceive the nations no more. Then the real millennium starts.[7] It is the time of the last preaching and of final grace. The Gospel will be preached to the ends of the earth. The whole world will hear of the triumph, the death, resurrection, and ascension of Jesus Christ, who rules in heaven as King of kings.

Whoever does not flee to Christ stands condemned with the prince of darkness. You either rise with Christ or you go down with the devil. This is the power of the apostolic Word which the Holy Spirit will confirm everywhere, and by which the world will be convicted. Everyone will have to acknowledge that Jesus Christ is King of kings, and if they will not do it to their joy in their life time, they will have to do it to their shame on the day of judgment.

There is a definite day of judgment. Satan already knows that he stand condemned. He cannot win anymore. If ever he fostered false hope in this respect, it is now gone. His time is short. This, of course, makes him very angry and more evil. "He is filled with fury, because he knows that his time is short."(Rev 12:12) He will seek to search and destroy whatever belongs to God. He will resist the Holy Spirit at every turn. Wherever the Gospel is preached, Satan will follow to snatch away the seed and to close the hearts of people. Satan has the whole arsenal of worldly weaponry at his disposal. He uses the cultures of this world, the technology of this world, the ideology of this world, and the artistry of this world. He uses all these things in his campaign against Christ.

There is escape

Were it not for the Holy Spirit, the Counselor, no one would escape judgment. All would remain in the grip of the prince of this world. But he will convict the world also of judgment, so that everywhere people do flee to Christ to find shelter and safety. When the great judgment finally

---

[7] See my publication, *Celebrating Salvation,* Premier Publishing, Winnipeg, 1997, pages 265-301, on Revelation 20.

comes, all people will have to admit with clear mind and sincere heart that it is just.

This is the work of the Holy Spirit in this world. Through the preaching of the Gospel, which is a power of God unto salvation (Rom 1:16), the Holy Spirit will convict the world. He will show forth the truth, convict of sin, righteousness, and judgment, because in this way the Triune God resolves the conflict of history, fulfills the hope of his people, and brings about the glory of the new heaven and earth. All this happens through Christ Jesus to the glory of God the Father.

We have seen this work in progress ever since Pentecost. It continues until it is completed, and then the end is here. The Holy Spirit is working towards that end with great longing, and therefore, as it is testified, the *Spirit* and the bride say: come, Lord Jesus! The Spirit who is here to stay and who works unceasingly in this world longs with the church for the appearing in glory of the Son of God, when all the counsel of God has been fulfilled and God is all in all.

Sovereign grace

We do not find here a doctrine of prevenient grace but the teaching of sovereign and triumphant grace, shown precisely in the ministry of the Spirit who works in and with the church through the Gospel to call all the world to salvation.

We still have here one more question. Is there in this text, as some suggest, a kind of a *method* to approach the world in mission or evangelism: first expose sin, then proclaim Christ's righteousness, and finally threaten with judgment? Some preachers have followed and do follow this method. The result is hell-fire and brimstone preaching. I would hesitate to build a method or system on one text. The danger of a system is also that it is easily closed and self-destructive.

But these three elements should not be missing in the apostolic ministry of the church also today. For in the end it is so clear and simple: we can be redeemed from sin only by the righteousness of Christ, which we embrace by faith. We must flee to Christ, who now is glorified, and if we do not believe, we are condemned already, and shall one day face the final judgment of God.

The Holy Spirit says: without Christ, there is no hope. But in Christ, life is secure. This is the catholic and apostolic doctrine of salvation.

IX

The Outpouring of the Holy Spirit

No, this is what was spoken by the prophet Joel: I will pour out my Spirit on all people. Your sons and daughters will prophesy, your young men will see visions, your old men will dream dreams. Even on my servants both men and women, I pour out my Spirit in those days, and they will prophesy.

(ACTS 2:17, 18)

A book on the Person and work of the Holy Spirit would be incomplete without dealing with the meaning of Pentecost. I dealt with the meaning of Pentecost in my publication *Celebration Salvation* (Premier Publishing), but I now deal with the meaning of Pentecost as prophesied by Joel and explained by the apostle Peter in his sermon recorded in Acts 2.

Some of the people of Jerusalem, who witnessed the effect of Pentecost, thought that the disciples were drunk. They heard these plain men speaking in other tongues, praising God joyfully, and they mocked, "They are filled with new wine." They are just a bunch of drunks, that's all, noisy, rowdy, and creating a public disturbance. Seeing the fact that in verse 14 a general plural is used, I think that many people immediately accepted that explanation: of course, they're drunk. These fellows are plastered. People readily accept the first plausible, negative explanation.

When the apostle Peter stands up to explain to the gathered crowds what really has happened, he's in a bit of a pickle. Damage control is required. He quickly puts down the idea of drunkenness, "These men are not drunk, since it is only the third hour of the day." Peter says: it's only nine o'-clock in the morning, and who is then already drunk? At this hour the real drunks are still sleeping off last night's binge. It is foolish to suggest that the disciples are drunk.

What follows now? Peter still has to explain what has really happened, but how do you explain something like the outpouring of the Holy Spirit, which has never happened before? How do you explain a totally new phenomenon?

The apostolic method

The apostolic method is always first to go to the Scriptures. There you recognize true preaching. It begins and ends with the given Scriptures, also on Pentecost. Peter says: people, if you want to understand what has happened here today, you have to go back to the Bible. New events are always part of that old-time religion.

When you go to the Scriptures, there is a wide range of possibilities. Peter could have referred to Moses' wish that all the people would prophesy. We find this in Numbers 11:29, "I wish that all the LORD's people were prophets and that the LORD would put his Spirit on them!" He could have referred to the well-known great prophets, like Isaiah, Jeremiah, and even Ezekiel, who all spoke so eloquently of the new era which would dawn with the coming of the Messiah.

Instead Peter quotes from *Joel*, one of the Minor Prophets, and perhaps even from a somewhat obscure book that is very difficult to date accurately. Some of the hearers may have been a bit stunned to hear a reference to Joel.

Have you ever read the book of Joel? The prophet Joel was famous for his grasshoppers or his locusts. What Joel essentially describes in his book is how a plague of locusts comes over the land of Judah and devours everything as an exercising of God's judgment. There is in the book of Joel also a reference to a time of relief and salvation, but it is all against the background of that terrible destruction by these locusts. Joel ends with a general description of the great Day of Judgment. He calls it: the day of decision, D-day.

Pentecost and locusts?

Therefore we ask ourselves the question: what is the connection between locusts and Pentecost? Locusts destroy everything in their way. When they are through with the crops, there is no harvest. Pentecost is the feast of the harvest, of joy and thanksgiving for God's blessings. How can a feast of joy be associated with a plague of doom?

When Peter says: this is what was spoken of by the prophet Joel, the whole matter of Pentecost is put in a very serious perspective. For this outpouring of which Joel speaks is preceded and followed by great judgment and leads to a final day of reckoning. The outpouring of the Holy Spirit on Pentecost, therefore, tells us first of all that we are in very urgent times, and that God's judgments will commence. These judgments begin always at the house of God, at the temple itself (cf. I Pet 4:17). If anyone still is to be saved, it is now by the power of the Holy Spirit. We have come into a decisive and final stage of history when everything is escalating towards its definite end.

Are these people drunk? No, says Peter, but you will soon be dead, unless you repent from your evil way and turn to the living God. What you see here is the outpouring of the Holy Spirit, and that is the only way of hope in a world bound for destruction. Think of the prophet Joel. There is your Biblical basis and precedent. Pentecost opens the only avenue of escape in a world that is headed towards its doom. We have entered, as Peter says in verse 17, in the last days, the definitive phase of history. It's now or never. If people now miss the boat, they'll go under in a sea of perdition. Pentecost opens God's last action of salvation in a desperate world.

We see in Joel's prophecy the width, the depth, and the height of this action of salvation.

All flesh?

Notice how Joel prophesies first of the width or the wide extent of God's action of salvation: I will pour out my Spirit upon *all flesh*.

The explainers differ on the exact meaning of these words. Some say that this only means that all Israel will partake of the Holy Spirit. All flesh is then interpreted as the fullness of the people of Israel. These explainers see their interpretation confirmed in the fact that Joel immediately thereafter speaks about "your sons and your daughters shall prophesy...." Your sons and daughters would mean *Israel's* sons and daughters.

But it is more simple and logical to conclude that the expression *all flesh* means more than just Israel. All flesh is the term commonly used for all mankind. Pentecost means, as we know from the New Testament, that God's action of salvation goes world-wide. God's work of rescue has global significance.

This world-wide action (all flesh) may in the next words be somewhat restricted (your sons and daughters) but it fits fully in the general scheme of things: the Gospel will now go world-wide, even if the order will still be first the Jew and then the Gentile (Rom 1:16). The Gospel will go, as the Lord Jesus said, from Jerusalem, to Judea, to Samaria, and from there to the ends of the earth (cf. Mat 28:19).

Catholic dimension

The prophets of old always had a world-wide, catholic dimension to their words. The Psalms speak of it as well. Jerusalem shall be lifted up, and all nations shall flock to it. Pentecost indeed means that the wall of separation between Israel and the nations is now broken down (Eph 2:14). The Gospel will go to the ends of the earth.

This is in keeping with the whole scheme of Joel's prophecy. Since the coming judgment will be world-wide, the preaching of the Gospel and the sharing in the Holy Spirit will also be world-wide. God will yet open to the world the treasures of the covenant with Abraham, Isaac, and Jacob before he finally closes the file of the sins of this world.

There are many contrasts in Joel's prophecy. One is the width of God's action: from Israel God seeks the world. No longer is one people privileged above another. All elements of race and nationality fall away. Christ Jesus transcends all nations and all tongues. That is why on Pentecost the languages of all flesh are heard, and everyone hears in his own language the mighty works of God.

This also means that Pentecost opens up a hitherto unknown possibility and calling: proclaim the Gospel to the whole creation. Set your scopes wide. Promote and further the work of God wherever you can so that all flesh may hear of the glory of Jesus Christ. Since Pentecost, there is a strongly global vision which permeates the life of the church. That is why, for example, local churches are also members of an International Conference of Reformed Churches, where faithful churches from all over the world meet to help and assist one another. The basis for this catholic unity lies also in the prophecy of Joel, quoted here by the apostle Peter.

Universal proclamation

Notice how the Lord says: I will pour out my Spirit upon all flesh. It is not so that all people now themselves have the potential to be saved. That is Arminian thinking. God remains sovereign in initiative and effect. It means simply that God will work everywhere through the Holy Spirit, and where he works, people will be saved by his power and grace, and will respond to his Word.

It means that we must have an eye for what the *Canons of Dort* so beautifully call "the universal proclamation of the Gospel" (Chapter II, paragraph 5). The Spirit is poured out over all flesh. The Canons say it as follows, "The promise of the Gospel is that whoever believes in Christ crucified shall not perish, but have everlasting life. This promise ought to be announced and proclaimed *universally and without discrimination to all peoples and to all men* to whom God in His good pleasure sends the Gospel, together with the command to repent and believe."

"All flesh" is the width of Pentecost. God seeks the world in one last campaign before the great Day of Judgment.

The depth of Pentecost

The Gospel is no longer reserved for one people or one race. But there is another element here, which I call the depth of Pentecost.

Notice how Joel speaks of the fact that the Spirit will be poured out over three categories: sons and daughters, young men and old men, and menservants and maidservants. The Spirit comes over people irrespective of sex, age, or status. Not only do geographical borders fall away on Pentecost, but also other lines of demarcation are removed. It does not matter anymore whether one is male or female, young or old, slave or free; all people may share in the gifts of the Holy Spirit. That's how deep it goes.

The Jews, who heard Peter quote from this word of Joel, may not immediately have understood the ramifications. As we noted already, under the old dispensation restricted to Israel, the Spirit of God was only given to some special people, not to all the people. These special people were mostly prophets, priests, and kings, men who held a high office in Israel. Call them if you wish the clergy. The Spirit was for the clergy, and not for the common folks or the laity.

There were exceptions to the rule. We know that in the days of the Judges, there was a prophetess called Deborah. But she is an exception who prophesied almost by default, because the men were so far removed from the LORD (Judges 4). Prophesying was generally not done by women.

Age was also an important factor. One did not give important tasks to the young. They lacked experience and wisdom. You had to be of age before you became an elder. In Israel all things were decided in the council of the elders, where the young men had no say.

The menservants and maidservants (literally "slaves") had nothing to say whatsoever. Most slaves in Israel were foreigners. As aliens they had no legal position. They had to be cared for and treated well, but they had no real status. Israel would never be led by a slave. Slaves had to be quiet, and simply do their work with no questions asked. Often these slaves were outrightly despised.

A new era begins

Perhaps you know of the famous prayer of the Rabbi's: I thank you, LORD, that you have not made me a woman or a slave. Women and slaves had no status and few rights. The Holy Spirit was associated with the clergy and the aristocracy, and not with the masses who did not know the law.

But Pentecost goes deep. All these social distinctions fall away. The Holy Spirit came over all the church. It says clearly in Acts 2:4, "And they were all filled with the Holy Spirit."

It really is the beginning of a new era. Suddenly all members, not just some of God's church, are anointed. The distinction between clergy and laity falls away entirely. All are now prophets, priests, and kings. All may now enter into the holy of holies to worship God there in Christ Jesus. The old temple, with its private priestly quarters and its sections that were off-limits to aliens and women, doesn't function anymore.

The depth of Pentecost is that all members of Christ's church share in the anointing with the Holy Spirit. The youth take in an important place. The church is not a society of elders. The women take in their own place. The church is not a restricted men's club. The slaves have something to contribute, for in Christ everyone is a free person. Paul wrote about this in Colossians 4:11, "Here there is no Greek or Jew, circumcised or uncircumcised, barbarian, Scythian, slave or free, but Christ is all, and is in all."

Not revolution but reformation

Pentecost goes deep. Not one member is passed over. Everyone receives his own place and task in the office of all believers. Gender, age, and status are no barriers for the Holy Spirit, for he mobilizes the *entire* church in the service of Christ.

Does this mean that age no longer plays a role? Of course not, for the enthusiasm of youth must still be guided by the wisdom of the elders (cf. I Pet 5:5). Does gender mean nothing? Is here the basis for Christian feminism? Of course not, for men and women retain their own specific place in the church. The offices are not opened to women (cf. 1 Tim 2:11-15). But

women are given, besides men, a lawful place as prophets, priests, and kings. Does status mean nothing anymore? Is slavery immediately abolished? Slavery will disappear gradually in society, but the slave is now as a Christian treated as an equal in the church (cf. Phil:14-16).

Pentecost is not a revolution, but a *reformation*. In a revolution everything is suddenly turned topsy-turvy, but a reformation means steady renewal from the inside out. The youth take in their place beside the elders. The women serve beside the men. The slave has equal rights beside his master. We all are equal before the Lord, as we saw from Colossians 4, for in Christ there is not male or female, slave or free, Jew or barbarian, but we all belong and contribute there where the Lord has placed us. Everyone is a partaker of the one anointing of Jesus Christ.

Long-term ramifications

This does have long-term social ramifications. In the Christian Church children will be cherished in the proper manner. In the Christian Church, women will not be discriminated against or abused, but esteemed. In the Christian Church there will be no partiality for the rich over against the poor, and slavery will be abolished. What is sometimes accepted in society, namely, exploitation, abuse, and discrimination, may never be tolerated in the church.

That's the depth of Pentecost. Everyone belongs, also the youth. From the beginning of our life we all have a place and a task in the church. That's the meaning also of infant baptism. Men and women have a common calling in the church. Do not think that a male may dominate or that a female has nothing to contribute. Both are anointed and are co-heirs of the grace of life. Rich and poor meet together at one table. We have no privileged class in the church, no aristocracy or clergy, for we are all office-bearers for Christ, and we all contribute according to our talents and blessings. This is the only way in which we can properly approach the world: as one people, where we all belong and have our own place and task.

The world will stand amazed, for people have never seen anything like this. The world operates on the basis of self-interest and conflict: young versus old (the generation gap), male versus female (the gender conflict), rich versus poor (the class struggle), but in the church this is overcome by the power of the Holy Spirit. We may not follow the conflict model, but must activate the communion of saints, being one, together in Christ. That's the depth of Pentecost.

The height of Pentecost

Then we also see the height of Pentecost. To what heights does the Holy Spirit lead us? It says: your sons and daughters shall prophesy, your young men shall see visions, old men dream dreams, and the menservants and maidservants shall prophesy.

That's the height. The church becomes a body that stands on the pinnacle of prophecy. The church will speak out as a professing church. A mighty witness and testimony will sound forth from out of this church to the entire world: Jesus Christ is Lord and King.

We read of visions, dreams, and prophecies by young and old, male and female, slave and free. What does that mean? Visions, dreams, and prophecies are typically in the Bible the ways and means to receive God's revelation. The church, filled with the Holy Spirit, will receive the full revelation of God, and will speak that Word to all nations. That's basically what it means.

I do not have to deal now with the question whether there is until Christ's return ongoing revelation. Some Pentecostal movements interpret the text in this way. Still today, they say, we receive visions and dreams and prophecies. New revelations come daily. But the Bible does not speak in that manner.

The apostolic time is the era in which the revelation of God is fulfilled and completed. That is what Joel means. The emphasis here is on the verb to prophesy. It is used twice in the text. Prophesying is the emphatic, ongoing element. From the complete data in the New Testament we learn that prophesying especially means *to proclaim* the Gospel. Prophesying is not fore-telling, but forth-telling, pro-claiming.

Personal testimonies?

Sometimes we meet people who do claim to have received direct messages from the Lord through dreams, visions, or experiences which they feel compelled to share with fellow-believers. What are we to think of this? It is not wise to call such people liars. They genuinely believe to have received some special message. We might gently remark to them that the Bible does not teach ongoing revelation.

It is of greater importance to inform such persons that whatever message they think to have received is very personal for them alone. We did not receive the same message. There is no way that a personal, subjective message can be properly verified in the church. All that we need to know has

been revealed in the Bible which is our only norm. Therefore such persons do best to keep their private messages to themselves.

This also means that personal testimonies really have no place in the worship services of the church. Promoting such testimonies is contrary to the teaching of Scripture. The Holy Spirit binds us only to the Word of God given in the Scriptures. Whatever impulse or guidance God has given to one person is neither normative for others nor illustrative of God's power. We do not believe on the basis of other people's testimonies, but only on the basis of God's given Word. These remarks are important especially in the light of the prophecy of Joel.

An urgent message

The church of Pentecost will be a prophetic church in this way: it will speak of Jesus Christ, the risen and ascended Lord, who is coming to judge the living and the dead. Remember the locusts of Joel. There is a day of reckoning, and now there is still escape in Zion, in the church of Christ. Pentecost means that the locusts are gathering for the final destruction, and that there is only one avenue open for escape: in the Lord Jesus Christ.

That's the urgent message which since Pentecost will sound forth from the church, from all its members, irrespective of age, gender, or status. We have one Word for all the world, and we must all speak that word. God places each one of us on this height that we are all confessors of Christ, prophets, who prophesy constantly and urgently of the coming of Jesus Christ.

Read the end of Joel's prophecy that is quoted by Peter (Acts 2:20, 21): the day of the Lord comes, the great and manifest day. And it shall be that whoever calls upon the Name of the Lord shall be saved. There is still in this age the possibility of salvation. But the time is winding down. We are called to prophesy, even more so as the end is drawing near.

Take the high road

No one in the church may come down from this height. We all have to take the high road. One may not say: well, I'm young, I'll wait till later; leave it up to the elders. One may not say: I'm just a woman; leave it to the men. One may not say: I'm only a hired hand; leave it to the boss. It is the task of everyone to prophesy and to testify in words and deeds that there is salvation. We must embody that salvation and show forth the power of Jesus Christ. We are all called to "shine like stars in the universe" as we "hold out the word of life..." (Phil 2:16). There is no higher calling than this.

Christ placed his church on that height. His action of salvation now goes through the church, which is called and enabled to do this by the Holy Spirit. The church of Christ, filled with the Holy Spirit, the church with the completed Word, is now the only hope for this world. What an immense height. Elsewhere we read that the church is a light on a candle stick and a city on a mountain (Mat 5). A light and a city are clearly visible, seeking the world with the Word.

The grasshoppers are coming. But the Gospel comes first. Destruction is nigh. But the proclamation of grace precedes it. Peter could not have picked a better text from the Old Testament. Now we know how serious the times are and how high our calling is. It has been Pentecost. Now is the time of decision for all flesh.

Let us speak then of God's awesome acts of strength that men may remember his goodness (Psalm 145) and that it is experienced by many: whoever calls upon the Name of the Lord in the land of the locusts, will be saved.

X Growth through the Holy Spirit

Those who accepted his message were baptized, and about three thousand were added to their number that day. They devoted themselves to the apostles' teaching and to the fellowship, to the breaking of bread and to prayer.

(ACTS 2:41, 42)

The work of the Holy Spirit in the new dispensation gives us reason to set our scopes wide and far. I mentioned how the outpouring of the Spirit marks the beginning of world-wide preaching and gives us a broad and panoramic view from Jerusalem to the ends of the earth. It is the view of which Psalm 87 speaks: many tongues, one God, one faith confessing. The macrocosm is filled with God's praise.

But the work of the Holy Spirit also has to do with what happens deep inside the heart of a person, in the microcosm of the human soul. The Holy Spirit comes to dwell within us. We need to pay proper attention to this in-depth work of the Spirit of God.

On the day of the outpouring of the Spirit, as described in Acts 2, there is a miraculous growth in the numbers of the church. In Acts 1:15 we can read that the church before Pentecost numbered about one hundred and twenty persons. That is not a great amount, when you look at the power of the ministry of Christ during his stay on earth. His many sermons and miracles led to a little more than one hundred members. But in Acts 2:41 we get quite a different picture: there were added that day about three thousand souls.

Imagine, three thousand persons are added in one day. If that happened today in any average sized church, the elders probably couldn't handle the influx. Just the idea of baptizing three thousand people on one day is phenomenal. We are not told how this was done or if this was done right away.

Now we are not concerned with numbers as such. We are not fixated on numbers, as is the case with exponents of the church-growth movement. A church does not always increase in numbers and sometimes in fact decreases in membership. Still we do appreciate church growth. What is more important is how this growth comes about and to what this growth leads.

Repentance and Faith

It is remarkable how the work of the Holy Spirit is always connected with proclaiming the Truth and hearing the Word. Where the Spirit is, there is always preaching and hearing. It is by these two means that the Holy Spirit works faith in our hearts.

In his sermon on the day of Pentecost, the apostle Peter makes no bones about the real situation: the hearers have crucified Christ, but he has risen from the dead, and has poured out his Spirit. The demand of the Gospel is rather simple (verse 38), "Repent, and be baptized every one of you in the Name of Jesus for the forgiveness of your sins; and you shall receive the gift of the Holy Spirit."

The preaching is an exposition of the riches in Christ and an exhortation to receive these riches through repentance and faith. The exhortation to repent and believe is very urgent and strong. See verse 40: with many other words Peter exhorted them, saying, "Save yourselves from this crooked generation."

Save yourselves? We should not misunderstand this saying of Peter. He is not suggesting at all that our salvation depends on any prior act of ourselves. Every Christian should know that he can not save himself. Salvation is the result of the powerful working of God's sovereign grace in our lives.

The responsibility to respond

But this truth does not do away with our responsibility to respond to the call of the Gospel. We are confronted with the Word and we are called to heed carefully what is said. This involves the activity of the mind and the will. The word *repent* indicates a complete mental and emotional (spiritual) change. Preaching always addresses both the mind and the conscience of the hearer.

We can sit in church and listen to the preaching of the Word, but all this must lead to action from our side. This action is called in this passage *receiving*: "So those who received his word were baptized...." The same verse notes that many did receive the word. It also shows us that not everyone received the word. We do not know exact figures here, but three thousand out of a rather large population is not a huge number. In itself it is huge but in the context of possible numbers, it was probably not so large.

Many were converted. But others, who heard the same preaching, did not repent and receive the Word. This again demonstrates that preaching always leads to a two-fold reaction, either faith or unbelief. When confronted with the Gospel, some do receive it, very consciously and joyfully, while others reject it, also very consciously and with grim determination.

Receiving the Word

It took much effort from the side of Peter and the other disciples to persuade people to receive the Word. Verse 40 gives evidence of this struggle. People do not immediately accept what they are being told. It takes persuasion and repetition to lead hearers to faith and acceptance.

But there are those who do receive the Word. Receiving means to take up and into oneself what it being said. It has the notion of carefully weighing what is said, approving it as being true, and then admitting it into one's mind. Whatever questions or doubts may at this point still remain, these are not sufficient to reject what is being said. These people basically understand the message, agree with it, and are satisfied that this is the truth. That is the sense here of the verb to receive.

We must acknowledge that this receiving of the Word is a great miracle, even on the day of Pentecost itself. Whenever anyone receives the Word, it is miraculous, and this holds true also for the day of Pentecost. It means that a powerful change has taken place and is taking place within these people.

Made receptive

The verb to receive indicates that people have been made receptive by the Spirit and Word of Christ. God has convinced and convicted them. Receiving the Word is not a natural thing for people to do. As we noted, the first reaction of people is generally to reject what is being said. In Acts 2:13 we already learned that some people were very quick and easy with their judgment over what was happening. They said that the disciples were filled with new wine. Some were perplexed, while others were amused. But no one will of himself really accept what is being said.

Paul wrote about this later in his first letter to the Corinthians, "The man without the Spirit does not accept the things that come from the Spirit of God, for they are foolishness to him, and he cannot understand them, because they are spiritually discerned (2:14)." You need the working of the Holy Spirit to receive and discern spiritual things (cf. also John 3).

There are those who on the day of Pentecost do receive what is said. This is then precisely because the Spirit worked in these people a powerful change. The Spirit of God opened minds and hearts, and so these people were able to receive and to internalize what was being expressed to them.

Receiving is done by faith

Now the Bible does not here explain the inner working or the mechanics of this receiving. It simply notes the fact. The receiving of the Word is done by faith. People believe that what Peter is saying is true. The evidence is in the Pentecostal signs, and even more so in the Scripture which is properly opened and applied. Perhaps many of these hearers still vividly remember what Jesus taught and how he had died. Many of them may even have seen the Lord in the flesh as he ministered among them. What they now hear and see on Pentecost strikes a responsive chord, and they receive the Word by taking it into themselves so that it becomes a part of them. It is now a compelling and controlling factor in their lives.

For that is the consequence of this receiving. The Word becomes a part of you. The Word is so powerful that you start to think differently about very important matters. You begin to act accordingly. Receiving the Word means a decisive change in thinking and doing.

It is important to note this carefully. We can attend church Sunday after Sunday, week after week, and we may constantly hear the preaching of the Word, but do we really receive the Word? Does it become a part of us as a compelling and controlling factor in our lives? Does it change our thinking and in this way influence our action? Or do we just continue to do as we were doing, without showing any particular, visible effect?

Word and sacrament

The people described in Acts 2 did understand that receiving the Word has certain consequences. It says: those who received his word were baptized. This is the baptism in the Name of Jesus (verse 38), the very

Name that was officially cursed by the Jewish leaders. Through this baptism, they publicly acknowledged that they wanted to belong to Jesus and to his disciples, to his church. That was in those days certainly a very bold thing to do, not without risk or danger. We see that receiving the Word leads to a very conscious public act of being baptized. Through that baptism one became officially enjoined with the followers of Jesus Christ.

Preaching and sacraments go together. The sign follows the Word, and where people receive the Word, they also desire baptism. In this way the people are called to make a very important decision, and to do so plainly and publicly. They respond in great numbers to that call, for it says, "and there were added that day about three thousand souls."

Joining an existing body

Notice the word *added*. These people joined an existing body, the church of Christ. They did not on that day institute some kind of a new organization, but they were added to an established congregation, which was clearly associated with Jesus Christ. Repentance and faith do not mean that you establish something new, let's say, a new church, but that you join the church which is faithful according to God's Word.

Now one can say: if there were added that day about three thousand persons, one might just be part of the crowd and not even be especially noticed. You can easily hide in a crowd. Who kept an exact record? That is true in itself. When a movement suddenly becomes a mass-movement, it may even be fashionable to join it. Who would not be attracted to the church on the day of Pentecost? But make no mistake about it: the decision to be baptized would not be without consequence. Everyone close to you or important to you would soon know: you were baptized that day and added to the church of Jesus Christ. It is not just a hidden commitment in someone's heart, but it is a public commitment that is made visible to all.

The growth of the church is a matter of a powerful change and a public commitment in people's lives. Without this change, there would be no growth at all. But when the change comes, it means a complete and radical change. From then on one visibly belongs to and is associated with the church of the Lord Jesus Christ. This has now become the priority of one's life.

Whatever criticism one might have on huge evangelism associations like e.g. the Billy Graham Evangelism Association, it must be admitted that Dr. Graham certainly has seen one important matter very clearly: commitment to Christ must be a public decision, for you can not light a lamp and put it under a bushel. Everyone should be able to see that you have indeed consciously committed yourself to the Lord. That does not necessarily mean an "altar call," but it must be visible in your association with the church of the Lord. Unfortunately it is not usually specified which church a believer ought to join. One is called to the light but left in the dark.

Receiving the Word and undergoing baptism indicate that the old way of life is gone, and a new way of life has begun. The powerful change leads to a new beginning in life. And it is a very promising start.

Growing in the faith

For what happens here is only a start. All these people have only made a beginning which demands a further activity. We read in verse 42, "And they devoted themselves to the apostles' teaching and fellowship, to the breaking of bread and the prayers."

Obviously you're not done when you repent and are baptized. Now you have to grow in the faith. Therefore it says that they devoted themselves to the apostles' teaching. The word that is used here is very strong and emphatic. They devoted themselves to i.e. carefully held to, stayed with, focused on, and abided by the apostles' teaching.

The apostles' teaching denotes the authoritative proclamation of the Gospel, of the death and resurrection of Christ according to the verified facts and also as prophesied in the Old Testament. The apostles begin to open to these people the Scriptures, and they accept that teaching. We see that the prime ministry of the church is a preaching and teaching ministry, to equip the saints with the Word for a life of service. Nothing has really changed since then, has it?

Fellowship and celebration

The text also speaks of fellowship. It can mean the fellowship with the apostles, but also includes the new fellowship with one another. These people did not stand on their own, but they sought and found one another in and around the teaching of the apostles.

Fellowship means sharing. The church is a communion of saints. Where the believers gather to hear, that's where I also want to be. You see here something realized of what Psalm 84 speaks about: the longing for the fellowship with the believers, the joy, the peace, and rest of the new and true Jerusalem. One day in God's house of praise is better than a thousand days outside the courts of his salvation. They devote themselves to this new fellowship and they cannot get enough of it.

We also read that they devoted themselves to the "breaking of bread." Although this can mean simply a normal meal – and they probably did have meals together – it is also an expression which can denote the celebrating of the Lord's Supper. This is how I understand it here. The preaching of salvation is confirmed in the celebration of the Lord's Supper. The atoning death of Christ is fully central. They begin to "cherish the blessed memory of the bitter death of Christ" (Form for the Celebration of the Lord's Supper, *Book of Praise*, page 599). The cross is no longer for them a stumbling block but a reason for praise and glory.

A promising start

The text also says that they devoted themselves to the prayers. Notice the definite article: *the* prayers. The Jews had set times and contents for their daily prayers. The Christian congregation did not neglect this aspect. Does not the Spirit lead us to say "Abba, Father"? (Rom 8:8) The Spirit is the Spirit of praise, thanksgiving, and supplication. The Christian life cannot function without prayer, for it is the life-line and the thermometer of faith.

If you sum up all the above, you must agree: what a promising start. These three thousand people have a long way to go, but they have made a very clear and decisive beginning. And their devotion must continue, for it is a hallmark of the church of Christ: submission to the Word, seeking of the fellowship of the Church, using the sacraments, and engaging in constant praise and prayer. Here we see the true depth of Pentecost. The Spirit by the Word shapes and forms knowledge, fellowship, and worship.

Can you find yourself in this picture? For this is not merely a description of how it once was, but a normative prescription of how it always must be. The Spirit brings about an in-depth change, and this change is visible in joyous and sincere participation in the fellowship and worship of the church of Christ. Pentecost is the beginning of growth, but then an in-depth growth, a sharing fully in the life and joy of the congregation.

All these elements still stand central: preaching and teaching (the apostolic doctrine), worship, sacraments, and public prayers. Is this not what the church services are all about? Here beats the heart of the Pentecostal experience. Only in this way can the promising start continue and find solidity.

Continuation in the same line

These people need this ministry or they will stagnate spiritually and cease to grow in Christ. Otherwise they will soon drift back into their former way of life. Christ will not be in the centre anymore. Devotion becomes indifference. We see it also today; it still goes the same way. When people no longer are devoted to worship and fellowship and do not seek the apostolic teaching of the church, you can see them slowly disappearing beyond the horizon of Christendom.

There are also today those who make a promising start. But somehow they do not stick with it. Some may even present what they consider to be legitimate excuses and good reasons to leave, but the point is that their heart was never in it. There was no real change within and soon it shows to the outside. If you do not truly receive the Word, you will not devote yourself to the communion of saints. It's as simple as that. Personal faith leads to communal commitment, and where the one is lacking, the other also fails.

Personal not individualistic

People today like to speak much about the experiencing of the power of the Spirit. A lot of this is presented in individualistic terms. It is true, as we have noted, the working of the Spirit is very personal. No one should deny that at all. But the personal element is not loose from the togetherness, the communal devotion in worship to the Word of Christ, the preaching, praise, and prayers of the gathered congregation, as described in this passage.

Personal faith must be shown in a life of holiness and in devotion to worship in the fellowship with the church. In this way the church grows in faith and works. Pentecost is all about growth. We grow together in Christ to maturity of faith and the fruits of faith.

We may echo the sentiments of the Apostles' Creed, as summarized in Hymn 1B:3 (*Book of Praise*)

"In God the Holy Spirit I believe.
Through whom we are a new creation.
And I believe a catholic Church,
One holy Christian congregation.
The true communion of all those
Whom God once as his people chose...."

Personal faith and fellowship with the saints are gifts of the Spirit and fruit of Pentecost.

XI The Spirit Resisted

You stiff-necked people, with uncircumcised hearts and ears! You are just like your fathers: you always resist the Holy Spirit! Was there ever a prophet your fathers did not prosecute? They even killed those who predicted the coming of the Righteous One. And now you have betrayed and murdered him – you how have received the law that was put into effect through angels, but have not obeyed it.

(Acts 7:51-53)

There are in our time, also in Reformed churches, many questions concerning the person and work of the Holy Spirit. Some members desire to know more about the mysterious yet wonderful work of the Holy Spirit. Younger people, who grow up in a more open and expressive society, desire to have better insight into the work of the Spirit. This desire is good.

On the one hand, the Bible speaks in very encouraging and certain terms about the Spirit in our lives. We have seen that he is called our Comforter or Counselor, who always abides with us and fills us with the riches that Christ has earned for us. This must always be emphasized. The Holy Spirit came to stay. Yet on the other hand, we are warned not to grieve the Spirit or even quench the Spirit, and there is the implication that he may withdraw from us. Do we receive here *conflicting* messages?

A reference could be made to Acts 7:51, where Stephen accuses the Sanhedrin of *resisting* the Holy Spirit: you always resist the Holy Spirit. In explaining this text, this line of thinking is often followed: the Spirit has to reveal man's misery and create the desire for salvation. He also needs to convince people that God's Word is true and reliable. This work [of the Holy Spirit] however, is not a guarantee to salvation – apparently it is *resistible* grace.

105

Some think that especially in the early stage of the Spirit's work, man can resist the Holy Spirit. I am not sure what is meant by an early stage as compared to any later stage in which (I assume) the Spirit is not so easily resisted, but notice how the resisting of the *Spirit* is in one sentence equated with the resisting of God's *grace*. It is not irresistible grace, as we thought and taught, for Stephen infers that the Spirit can be resisted.[8] This is a flawed manner of thinking.

Invincible grace

I mention as a side-note that I do not anymore speak of irresistible grace, and therefore also not about resistible grace. This dogmatical terminology is insufficient to describe what is meant. We have learned to speak of *invincible* grace. Just as the Holy Spirit is almighty God, so the grace of God is invincible. God's sovereign grace is by nature resisted by everyone, and even true believers can sometimes lose the sense of God's grace because of their sins, but God's grace, as the Spirit himself, is invincible. To say it differently, when the Holy Spirit sets out to save us, we can resist but cannot overpower the Spirit, for he overpowers us. God remains stronger than man.

Which brings us back to this passage, then, and to the question: what is meant by this *resisting the Holy Spirit*? It is something that indeed demands our attention, for it would not be good it if was rightly said of us that like the Jews in the apostolic time we today resist the Holy Spirit.

Remember the context

Actually this is the only passage in Scripture where the term "resisting the Spirit" is used, and that should make us careful not to draw quick conclusions. It also should alert us to the fact that we are to understand the expression here very specifically in its *context*, for that is the first rule of proper exegesis or explanation of Scripture.

In the context of Acts 7 this resisting is not at all something which takes place during an early stage of our regeneration or sanctification. On the contrary, it is something that Israel has been doing for a long time, throughout the ages. Stephen says: you *always* resisted the Holy Spirit. He implies that the Jews still do so. Precisely stated, we do not stand here at the beginning of a process of regeneration, but at the end of a long history of hardening in sin.

---

[8]See e.g. Isaac Smit, *Praying For Rain*, Mt. Hope, 1998, p. 42.

This chapter in Acts gives us the account of a great *turning-point* in the history of Israel and the church of Christ. Until now there have been certain prohibitions to the Christian church and some brief imprisonments. The apostles were slapped on the wrists and told to stop preaching the name of Jesus (see Acts 4). But now it becomes very serious. Stephen is the first martyr and here the ways of Judaism and Christendom truly part.

Massive persecution

We must have a keen eye for these circumstances; otherwise we completely misunderstand the passage and text. The resisting of the Holy Spirit, which was evident through the ages in Israel's history, found its strongest expression in the rejection and crucifixion of Christ. Now it breaks loose against the church of the new covenant, and this will lead to great consequences.

As Stephen dies, massive persecution begins and the church at Jerusalem is scattered far and wide. Israel's resistance against the Holy Spirit comes to an unprecedented height. We must understand that through Stephen's testimony the Lord makes a final appeal to the Jewish Sanhedrin regarding Israel's sin of resisting the Holy Spirit. This passage speaks to us about the key element in this sin, the final evidence of this sin, and the only deliverance from this sin.

Vehemence and sharpness

This passage is remarkable for its sudden vehemence and sharpness. Stephen was going along at a leisurely pace, being nice to everyone, simply recounting the main moments of Israel's history, when suddenly there is this outburst: you stiff-necked people, with uncircumcised hearts and ears! One is almost taken aback by the sharp tone and strong language. We understand that the first hearers could hardly be pleased.

Please note two things. First, Stephen is addressing the Sanhedrin, the official Jewish court, on the charge of *blasphemy*. He is being accused of a terrible crime. Stephen knows, as do all others, that if found guilty, he will receive the death penalty, as did Christ Jesus. So he's not telling a fairy tale which might well begin with the words "once upon a time" but he is recounting a specific history.

Second, he does this from a certain perspective. What comes out time and again in his defense is that Israel has a history of *rejecting* faithful prophets. Joseph was sold as a slave to Egypt by his own brothers. Moses was betrayed by the very same people he was trying to help. Moses spoke about the coming of a great prophet, but they laughed at Moses. Later God gave them the Promised Land, and a place to worship him, but they did not appreciate it.

The defense of Stephen is precisely that Israel has throughout its entire history been a stiff-necked people with uncircumcised hearts. History is not neutral. It could be that the hearers were slowly catching on to this theme, and were starting to get angry. Sensing their rising displeasure, Stephen makes it very plain: you are a stiff-necked people with uncircumcised hearts and ears. Imagine, the man accused of blasphemy is now accusing his judges of resisting the Spirit.

Stiff-necked

Being stiff-necked is the sin of *human pride*. It is a refusal to bow before the Lord and his Word. The people of Israel never learned to depend on the Lord alone and to entrust themselves fully to his care, but they went their own ways and sought their own security. They fell into deep apostasy time and again, serving dead idols instead of the living God.

Stiff-necked also means that they would not bend under God's discipline. Instead of bowing before him and his servants, they became even more defiant. And this is because they have "uncircumcised hearts and ears." Circumcision was a sign of *renewal of life*. Sin had to be cut out. But for the Jews it became an outward ritual with no real spiritual meaning. They took pride in the *sign* of the covenant, but did not honor the *essence* of the covenant. This is a very serious matter, which must meet with God's wrath.

You would expect that the Jews in Stephen's time had learned their lesson. They had the Scriptures. They knew how God had punished his people in the past. Had not the prophets already warned them for uncircumcised hearts and ears? They would not fall into the same pitfalls as their fathers. They honored the very memory of the prophets killed by their fathers. They built impressive tombs and erected fancy memorials for the prophets of old (Mat 23:29, 30). They thought they were different and better than their poor, misguided, unrepentant, unspiritual fathers. They knew better....

Like your fathers...

But Stephen tells them unequivocally: you are just like your fathers. You come from them, think like them, act like them, and refuse to listen. You

always resist the Holy Spirit. Times change and generations come and go, but the sin of resisting the Holy Spirit is always the same. It is constantly present like an ugly birthmark. This sin stands out: you always resist the Holy Spirit.

It is remarkable that this is not said in general terms about the Gentiles, but about God's covenant people. Resisting the Holy Spirit is something of which especially covenant people have to be aware. The Holy Spirit may be resisted everywhere, but only among God's people can it be known *whom* they are resisting. I would say: it's not a sin found in the *world*, that does not know God, but in the *church*, where God has made himself known.

Can the Spirit be resisted?

What is this resisting of the Holy Spirit? Can the Spirit really be resisted? Indeed, he can be resisted. Resistance means that you do not want to give in or give up. There is no surrender or compliance. You go your own way, doggedly and stubbornly. We continue to resist, and if God does not powerfully break down that resistance, it will *kill* us.

Stephen does not say that there is any weakness with the Spirit, or any inability to break down human resistance, for the Holy Spirit is omnipotent and invincible God. The point is rather that we are so terribly stubborn and unyielding. Were it not for God's covenant of love and his enduring faithfulness, there would be no covenant people left. We are so incredibly stubborn and stiff-necked that God would not put up with us.

Stephen makes it clear that God wants to break through that stubbornness. God did not say: okay, have it your way, do what you want, I don't care. On the contrary, the LORD sent prophet after prophet. He came to his people with his holy Word. Through those prophets and in that Word, he proclaimed the promise of the great Messiah, who would save his people from their sins.

Rejection of the prophetic word

Stephen asks: was there ever a prophet your fathers did not persecute? It is a rhetorical question of sorts, because the inference is that all the prophets were persecuted, and many even killed. When God in his love sent prophets who spoke of the great Deliverer, the son of David, they would not listen to them either, but killed them as well. And finally in the greatest manifestation of their sin, they killed even the Messiah himself. Stephen says: now you have betrayed and murdered him. Not just killed, but murdered. Murdered, for he was innocent of all that was brought in against him. They wrongly accused Jesus also of blasphemy, and knowingly condemned an innocent man.

The resisting of the Holy Spirit is not some initial reluctance to be saved, let's say a natural hesitation on our part, so that God often waits to see what choice we will make, perhaps even nudging us along a bit in the right direction. It is something far more serious; it is the rejection of the prophetic Word of God which leads ultimately to the denial and rejection of Jesus Christ.

Stephen stands here before the Sanhedrin with his own life on the line, and he dares to say: you have always resisted the Holy Spirit. How? They have done so by rejecting the prophetic Word by which the Spirit came to them time and again, by rejecting even those prophets who spoke about the coming of the Messiah, and then finally, despite all his signs and his obviously authoritative and clear teaching, by murdering the Messiah himself, our chief prophet and teacher.

The resisting of the Holy Spirit is a denial or twisting of God's Word which leads to the rejection of Christ as the only and complete Savior. This is the inclination of all people, whether they are Jew or Gentile, as Paul writes to Romans, and it is most serious among those to whom the Holy Spirit has revealed and proclaimed the counsel of God concerning redemption.

The breaking point

Stephen makes clear that the breaking point has been reached. This is not open for discussion. There is a breaking-point with all who promote false teaching. You cannot negotiate on this point. The Sanhedrin must now recognize its sin and confess that sin, or the moment has come that the apostles and other members of the church go to the Gentiles.

Constant resisting of the Spirit ultimately means that God gives you over to your own devices. In this sense, there is hardly a way back. One explainer suggests that it comes very close to the sin against the Holy Spirit, consciously and willfully rejecting the clear testimony of the Word of God concerning the redemption in Christ.

Resisting the Spirit is not an initial human reaction which leads God to wait and see and to give you the benefit of the doubt, but resisting the Spirit is saying, after all the evidence is in and the Word has clearly sound-

ed, that there is a better way to be saved. Rejecting the way in Christ, we determine a way of our own.

Some people think that there is no breaking point with God and that people can go on resisting the Spirit indefinitely. But there is a breaking point. Stephen warns the Sanhedrin that this moment has now arrived. The Jews have doggedly charted out their own course and they are sticking to it.

Christ or the law

Stephen makes this quite clear as well. Just before they mob him and drag him out of the building, he says (verse 53), "...you who have received the law that was put into effect through angels but not obeyed it."

The Sanhedrin followed a way of salvation secured by doing and obeying the law. If you reject Christ, as the one who fulfilled the law in your place, the only way of deliverance is then that you yourself fulfill the law by obeying it. If Christ does not save you fully and perfectly, then you are left to yourself. How far will that get you?

Reject Christ as perfect Savior, and you will have to deliver yourself. It's the only way left over. Now Stephen does not deny that the law is important. He does not deny that the law should be obeyed. On the contrary, it is very important that there are good works as fruits of faith. The law is good and spiritual, as Paul would later write (Rom 7:13-20).

Stephen speaks highly of the law as having been put into effect *by angels*. This may seem like a cryptic reference, which is not supported by Old Testament evidence, but Stephen only speaks here of angels to show that the law came from God and by God's own messengers. It is not strange to think that when God descended on Mount Sinai, also many *angels* accompanied him and that these angels played a role in communicating with Moses. But that's not the point here.

It is clear that Stephen does not want to deny the importance of the law. The law is so important that if you do not keep it, it condemns you. Those who seek their salvation by the works of the law will be judged by the law. In rejecting Christ and resisting the Spirit, the Jews have made a clear choice for a man-centered and works-oriented salvation, stressing what we have to do in order to be saved. God will therefore judge them on this basis. Let it be clear then that they will not be saved in this way, for they have not obeyed the law. The only way of deliverance is by faith in Jesus Christ, and that means also by not resisting the Holy Spirit, but yielding to him and accepting the full testimony of the Word of God regarding his sovereign grace in Christ.

The only way: accept the Gospel

We should not resist the Holy Spirit. This means that we should fully and completely accept the Gospel which we have received, and so become wise unto salvation. Then we discover what the love of God in Christ truly means, how his grace is wondrously imparted to us, and that all our boasting is in the Lord alone.

Want to resist someone? The Bible tells us that we should resist the *devil*, and he will flee from us. [9] We can now by the power of the Spirit resist sin. The more our lives are governed by Christ's Spirit and Word, the less control Satan and sin have over our life. Then we start to obey God's commandments again. We try to keep his law, not for merit, but out of gratitude for the salvation received. Then we go the only way of deliverance that is truly open to mankind: the way of faith in Christ Jesus.

Just before he died, Stephen said it plainly: there is only one way of deliverance and that way is by faith in Jesus Christ. If you reject that, you are riding on your own merits right into hell, because you have not kept the law.

There is one way of deliverance. This is the way of the Gospel that was proclaimed and is being proclaimed all over the world. After Stephen's death a great persecution arose and the disciples were scattered all over, but the true Gospel had been maintained again before the Jewish Sanhedrin. It was God's last appeal to them in their official capacity as Jewish rulers.

Later Paul would appear before the Jewish leaders, the very same man who agreed with Stephen's execution at this point, but then it was before the Roman governors Felix and Festus. The members of the Sanhedrin were only false accusers and angry spectators. God did not again deal directly with them. There surely is a breaking point.

Through Stephen's testimony God still appeals to his people to be faithful, to stay on the one way of salvation of faith in Christ. It is the only way.

Do not resist the Holy Spirit, but yield to him. Let the Spirit direct the bride to Christ.

---

[9]James 4: 7; I Peter 5:9. . See also Paul's instruction about the full armor of faith required for this resisting, Ephesians 6: 10-20.

XII

Led by the Spirit

Because those who are led by the Spirit of God are Sons of God.

(ROMANS 8:14)

There is a question that comes up time and again in the life of a Christian. How can I know God's will for the decisions that I have to make every day from day to day? The passage above this chapter speaks of being *led* by the Holy Spirit, but how does the Spirit do this leading? How can we be sure it is the Spirit's guidance we are following and not our own insights?

Claims of being directly guided by the Spirit of God are highly suspect. This is especially true when someone claims to be led by the Spirit to do something which also involves *others*. Some easily say: the Spirit guided me to do this, or I felt guided by the Spirit, the Lord prepared and called me for this, God opened doors, God spoke to me, he laid this burden upon me etc., and therefore you have to do as I say.

I touched on this matter earlier but mention it now in this important context. What do you say in response to such claims? If the Holy Spirit led someone to a certain task, position, or insight, we had all better sit up and listen, right? Whoever dares to say that God has led him to become, for example, a leader in the church, affects everyone, for woe to the person who does not see or recognize God's leadership and guidance behind such a lofty claim.

Such charismatic persons are either special instruments of God, or they are supremely arrogant. Such persons are most often schismatic rather than charismatic. I read somewhere that we should never make our own decisions or feelings absolute, as if they have the force of divine

113

revelation.[10] All too easily people present their personal insights as God's guidance.

Difference between providence and revelation

What is this being led by the Spirit? Do we experience this in our lives? How do we detect God's guidance? Is this visible only, as is sometimes suggested, when we look back? Then we can say: in retrospect I see God's guidance. Is this guidance ever to be discerned in the present? Do we receive clear directions for the future?

In this passage Paul clearly infers that this being led (present tense) is an *ongoing* work of the Holy Spirit. The Spirit *is* leading us, today as he did yesterday. The question is how we are to discover this guidance and work with it.

It is important to note that there is a world of difference between revelation (God told me) and providence (God guided me). Revelation has ceased; providence continues daily. It is in the realm of God's providence, of his dealings with us in Christ, that we may understand this being led by the Holy Spirit.

An exclamation

In this passage the apostle presents the leading by the Holy Spirit as a great gift of God to his children. The text is actually in the form of an exclamation: those led by the Spirit are the sons of God! So we should not neglect Christ's work of spiritual leadership and divine guidance in our lives, but we should delight in it.

The Lord Jesus Christ leads us by the Holy Spirit to live as children of the Father. We must come to recognize the evidence and the assurance of this leading by the Holy Spirit. Then the leading by the Holy Spirit will in our lives not be a question mark but an exclamation mark. He does lead us!

Principle themes

In the letter to the Romans the apostle has explored and expounded the great principle themes of the Christian faith. He wrote about justification (chapters 3-5), sanctification (chapters 5-7), and glorification (chapter 8). Then many practical exhortations and warnings follow in the

---

[10] Donald Macloed, *The Spirit of Promise*, Christian Focus Publications, 1986, page 67.

chapters 9-16. The passage about being led by the Spirit is found in the section on *glorification*. One might even say, to be more exact, that it is found in the section that gives us the transition from sanctification to glorification.

These three main themes are presented by Paul in a marvelous, balanced manner. We are justified by faith, acquitted of guilt, but still there is death with which we have to deal. We are sanctified and being sanctified, the Spirit dwells in us, but there still is the effect of sin. We have conquered in Christ, share in his glory, and will as heirs receive full glory, but there is still the reality of suffering. See the strong lines: justification, and yet death; sanctification and yet sin; glorification, and yet suffering.

But we have triumphed and shall triumph in Christ. This triumph is seen and experienced in various ways. In chapter 8 the main theme is that those who are *in Christ Jesus* (and we want to consider that expression more closely later) are, see verse 9, "...controlled not by the sinful nature, but by the Spirit, if the Spirit of God lives in you."

Being in Christ

Notice the conditional phrase: if the Spirit of God lives in you. Paul continues in that verse: and if anyone does not have the Spirit of Christ, he does not belong to Christ. And again: but if Christ is in you, your body is dead because of sin, yet your spirit is alive...Verse 11: and if the Spirit...is living in you. We have at least four "ifs," which merit our attention.

The all-important fact is that the Spirit of God must live in us. As we head towards glory and long for it, and must persevere in suffering, the Holy Spirit must certainly dwell in us. He must lead and guide us or we cannot persevere.

In chapter 8:1 Paul writes about those who are "in Christ." To be in Christ means that we are a part of him and of his body, the church. It means that we embrace him by faith as our only and perfect Savior. It means also that we have seen our sins, confessed them, and broken with them. We are now fighting against them.

You cannot be in Christ if you *live* in sin. You cannot be controlled by the Spirit, if the devil governs your thoughts and actions. We are not to fool ourselves but to take stock of the real situation in our lives. Self-examination is constantly needed. Therefore Paul dares to write: *if* the Spirit of God is living in you.

Not meant to cast doubt

Reformed explainers agree that these four qualifications are not meant to cast doubt on whether the Christians in Rome have the Spirit or not. Rather they chart out the riches of having the Spirit and highlight the sad consequences of not having the Spirit. The point is not that the believers shall question whether they have the Spirit, but they must see the great and wonderful effect of having the Spirit in their lives. To that end they must repent wherever needed.

Notice how Paul also balances this aspect very carefully. The congregation is indeed to take stock: how terrible would it be not to have the Holy Spirit. His presence must be evidenced, but how wonderful it is that the Spirit has been given to the church: (verse 9) you, however, are not controlled by the sinful nature, but by the Spirit... Verse 15 also, following the text: for you did not receive a spirit of slavery... but the spirit of sonship. Paul is convinced that the Roman Christians have received the Spirit of sonship.

Paul bases his writing on the notion that the believers in Rome indeed have received the Holy Spirit. So he can write in verse 12, "Therefore (because the Spirit lives in you) you have an *obligation*...! His point is that having the Holy Spirit leads to a great obligation.

Spiritual obligation

We know the word obligation to be a covenantal word. At baptism we say in the Form adopted for that occasion[11]: a covenant has two parts, a promise and an *obligation*. In Romans 4 Paul has written extensively about the *promise* given to Abraham and all his offspring – which also includes us, as Paul emphatically states. The promise comes by faith and is given only out of grace. God has fulfilled his covenant promises to Abraham and to all whom he has called, and now there rests upon us an *obligation*.

We are obligated to put to death the misdeeds of the body (verse 13) and so we will live. This is possible *because* (verse 14) those who are led by the Spirit are sons of God. The Holy Spirit enables us by his indwelling and leadership to put to death the sinful nature and the misdeeds of the body.

Notice the word "because" here. The obligation that rests upon us is not something that we have to fulfill by ourselves or in our own strength. We

---

[11] *Book of Praise*, page 594.

can put to death the misdeeds of the body and we will live *because* those led by the Spirit are sons of God. God enables us by his Spirit as his children to put to death the misdeeds of the body. We are under a covenantal obligation, but we can meet it by God's Spirit as his children. This is the line of thinking followed by Paul.

What is meant by leading?

We are led by the Spirit. How are we to understand this leading? The word has various connotations which might all be important, but I want to focus on the translation "led." It does not mean that the Spirit goes ahead of us and that we then decide if we will follow. That's often how leadership is understood or experienced. We choose someone as a leader and then we follow the leader, or not.

The word used here is, however, somewhat stronger. Some translate with *driven*. We are driven by the Spirit. What I like about this translation is that it does give due recognition to the Spirit's power in his leading. But it should be clear that the Spirit does not force us to do things against our will. Instead he renews our will so that we want what God wants. Where he leads, we faithfully and heartily go.

This leading is a steady going ahead of us, always being there, giving constant guidance, so that we follow and even find joy in this following of the Spirit. It means from our side a growing in submission and discipleship.

How does the Spirit do this leading? Where is the real *evidence*? We can say or think that we are being led by the Spirit, but how do we know for sure? Do we hear a voice? Is it a feeling that grows into a conviction? Are special messages imparted to us by certain signs, by dreams, or by natural occurrences? How does it work?

The Spirit uses means

The question is whether this leading by the Spirit is *immediate*, that is, without any certifiable means. Does the Spirit come directly to give us guidance and leadership, or does he come to us by various means which he has preordained? The latter is indeed the case. Direct revelation has ceased. Those who claim to have it, have founded sects, not built churches, and have misguided believers, not put them on a better path.

The Spirit leads us by various means. This is first of all the means of *God's Word*. If a self-professed leader tells us that God's Word is unclear or insufficient, and that we are therefore to be guided by feelings, sensations,

signs, convictions, and dreams (as happened of old), and must follow especially his own ideas, you can be sure that an imposter is at work. It is remarkable how our Lord Jesus himself built only on the given Word. He said time and again, "It is written...."

If anyone comes with a teaching that is contrary to God's Word – or something that goes above and beyond God's Word – we can be sure that this is not a result of the Spirit's leadership. The evidence of true spiritual guidance lies in the Scriptural nature and content of what is taught.

It is impossible that the Spirit would lead us against God's own Word. Instead he gives us "illumination," the light to understand God's Word even better.

The Spirit also leads through lawfully given office-bearers who are faithful to Scripture and can properly apply God's Word. When Paul writes in the letter to the Ephesians that the ascended and glorified Christ gave gifts to men, these gifts are specified as being apostles, prophets, evangelists, pastors, and teachers. They will build up the church in the true knowledge of the Son of God.

Leadership in communion

This brings us to another important point. The Spirit gives leadership not just by one person who stands alone and above the crowd. That is typically sectarian. The Spirit leads through the fellowship and the communion of the holy catholic church.

The apostle Peter refers to this when he writes (I Pet 2:4) that we are like living stones being built into a spiritual house. The church is the house, the temple of the Spirit, and we have to be part of that house as a living stone if we wish to be led by the Spirit. Spiritual stones are not rolling stones. This same church, this spiritual house, is called by the apostle Paul the "pillar and foundation of the truth" (1 Tim 3:15). We are led not just by ourselves, loose from the flock, but we are led together as communion of saints with the church of all ages, to be faithful to the teaching once for all delivered to the saints (Jude:3).

If someone, then, decides to close the confessions and ignore the historical foundation of the church, how can there be any leading by the Spirit? There is in the leading by the Spirit the use of the lawful ministry of reconciliation, the fellowship of the saints, and so growth together in the truths of the Word. We let ourselves be corrected by the evidence of Scripture. We humbly submit to the faithful discipline of the church, as we have promised.

I find it very telling that many of those who claimed to be particularly led by the Spirit deeply rejected the spiritual discipline of the church and lacked the humility which characterizes faithful children of the Lord. They always knew better, and they alone knew the truth. Leadership that acknowledges the wisdom of others and does not lord it over others is leading in accordance with Biblical rules.[12]

Thinking Spiritually

The Holy Spirit guides us clearly in the Scriptures. In the day to day decisions that must be made we apply the norms and rules of Scripture as best as we can. It is sad to observe how we sometimes in our daily life knowingly make decisions that clearly and directly go in against God's Word, but we refuse to be led by the Spirit. Paul speaks about the "misdeeds of the body," giving in to sinful desires, despite the consequences that come, neglecting to do what we should do, and going consciously in against the leading of the Spirit.

I must add that the Spirit's leadership does not mean that we should not apply with Scripture the principles of nature and the rule of common sense. We have to use our minds and learn to think spiritually and responsibly. God did not create us without a mind, but he by his Spirit *renews* our mind.[13] Think biblically, speak with others, listen to their insights, and come to a sensible conclusion.

What strikes me when it comes to self-evaluation is that some people overestimate their gifts. They think highly of themselves, even though this is hidden under a thin veneer of pseudo-humility. But there are also people who tend to underestimate their gifts, do not see their talents, and therefore do not multiply them. The Spirit leads us properly to esteem the gifts, abilities, and talents that we have been given, and then we are to exercise sober judgment (Rom 12:3) and appreciate the input of fellow members of the church.

---

[12] In Proverbs 11:14 we read, "For lack of guidance a nation falls, but many advisors make victory sure" (NIV) or "...in the multitude of counselors there is safety." (KJV). Leadership may lie ultimately in the hands of one person, but he needs many advisors to rule wisely.

[13] Ro 12:12, "...be transformed by the renewing of your mind...."

Is what we do edifying?

Being led by the Spirit means that God involves us to examine our heart, motives, gifts, feelings, and even to open our lives to the views of those who are faithful to the sound doctrine. This leading by the Spirit always guides us to do what is *edifying*. Paul has written in I Corinthians 6:12, "...everything is permissible, but not everything is beneficial" (edifying). The Spirit leads us not to offend others, not to cast stumbling blocks, not to cause division, but to seek what is up-building for all without compromising the Word of God. The purpose is not to demonstrate that we are right, but to consider how something we do benefits the church of Christ.

Being led by the Spirit means that we grow in the wisdom of Scripture. We must prayerfully meditate on God's Word every day. We must be renewed in our thinking, that is, approach all questions with a mind ruled by the Spirit, use our given talents as well as our natural abilities and common sense – which have been reshaped by the Scriptures – and listen to the brotherhood in whose midst we live and function.

The leadership of such persons will be accepted by the holy Catholic Church.

Never forget prayer

In this process, we may never forget *prayer*, the ABBA, Father! as the Lord Jesus taught us to pray. Being led by the Spirit is evidenced through a close walking with the Lord, in humble but persevering prayer, asking him to bless and to give wisdom and insight. I will elaborate on the relation between the Holy Spirit and prayer in another chapter, but let it be said now in connection with being led by the Spirit: whoever does not pray in accordance with the Word, can not be led by the Spirit. But by prayerfully mobilizing all the gifts that God has given us, we can progress in knowing and doing God's will.

Will we then never make mistakes? Will we sometimes not fall into sin or error? Does this leading by the Spirit make us virtually invincible and untouchable? It does not. The Spirit does not *replace* our nature with another one, let's say a flawless one, but he *renews* our nature. That is not a single event, but an ongoing process. And it is on this way also that we receive assurance of being a child of God. Paul writes: you will live, because those who are led by the Spirit are sons of God.

Not become sons but are sons

Notice that Paul doesn't write: those who are led by the Spirit *become* sons of God. He writes that they *are*. This being led does not bring us to hope or speculate or assume that we are God's sons, but it gives us the assurance that we are God's sons.

Some would have it this way: if we really try hard and climb up to a certain level of obedience, then we might become sons of God. It takes a lot, and it can also be lost, if we are not very careful. There is very little lasting assurance here, for we can tumble out of every state of grace. Those who are led by the Spirit, it should read then, are for that time also sons of God, but not when they tumble and fall. This is the Arminian position which denies the perseverance of the saints.[14]

But we may say: if we by the Spirit put to death the misdeeds of the body and if we are in the process of true sanctification, we are also on our way to *glory*, because those who are led by the Spirit are the sons of God. Justification leads to sanctification, and that is part of our glorification. It will culminate in the full manifestation of our being sons of God.

The Spirit leads to Christ

Even though we are led by the Holy Spirit, we can still fall into grievous sins. Remember that sin is with us until glorification is realized. Sometimes we might even come to doubt our sonship. The devil can accuse us, as well as our sins and our own conscience, and we can despair, "Am I really a child of God, when I am still capable of terrible sins?"

Our sins should shock us. I read somewhere that it's like being in a dark tunnel, where we never should have gotten into, and then seeing there is light, not at the end of the tunnel, but all through the tunnel. This happens when our sins alarm us, and teach us to watch and pray, to flee to Christ alone for forgiveness and renewal. This is what the apostle Paul calls "godly sorrow" (2 Cor 7:10).

For the Spirit in his guiding always leads us *to Christ*, to Golgotha. The Holy Spirit is one-directional. He is not one dimensional, so to speak, but one-directional. He always leads us back to the Lord Jesus, from the cross to the throne. He assures us of our inheritance in the Lord Jesus. We receive the inheritance not on our merit or because we

---

[14] This is also the classic position of John Wesley, which has permeated much of British and American theology.

were so faithful and fruitful in God's service. But we receive it through the Son of God alone.

Son ship means inheritance

Notice how Paul writes, "…because those who are led by the Spirit are *sons of God"* I hope that women who read this book are not offended by this apostolic way of speaking. Paul uses the word *sons* at this point because he wants to emphasize the *inheritance.* The sons received the first right to the inheritance. But this includes all who are led by the Spirit. In verse 10, after having established who the lawful heirs are, he uses the expression "God's children." Being a child of God is not a matter of gender but of faith.

When it comes to the inheritance, there is only one point that matters: are you an heir of the kingdom of heaven? Do you belong to the covenant of God? Are you his child, and was this evidenced by the Spirit? Are you assured in Christ of the inheritance itself?

For the Spirit drives us to Christ, to the Son. The same Spirit assures us by Christ's cross that indeed we are children of God. We may grow in that assurance, also when we come to repent of grievous sins, and we may know: I am (still) an heir to the promises of God, I shall again take upon myself the obligation in the covenant, for I have a renewed desire to put to death the misdeeds of the body.

Then life becomes new again. There is no experience of greater joy than to have broken with a certain difficult sin by God's grace and power, and to live again in the assurance of salvation: I *am* a child of God. How wonderful it is to experience the riches of the comfort of Christ and to see again how the way of justification is the way of sanctification and also the way of glorification.

Where does he lead? In the Lord's house I shall dwell forever (Psalm 23).

XII

The Inward Testimony of the Holy Spirit

The Spirit himself testifies with our spirit that we are God's children.

(ROMANS 8:16)

Earlier I dealt with the previous verses in Romans 8 which speak of being led by the Holy Spirit. We noted that this leadership is given by the Spirit in the way of the means of grace, through the preaching of the Gospel and the use of the sacraments, and also through the work of the office bearers and the communion of the church. Of course, we may not restrict the leading of the Spirit to these means, for there is also his omnipotence and providence, but we certainly do appreciate what God gives us in the means of grace.

The question, however, still comes up if there is not a direct, immediate working of the Holy Spirit in our hearts. In the above-quoted passage we read about the fact that the Spirit himself testifies with our spirit.... How are we to understand this testifying or testimony? Does it appear from this text that this testifying is something beyond or besides the Word or the preaching of the Word? It seems to be some *inward* testimony, since the Holy Spirit testifies with *our* spirit. Does this indicate that some conscious experience takes place within us? It would be rather strange if the Holy Spirit testified with our Spirit, and we did not notice this or experience it.

Experiential?

Do we read here about what some have called the *experience* of faith, or the experiential aspect of faith? It has been said that the experiential

123

side of faith is not stressed enough (if at all) in many Reformed churches. We sometimes hear that in Reformed preaching there's often an element missing, and that is the emphasis on the inward working of the Holy Spirit. We should be sensitive to this criticism.

If we are controlled by the Spirit (verse 9), if the Spirit of Christ lives in us (verse 11), and if we have received the Spirit of sonship, then certainly we must have some experience of this. These things cannot happen without us noticing them, and therefore Paul can write that the Spirit himself witnesses with our Spirit.

We may say that the inward testimony of the Holy Spirit assures us that we are children of God. This testimony is not any new information but it is a true confirmation of what we have embraced by faith.

Testifying

We must be clear from the start when we speak of "the testimony of the Holy Spirit," that we are not speaking of something that is totally new, that Paul has not referred to earlier in this letter. It now comes out more clearly and powerfully, and there is a reason for that, but the matter itself is not new.

Our Lord Jesus in his farewell conversation with his disciples already spoke about the testifying of the Holy Spirit: he will testify about me (John 15:26). The Spirit is the Spirit of *testimony*. He officially witnesses that something is true and credible, and therefore it must be accepted.

In John 15 there is a noteworthy connection: the Spirit comes to dwell in the disciples and testifies to them about Jesus, and this leads the disciples, in turn, also to testify about Jesus. So whatever it is, this inward testimony of the Spirit is evidenced by external testifying in mission and evangelism. This stands to reason. How can we have the Spirit testifying within us, and we do not speak of it to others?

The Spirit testifies

Before we go back to Romans 8, let us at this point look closer at 1 John 5. In verse 1 John writes that everyone who believes that Jesus is the Christ is born of God. It is the Lord Jesus who came by "water and blood," and this refers both to Christ's baptism and his crucifixion and death. Christ's entire public ministry (from baptism to death) was one of intense suffering. John repeats the element of the "blood" because it emphasizes that Jesus really died and in a terrible manner.

Then we read again (verse 6) about the Spirit: it is the Spirit who *testifies*, because the Spirit is the truth. Almost the same verb is used as in the passage we are examining in Romans 8. The Spirit testifies. Testifying is apparently a prime work of the Holy Spirit.

A few verses later we read that the testimony of the Spirit is the testimony of *God*. And the testimony of God is greater than that of anyone else. John continues in verse 10: anyone who believes in the Son of God has this testimony *in his heart*. Consider also verse 11: and this is the testimony, God has given us eternal life, and this life is in his Son.

The Spirit of testimony

It is clear from all these passages that the Spirit is the Spirit of testimony, and that this testimony is the testimony of God. This testimony is true and reliable, and must be believed by all. Whoever rejects it, calls God a liar.

The testimony of the Father and the Spirit is that Jesus Christ is the Son of God and in him is eternal life. We see here again something of the unity in the Trinity.

There are many things that testify to the fact that Jesus is the Son of God, the Messiah given by the LORD. There are the words of Scripture. There are Jesus' own teachings. There are the facts of his life and death, notably his resurrection and ascension. There is enough evidence to clinch the case, as it were, but the greatest evidence, the most credible testimony is given by the Holy Spirit himself. All those other things cannot really convince anyone, but the Spirit's testimony, in and through these things also, completes the others and renders them fully trustworthy.

The Spirit testifies. He is an expert witness, so to speak. He is the most credible witness of all because he has outstanding, perfect credentials. He presents all the evidence – and also examines the evidence given by others – and he says: yes, this is true indeed. It is this testimony of the Holy Spirit that convinces everyone of the *truth* of the matter.

True and factual

Sometimes in an important trial or court case, everything hinges on the testimony of *one* crucial witness who has seen all and can tie all together. The defense lawyers try to get at this witness, to confuse him, to catch him in contradictions, and so to discredit the witness. If you can discredit the main witness, you stand a good chance of getting your client off the hook.

The Holy Spirit is the prime witness. He testifies that Jesus is indeed the Christ, who has paid for all our sins by his death, and who is now raised in glory and lives in heaven. The Holy Spirit says to all: this is exactly how it went and how it is. So the Holy Spirit testifies *about God*: he tells us exactly what God had in mind in the life and death of Jesus Christ, to redeem us from our sins, to deliver us from slavery, and to makes us again children of God. The Holy Spirit testifies that all this is absolutely *true and factual*, so that everyone has to believe and accept it. This is one witness whom no accuser can rattle or disprove. No one can get around the power and the truth of this testimony.

Convince and convict

While we are on the subject of testimony or witness, I mention as a side note that in the *Belgic Confession* the work of the Holy Spirit in this respect is also mentioned. Let's look at Article 5 [15] about the authority of Scripture. We confess there that we believe without a doubt all things contained in the Bible. Why do we believe this? It says, "...not so much because the church receives and approves them as such, but especially because the *Holy Spirit witnesses in our hearts* that they are from God...." The Holy Spirit witnesses of the truth of the Bible in our hearts. How does he do that?

Meanwhile it becomes clear from Scripture that the prime work of the Holy Spirit is *witnessing and testifying to the Truth*. In this way the Holy Spirit also *convinces and convicts*. Only the Truth is convincing and only the Truth will set you free. The Holy Spirit does this so that there is no doubt left whatsoever in our minds and hearts that the Bible is true and Jesus is our Savior. Therefore we believe in him, are saved by him, and God is our Father. All this rests on the testimony of the Holy Spirit.

No new information

We have not yet considered how the Spirit testifies *with our spirit*, but that can be done only in a proper manner when we realize on the basis of what has been said thus far that the Spirit really does not give any *new* information. Sure, he is the Spirit of *revelation*, and he has revealed all things that we need to know for our salvation in the Bible. The truth is given in all

---

[15] *Book of Praise*, page 443.

that is written by the prophets and the apostles, and we now neither need nor receive new information.

Jesus said: [the Spirit] will glorify me. He will take what is mine – what I have earned – and will give it to you. There's nothing new here that has never been said before. This is now especially true in this age in which God's work of revelation has been fully completed. There is no new information. It's back to the cross every day again.

I think that this is important for our understanding of the work of the Spirit. There are those who teach that revelation still continues today, and that new messages are received by some internal process. Some think of dreams, for they believe that God still communicates sometimes by extra-ordinary means.

This would happen especially on the mission field where the added testifying of the Spirit, above and beyond the preaching of the Gospel, may be required to convince people. Perhaps events occur that are unusual or even miraculous. But this is not revelation.

Pre-scriptural revelation?

I came across the term "pre-scriptural revelation." This term sounds impressive, but it is utter nonsense. It conflicts with what we know of the testimony of the Spirit. There is today no new or pre- or extra revelation. There is in terms of revelation nothing "pre-scriptural." It's simply a wrong and dangerous use of the word revelation which only furthers the erroneous claim that God reveals himself (today still) outside of the Holy Scriptures.

There are those who suggest that God by the Holy Spirit must first prepare the soil so that the seed can be taken up by the soil. A fitting reference here, they say, is the parable of the seed that falls on rocky soil, on soil with weeds, and in good soil. The soil is then made good by "pre-scriptural revelation."

But let us not get mixed up between the soil *and the seed*. The seed, the Word that is revealed, is in all cases *the same*. The soil is different, indeed, and one must understand the parable in its context and entirety to understand the differences in the soil and what these mean, but let us not be confused about the seed: everywhere the same seed was sown. There is no pre-scriptural revelation, no message behind the words, and no text between the lines.

The testimony of the Spirit is not new information, for the Holy Spirit directs us always to the *given* information. Only the Word of God as

revealed in the Scriptures is normative. The Spirit brings this normative word to us, confronts us with its powerful truth, and then proclaims by it: believe and be saved; reject it, and remain condemned.

Confirming, not informing

Therefore we can only go in one direction here. The testimony of the Holy Spirit *confirms* the testimony and evidence given in the Word. When the Belgic Confession speaks about the fact that "the Holy Spirit witnesses in our hearts that [the Scriptures] are from God," this is God's sovereign and powerful *confirming* to us in our hearts that God's Word is *true* and fully sure. Confirming is something quite different than informing. It is very important that we appreciate this difference.

The Spirit witnesses in our hearts. As we are reading Scripture and meditating on it, or listening to it being read and expounded, the Holy Spirit by that very Word convinces us deep in our hearts that what it says, gives and demands, is *true*, not just true in general or in a scientific sense, but true for the reader or hearer.

When I read the Bible I know deep in my heart that it is true. It is true for me personally as well. Every single word is true. I do not doubt the truth of what is says, not once, not ever. I may not always understand each and every sentence or section, but that's another matter. It is absolutely and completely true. This is not my own conviction, for by nature I would have rejected the Word, like so many others do, but this is the convincing of God, the witness of the Holy Spirit.

The Spirit himself testifies with our spirit

This is also how we now understand what is written in Romans 8:16: the Spirit *himself* testifies... Notice the word himself. There is in the original some emphasis on this word himself. Paul is at this point not writing to people who do not believe, and who are objects of mission or evangelism, but he is writing to believers about their joy and certainty. He then writes: it is not because we have all kinds of wonderful feelings that we believe. The Spirit does not necessarily give you goose bumps. Faith is not some kind of a midway thrill. Do you know what really happens? The Spirit himself – and no one else, not any human being, that's for sure – testifies *with our spirit*!

Please note that it does not say here that the Holy Spirit testifies *in* our spirit or *to* our spirit, but *with* our spirit. We are here not dealing with people who are in the process of coming to faith, or must still believe, but we

are learning about people who already believe and whose faith must be confirmed and strengthened.

How does this strengthening take place? It happens in a very close bond with the Holy Spirit. We testify that we are God's children. We do this by faith in response to God's Word. Somebody may ask: are you sure? Satan may accuse us, and say: you are not. Our own consciences may testify against us: are you really? But my spirit says: Yes, I am. Despite all, through all, I may cling to Jesus Christ, and I seek cleansing and renewal in him alone.

This is how the Holy Spirit himself *testifies with our spirit*. The Holy Scriptures are applied to us. There is a deep, inner conviction, calm, peace, and love that knows one thing for sure: I am a child of God.

We need confirmation

I emphasized that the testimony of the Spirit does not give anything new. It is not something that I now am convinced of for the first time. It is a confirmation that Scripture is true for me. I badly need this confirmation, too.

I had to think of what is sometimes said when we plan a trip. We need to have our flight *confirmed*. We have the ticket, the seat is ours, and the reservation has been registered. The arrangement is legal and valid. Yet even then, when we have the tickets, some hours prior to the flight itself, we phone the airline company, just to make sure, and we have our trip confirmed. I am booked, am I not?

I have traveled often, and then you come to the point that you do not bother always to confirm the flight. You take your reservation for granted. But it does leave you with a little uneasiness: maybe I should have had it confirmed. In some places you simply have to get your flight confirmed or you won't get off the ground.

When it comes to this most important matter of all, whether I am a child of God, I need *confirmation*. I have to know for sure. I cannot live in uncertainty on this point. I cannot function without being a child of God. For then I fall to pieces.

Here's where the Spirit comes in. Now we have to backtrack one verse. The Spirit is not a spirit that makes me a slave again to *fear*, it says, the fear that I am condemned by my sins and weaknesses, that I might lose my salvation through misdeeds of the flesh, and that the law of God will crush me. What does the Spirit do? He is the Spirit of *sonship* who assures us that we are God's children, and leads us again to the Father.

It says in verse 15 (end): and *by him* (the Spirit of sonship) we cry ABBA, Father! Here I am, struggling with my obligations, knowing that I am not worthy, have not kept God's law as I should have, and I fear sometimes that God will reject me, but when I feel that way, the Spirit comes into action, and confirms: you are God's child, come let us together go to the Father. And I cry ABBA, Father. Paul uses the verb *to cry*, and that is not necessarily a loud screaming, but it is a sincere pleading that comes deep from the heart, ABBA, oh my Father, I cannot live without you, do not cast me away, cover my sins, and show me your grace.

In and by that prayer the Spirit works the assurance of faith. He testifies because he knows the truth. He testifies with my spirit, which does believe but is so weak and failing. He testifies with my spirit, strengthens it and fills it with God's love. He focuses my faltering spirit on Jesus' grace, calms it with his fellowship, and I am convinced again that I am a child of God. It is confirmed.

Incredible peace

Then there is this incredible peace in which we rejoice that there is no condemnation for those who are in Christ Jesus (Romans 8:1). Then there is this testimony (I John 5:11): God has given us eternal life, and this life is in his Son. The storm is stilled, I am where peaceful streams are gently flowing (Psalm 23). If this is called experiential, let's have it, indeed.

Notice also that it says: the Spirit of sonship, and by him *we* cry, Abba, Father. The word "we" means you and me and all of us. It is not an experience unique to one Christian. It is not something that God gives only to certain members, but to *all*. Let us beware here of haughty individualism. We cry. We are part of the church. Ephesians 4:4, 5: there is one body and one Spirit, just as you were called to one hope when you were called, one Lord, one faith, one baptism, one God and Father of us all. We cry. We do it sometimes even *together* in communal prayer in the worship services. We cry out, loud and clear, and without fear: Abba, Father! He is near. Paul writes about it in terms that the Romans, too, can say: we know what you are talking about.

We are God's *children*, it says in verse 15. In the preceding verse 14 it says sons. We looked at this in the previous chapter and said that the word sons also includes the daughters. Let me now add that the word son is a more formal way of speaking, while the word child is more intimate. It is a close bond: *Abba, my Father. Yes, my child.* It emphasizes that God himself brought us forth, gave us birth and rebirth, life and eternal life. This life is

in his Son Jesus Christ. We can always flee to him and experience the tenderness of his mercy. He calls me his child. I call him my Father. And I feel I have come home again.

Ongoing testimony

Allow me one last remark in this connection. The verb to testify is in the present tense. It indicates that this testimony is *ongoing*. The Spirit constantly is working in us prayer and leading us to conviction through prayer. It is not a one-time event, as some would have it, but it continues throughout our whole life. He abides with us forever, and he always works in us the knowledge that we are God's children.

We need this experience throughout this difficult life with all its ups-and-downs. We cannot walk one day in faith without the Holy Spirit. Every evening as I review the day's events, I may say through the Spirit of sonship: Abba, Father! Then I can rest in the love of God, in the grace of the Lord Jesus Christ, and in the fellowship of the Holy Spirit. I can face another day.

XIV

The Spirit of Intercession

In the same way the Spirit helps us in our weakness. We do not know what we ought to pray for, but the Spirit himself intercedes for us with groans that words cannot express. And he who searches our hearts knows the mind of the Spirit, because the Spirit intercedes for the saints in accordance with God's will.

(ROMANS 8:26, 27)

The main theme of the apostle in Romans 8 is life through the Spirit. In the last two chapters, I concentrated on the fact that we have received the Spirit of sonship, the Spirit who testifies with our spirit that we are children of God. In Romans 8:17 the apostle tells us that we will share in the *glory* of Christ. That is ultimately the inheritance which awaits us as children of God. The counsel of God concerning our redemption is completed only when we are glorified.

We find this same line in Romans 8:30, "And those he predestined, he also called; those he called, he also justified; those who justified he also *glorified*." The apostle does not give here an exact scheme with each and every phase in God's order of salvation, but he shows us key lines from calling to glorification. Until we are glorified, the work of redemption is not yet perfected in us.

Reality check

Therefore a reality check is in order. We are not yet glorified, but live in a creation that is in bondage, under present sufferings. Sometimes we are like sheep being led to the slaughter, as Paul quoted from Psalm 44. It is comforting to look at the great and glorious future that awaits us, but first we must contend with the present sufferings of this world.

133

With the word "sufferings" Paul does not just mean the situation of his time, which was becoming increasingly difficult for Christians. He looks at the entire last age, connects that in verse 22 to previous times, and realizes that in many ways for the believers the worst is yet to come. How will we stand as believers in the ever-deteriorating situation of the last ages, when Satan will be loosed (Rev 20) and the man of lawlessness will appear (2 Thessalonians)?

Groaning

If there is a word that connects the entire passage on which we focus, it is the word *groaning*. Verse 22: we know that the whole creation has been *groaning* as in the pangs of childbirth. Not only this, but (verse 23) we ourselves *groan* inwardly. And then in the text printed above: the Spirit himself intercedes for us with *groans* that words cannot express. Creation is groaning, we are groaning, and the Spirit is groaning. How are we to understand this groaning?

The word groaning indicates deep misery and great suffering. Often when there is groaning, there are no clear words spoken, just sounds uttered that come from deep within. It is significant that life is characterized as groaning, for this clearly indicates that life in this world is one of deep suffering.

I once read a description of how an army surgeon entered a military hospital ward, and he heard only groaning, a clearly audible but incomprehensible sound. He suddenly realized that many of the wounded were beyond help, already crossing the threshold of this life with incessant groaning.

But here it is not a groaning without hope. The groaning of creation is compared to the pangs of childbirth: I can see a new tomorrow coming on. At the end of this process is new life. We groan, it says, but inwardly as we wait eagerly for the redemption of our bodies. The Spirit's groaning is not without purpose and effect. The groaning is done in *hope*, see verse 24: if we hope for what we do not have, we wait for it patiently. In this light also we understand the work of intercession which the Holy Spirit does on our behalf.

The Holy Spirit intercedes for us in the hope of salvation. We learn about the need for this intercession. We may be assured of the depth of this intercession. And finally, we may find joy in the effect of this intercession. When the Spirit intercedes for us, he does a wonderful work.

We have two Counselors

We know that we have a sympathetic high priest in heaven, our Lord Jesus Christ, who can fully understand our predicament because he himself was here in the flesh, knows this world, and knows us intimately. We know that in his love he intercedes for us with the Father, that is, he pleads our cause at God's right hand.

What is remarkable about this passage is that we learn here how the *Holy Spirit* himself also intercedes for us. Christ in heaven and the Spirit on earth in us both intercede for us. We do not have one Counselor, but we have two Counselors, one in heaven and one on earth. We noted this earlier, but with this passage we bring to mind once again this deeply comforting reality.

Why the intercession of the Holy Spirit?

Why do we have or do we need this intercession of the Holy Spirit? Let me begin with the indication in the text itself. It says: in the same way the Spirit helps us in our weaknesses. Note the expression: in the same way. What way is meant?

The apostle has written about birth pangs. A woman who is about to give birth needs much support and help. At the end of the birthing process, human resources are almost empty. We, too, who eagerly await the redemption of our bodies, are sometimes at our wits end. There is the danger that just before the new dawn breaks, we give up and give in. We need to have hope. Hope springs eternal, keeps the fires burning, and the hearts beating expectantly.

This is now exactly the work of the Holy Spirit. He is the Spirit of hope whose great joy is to give us hope and perseverance. Therefore he intercedes for us. You have to see the need for this intercession; otherwise you will not appreciate it or even despise it.

Our weakness

It says: the Spirit helps us "in our weakness." Here again, as so often, the Lord gives us a proper evaluation of our activities and possibilities. We cannot stand on our own, not even for a moment. If God did not sustain us every moment of the day, we would perish utterly. We'd be crushed under the harsh reality of life that is cursed by sin.

I think that Paul here, however, means more than just our weakness as human beings. There is a strong connection with the next sentence: we

do not know what we ought to pray for, but the Spirit himself intercedes for us... Now the apostle is speaking not about the style or the manner of our praying, but about the *content*: we do not even know *what* we ought to pray for! We may ask many things, but in our praying we miss the real need and overlook the true essentials.

The disciples once asked the Lord: teach us to pray (Luke 11:1). Then he taught them the Lord's Prayer. That prayer is a basic model. But how are we to pray these things in the ebb and flow of daily life? It is not so easy. We do not even know what we should be asking for. This shows how limited we are. We lack the proper self-knowledge for a God-pleasing prayer. We either estimate ourselves too highly or too lowly. Often specific character weaknesses are seen only by others and not by ourselves.

Besides, we cannot properly fathom our circumstances. We fail to see where the real dangers lie and where the true opportunities are. There is a tremendous lack of insight in the complexities of life. We do not know what will happen tomorrow. We look through a dark glass, and sometimes we, indeed, come to the point where we do not know anymore what to pray. Ever had the experience that you simply don't know anymore what to say to the Lord?

The Spirit knows

Paul speaks here inclusively. This happens to all Christians. There is a great need here that pertains to everyone. Our life of prayer is insufficient, lacking in depth and conviction, often so much a manner of custom that it fails utterly as a prayer. I am not trying to put anyone down, especially not those who think that their prayer life is very advanced, but this is the Biblical assessment of our prayer life: we do not know what we ought to pray for.

This sad situation is one that the Holy Spirit, who dwells within us, fully comprehends and tackles. It says: we do not know what we ought to pray for – we have our priorities all mixed up often – *but* the Spirit intercedes for us... The Spirit who knows all, who accurately assesses our present condition, and who knows our character, our God-given strengths and our natural weaknesses, intercedes for us.

This is truly astounding. As mentioned, we know that Jesus Christ intercedes for us in heaven, at God's right hand. But now we read that the Spirit himself (emphasis on his person) intercedes for us as well. This interceding has a judicial element. It is based on God's *law and justice*. The Holy Spirit functions as a "counselor," as an advocate, an attorney-at-law,

and he presents to God on our behalf the real *facts* – the saving work of Christ – and he points out the real *needs* – that we need to persevere in hope. The Spirit urges God to listen, even to the things that we do not say or cannot say. The Spirit points to the lawful basis for this, namely the death and resurrection of Christ, and he pleads: forgive your children, help your children, renew your children, and do not let them fall. As in heaven through Christ God speaks to God, so the Holy Spirit within us on earth carries the embattled and beleaguered believers before the throne of God, and pleads on their behalf. On earth through the Spirit, God speaks to God.

Our prayer not replaced

We must be clear on one important matter here. The Holy Spirit does not replace our prayer. It does not say that the Spirit intercedes *in* us, or *with* us, but *for* us. I may not say: the Lord Jesus intercedes for me in heaven and the Spirit intercedes for me on earth, so now I can sit back and do nothing. After all, with such intercessors, what weight will my feeble prayer possibly put on the incense scales of heaven?

It does not say at all that we should not pray or intercede for one another. The Holy Spirit does not push us aside, and say: you're making such a lousy job of it, here, let me take over. On the contrary, Paul, for example, later asks for the intercession of the Christians in Rome that he may come to them (Rom 15:30, 31). The intercession of Christ and the Holy Spirit are meant to undergird and fortify our own prayers and intercessions. We can even say: our praying makes sense, despite its many weaknesses and shortcomings, because the Holy Spirit himself intercedes for us. He asks the Father: please listen to them as they pray, for I know their needs, their trials, and their hopes. I live in them.

The Spirit's praying does not cancel our prayer but strengthens and furthers it.

No superficial request

The intercession of the Spirit is not some kind of superficial or off-hand request that the Holy Spirit makes on our behalf. We sometimes also plead for somebody else in needy circumstances but our heart is not always in it, and we try once but then give up. Then we sometimes even dare to say: I did my best for you, but it did not help. Our intercession is perhaps well-meant, but is always weak.

But it is said here of the intercession of the Spirit, "(the Spirit himself intercedes for us) *with groans that words cannot express*" (verse 26b). If our groans, as I suggested earlier, are mere sounds, that come from deep within us and express our anguish wordlessly, how much more will this not be said of the Holy Spirit?

As a matter of fact, it actually says: the groaning of the Holy Spirit cannot be expressed in words. That's how deep it goes. Our language, colorful as it may be, simply does not have the words that can adequately catch and convey this groaning of the Spirit, what he is saying and why.

A bond of solidarity

What is the meaning of this groaning of the Spirit? In what way is it helpful for us to know this? First of all, it shows us something of the depth of the Spirit's involvement in every situation and in our lives. He is here, indwelling in our hearts, but we should never take this to be a cold and lifeless presence. The Spirit knows what we feel, what we need, and also knows that we cannot express this properly ourselves, and therefore in his interceding for us there is a bond of solidarity that goes beyond our understanding.

Reformed explainers, and others also, refer to this as a mystery, that is, something which we know about, but cannot understand. It goes far beyond our mental and spiritual capacity.

It means surely that the Spirit who helps us in our weakness is very personally and intensively involved in every aspect of our lives.

What we cannot express to God, he expresses on our behalf. He makes clear what deep need we are in. He explains how sad and defeated we can feel. He also testifies to the remorse over sin that there is in our hearts, and he pleads with the Father in heaven that he graciously for Christ's sake grants us what is necessary. In this way he adds what is lacking in our prayer. He expresses what we cannot express. My weak and sinful prayer, which is often not to the point of real need, is carried to heaven by the groaning of the Holy Spirit, and he makes it into a proper, even a perfect prayer.

In prayer we are not alone

Here we see the depth of the intercession by the Spirit. Creation groans. We, too, groan. But the Spirit also groans! He is not an uninterested observer, who has no bond with us and with this creation, but he longs for the day of complete renewal and perfection, the liberation from all

bondage and the glorious freedom of the children of God. The Spirit is the Spirit of *freedom* (2 Cor 3:17) and he wants us all to be free forever from all sin and effect of sin.

This deeply motivates the Holy Spirit, and when we pray such prayers, our prayers fully touch the Spirit, and he groans also in a longing that goes beyond our longing, for the longing of the Holy Spirit is greater than ours, as we learn also in Revelation 22: the *Spirit* and the bride say: come, Lord Jesus. The bride says come, but only because the Spirit says it first, and teaches the bride to say this.

We see here how the Father, Son, and Spirit together long and work for the renewal of all things, of creation, and of God's children, so that God will be all in all. The Father works his counsel, the Son pleads on our behalf as heavenly high-priest, and even the groaning of the Spirit ascends on our behalf before the throne in heaven.

So when I pray, I am not alone. When you pray, you are not alone. We are not alone when we pray together. For the Spirit also prays. He intercedes for us with groans that words cannot express. He takes our feeble prayers, and makes them strong. He takes our unfinished prayers, and perfects them. He makes our groans his own and deepens them. We must learn this, reckon with this, and work with this knowledge. It's not revealed here to be ignored. Focus in your praying on the Spirit also, knowing that he lifts up your prayers to heaven by his intercession from earth, and then in heaven Christ receives them, sanctifies them, and offers them to the Father, who listens and understands. In this way prayer becomes so uplifting, comforting, and encouraging that you can not, will not, do without it. Your own praying will become deeper and stronger, because of the work of the Spirit in you, and the bond with God will grow.

No deceiving of God

There is one more question here. If the Spirit intercedes with groans that words cannot express, and if they are unintelligible sounds, how can God make any *sense* out of them? How can God possibly understand and hear such groaning, much less respond to it?

We read in verse 27 exactly how this goes. It says: he who searches our hearts knows the mind of the Spirit. These are important words. He who searches the hearts is *God*. God is always searching our hearts. He looks deep into our hearts, especially when we *pray*. When we talk to him, tell him our problems, and ask for his blessing, he looks deep into us to test our true motives and real desires.

That's why we cannot deceive God with our prayers. We sometimes perhaps subconsciously think that we can fool God. We pray, but our heart is not right. Our motives are wrong and self-centered. We use the means of prayer, knowing that God cannot be pleased. And God knows, because he made us. He is our Creator. Although we are different, for he is God and we are human, he sees right to the core of our hearts. Nothing is hidden before him.

We must remember this when we pray. We should not try to hide things or conveniently forget to mention important matters. When you speak to God, he listens, and he does so better than anyone else, for he listens to the heart. He knows if our groaning is real or feigned. You cannot fool the Lord God.

The mind of the Spirit

He searches the hearts of men. But it also says: he knows the *mind of the Spirit*. The Father, Son, and Spirit are one, also in their thinking. God knows what the Spirit wants. God knows what the Spirit is aiming for. The groaning of the Spirit may be without words, but the Father and the Son do not needs words to understand exactly what the Spirit is conveying.

The *effect* of the Spirit's intercession therefore is immediate and powerful. God does not have to check it out to see if it fits or to analyze it to see if it is proper. You only have to check out requests if you are not sure about their truth, their sincerity, and their motive. Then you must try to ascertain whether everything is in accordance with God's will. God does not answer petitions or intercessions which are not in accordance with his will. Therefore we must remember always to pray according to God's will only; your will be done.

This explains why Paul writes that the Spirit intercedes for the saints *in accordance with God's will*. Since our petitions are not always proper, God does not accept them or hears them differently than we expected. But the Spirit's intercession is always heard, for the Spirit intercedes only in accordance with God's will. Every intercession of the Holy Spirit is timely, proper, and exact. Whatever he asks is always in full harmony with the will of God. So when the Spirit intercedes for us, we know that it will be heard. The intercession of the Spirit is very effective.

Perfect and true intercession

If the hearing of prayer depended on my motives and my sincerity, I think that many of my prayers would not go halfway to heaven. Our prayer-life is poor, lax, and off-hand. Sometimes when we pray, our mind is even on totally other things. This must be very annoying to the Father.

But the Spirit's intercession is perfect and true. He knows God's will. He applies that will to us in his intercession. He knows that what God decides is good, what God does, is excellent, and that in all this, we are bound for glory. The Spirit in this way helps us to bear our burdens, to accept our trials, and to look forward in hope, because in all these things we are more than conquerors through him who loved us.

The Spirit gives us the sense, the knowledge, and the anticipation of complete victory, when also our groaning and yearning will be stilled in eternal peace. It is because of Christ's work of atonement and through the Spirit's work of intercession that our prayers become possible and make sense. When thus grounded in Christ, our praying, too, makes sense and is sent to heaven by the Spirit. In this way our prayer becomes powerful. Our prayers have full effect as well. Our prayers are restored, empowered, transmitted by the intercession of the Holy Spirit. Our prayers do not loose strength but gain it by the effective intercession of the Spirit within us.

I can pray, and the prayer of a righteous person is powerful in its effect, because the Spirit intercedes for me and for you, and for all who call upon God in faith through Jesus Christ.

XV

The Lord is the Spirit

Now the Lord is the Spirit, and where the Spirit of the Lord is, there is freedom.

(2 CORINTHIANS 3:17)

The passage that we wish to discuss in this chapter is considered to be very difficult by many explainers, perhaps one of the most difficult in the New Testament. But despite some degree of difficulty this passage shows us in very clear terms the close relationship between the Holy Spirit and the Lord Jesus Christ.

This text is not per se required as a proof-text for the biblical doctrine of the Holy Trinity. Still, that is the basic background here. In this passage we read about the Lord, and seeing the entire context, that must mean, the Lord Jesus Christ. When we read about the Spirit in the same passage, we think of the Holy Spirit. There is here a very close relation between the Son and the Spirit to the point where Paul can even write: the Lord *is* the Spirit.

Now this does not need to confuse us. For we know that the three Persons in the Trinity, the Father, the Son, and the Spirit are distinct and yet never separate. There is only one God, and therefore a very strong and close identification is made. Just as Christ himself once said: I and the Father are one, and, if you have seen me, you have seen the Father (John 14), so Paul can write: the Lord is the Spirit. Not that the Lord and the Spirit are the same Persons, but they are of the same Being, one divine essence. There are three Persons, but there is one divine Being. This is consistent Biblical teaching.

Difference between Old and New Testament

Yet all this is not the issue in this passage of Scripture. Paul is explaining the relationship that exists between the Lord Jesus and the Holy

Spirit, and what this means since Pentecost (the outpouring of the Spirit) for the church. The close connection between the Son and the Spirit has great meaning for us as New Testament church. In this entire section of Scripture Paul is contrasting the difference between the old and the new covenant. Let us see in what terms the apostle contrasts the two.

The old ministry or dispensation (of the Old Testament) is described as follows. Verse 3: it was written on tablets of stone. Verse 6: it was a covenant based on a written code. Verse 7 (even stronger): it was a dispensation of death. Verse 9: it was a dispensation of condemnation. Verse 14: it was a dispensation with a veil. In short, the old covenant is a covenant of the law, written on stone, and it brought death and condemnation, while it did not allow people to see clearly and fully the glory of God.

But the new dispensation (of the New Testament) is vastly different in this sense: it is written on human hearts (verse 3), is new (verse 6), and gives life. Therefore it is called the dispensation of the Spirit, even the dispensation of righteousness.

The two are quite remarkably different. The difference lies at bottom in what Jesus Christ has done in his work of atonement as the Mediator of the new covenant. Through this work, the covenant has become new and has taken on a much broader, deeper, and spiritual dimension.

What is a dispensation or ministry?

We read of the ministry of the Holy Spirit. The *Revised Standard Version* still has the expression the "dispensation" of the Holy Spirit (2 Cor 3:8). This is now the dispensation in which the church lives and functions. Therefore we need to understand the heart and the glory of this dispensation. We live today in what is called the dispensation or ministry of the Spirit.

The first question that must be answered is this: what is a "dispensation" or a "ministry"? In verse 7 the word is also used: the "dispensation" (ministry) of death. That is the obvious contrast, the one (former) dispensation or ministry brought only death, but the other (present) dispensation of the Spirit gives life. What is a "dispensation"?

The verb "to dispense" means "to hand something out." When you dispense something, you give something to another person. When you, for example, go to a drugstore to buy prescription drugs, you must pay what is called a dispensing fee, which is the administrative cost attached to the selling of that particular product. You need a prescription for this drug, and the pharmacist must follow certain rules in handing out the medication. Dispensing then is the required and official way of handing out certain products.

The old dispensation was inadequate

The word "ministry" means basically the same. We administer medication to another person. That means we give it under lawful and controlled conditions in the right manner. This is also the case with the manner in which salvation is dispensed, administered, or given. Under the Old Testament salvation was dispensed, given, by means of the written code, the law given through Moses. This was the law of God, and by keeping the law, you were saved, reconciled to God. So the giving of salvation was inseparably connected to keeping the law and its many ceremonies.

But it is clear from Scripture that this old dispensation did not achieve what it wanted to do. Instead of bringing to people salvation and life, this dispensation of the law actually brought condemnation and death. Because people could not keep and did not keep the law, they received not the reward of obedience, but the just reward of disobedience. So let's say: the old manner of dispensing salvation was inadequate or insufficient, and it did not really achieve what it wanted to achieve. This is not because the dispensation itself was wrong, but because of our human failure to meet the conditions of that dispensation.

Yet that old dispensation did have its glory. Despite all its shortcomings, it still functioned to show forth the glory and grace of God. Paul uses the example of Moses to show something of this glory. When Moses came down from the mountain or whenever he went into the tabernacle and came back out, his face shone with heavenly splendor, a light so bright that people could not bear it. Moses therefore had to cover his face with a veil.

Insufficient and Temporary

The old dispensation certainly had its moments of splendor. It is therefore quite striking that the new dispensation has much more splendor. For the manner in which salvation is now handed out and dispensed to us is not via the Law of Moses but through the perfect atonement of Christ. He has fulfilled the law in our place, and now because of this atonement, the Holy Spirit has been poured out, and we may through the Holy Spirit for Christ's sake have direct access to all the riches and blessings of God.

Because the old way of dispensing salvation was insufficient, Paul can write that it was also temporary. It served only for a time despite its moments of splendor, and it had to make way for something infinitely more glorious, the new dispensation, which is the dispensation of the Spirit.

Actually, the old dispensation already pointed clearly to Jesus Christ and his work of atonement. However, the people did not understand or see this. Just as Moses needed a veil to cover his face, so the people of Israel could not see clearly: it was as if a veil (a covering) lay over their minds. The only one who can remove this veil is Christ. He alone can and does show us the true meaning of the covenant, how it worked under the old dispensation and how it has been arranged under the new dispensation. To understand how salvation is given, we must go to Christ.

The veil removed

In the words that immediately precede our text we read (verse 16), "But when a man turns to the Lord (Jesus) the veil is removed." We can say: I can see clearly now, the veil is gone. Now I truly understand how salvation is given and administered. Christ has made full atonement, and each Christian builds on that foundation. Christ fulfilled the law. He also gives insight into the real meaning and function of that law. When someone turns to Christ, he sees clearly the way in which salvation is given.

The sad thing that Paul encountered in his ministry was that many of his fellow-Jews refused to acknowledge the Lord Jesus Christ. Every week in their synagogues, they read the books of Moses, but they did not really understand what they were reading. It is still as if there is a veil over what they read. They do not have the proper spiritual approach to the Scriptures. Paul suffered much from the rejection and opposition of his fellow Jews.

But he writes: when a man turns to the Lord and receives Christ as the great Mediator, the true Messiah, and the only Savior, the veil is removed. Then he really begins to see and understand the meaning and beauty of the Scriptures of old. He also sees that the new dispensation is far richer and has much more splendor than the old dispensation. For Christ is the heart of the new dispensation. It all now – as it did basically in the old, but then not so clearly – focuses on him. What was not so clear before is now abundantly clear and true.

In that context follow the words of this text, "Now the Lord is the Spirit." This sentence refers to the previous one, "when a man turns to the Lord, the veil is removed." Paul's point is: if you want to see what the new dispensation is all about, you must begin with the Lord Jesus Christ. Accepting Christ as Savior, you also share in the gift of the Holy Spirit. Then more light dawns. For the way to understand the very heart and function of the new dispensation is through the Holy Spirit. We receive this Spirit only when we acknowledge Christ.

The Lord is the Spirit

That's the sense of the words "now the Lord is the Spirit." Paul does not write vice-versa: the Spirit is the Lord. The very point is that the key to understanding the new covenant is the Lord Jesus. When you turn to the Lord, you receive access also to the gift of the Holy Spirit and only by the Holy Spirit do you begin to see and appreciate more and more what great riches you have in Christ.

Paul does not simply identify the Lord Jesus with the Holy Spirit, as if these are the same Persons. He makes very clear: if you want the Holy Spirit, you must acknowledge Christ, for the Lord is the Spirit. The one (the Holy Spirit) only comes together with the other (the Lord Jesus). Their relation is so close and their unity is so deep and essential that you can not have one of the two. You must have both.

The heart of the new covenant is Christ Jesus. He is the Mediator of that covenant, greater than Moses. He is the image of the invisible God, his only-begotten Son. And when you turn to him for complete and full salvation, you receive also the gift of the Holy Spirit, for the Spirit comes with Christ, and in that sense, Paul can even say: the Lord *is* the Spirit.

The Spirit guides us to Jesus Christ

You cannot have the Holy Spirit except by turning to Christ. And when the Spirit comes, he directs you always to Christ, the Savior, the great Mediator of the new covenant. The Holy Spirit opens for you the Scriptures and guides you in a proper understanding so that you increasingly see how your entire salvation rests on the work of atonement realized by the Lord Jesus. Salvation is dispensed now solely and exclusively by Jesus Christ and through the Holy Spirit. There is here a *reciprocal* relationship between the Son and the Spirit.

The Spirit always and constantly guides us to the Lord Jesus. For Christ is the heart of the new dispensation. He fulfilled the demands of the law. He bore the penalty of the law. He took away the curse and damnation of the law. He gave us life unending. He binds us to the Father. Through Christ we may see the true glory of God. When you turn to this Jesus, you begin to see things as they really are. The Holy Spirit guides you in this process and the veils are lifted, the shadows are removed, and the full light begins to shine.

He will glorify me

Christ himself spoke of this when he was telling his disciples that the Spirit would come. He said about the Spirit (John 16:13-15), "When the Spirit of truth comes, he will guide you into all the truth; for he will not speak on his own authority, but whatever he hears he will speak, and he will declare to you the things that are to come. He will glorify me, for he will take what is mine and declare it to you. All that the Father has is mine, therefore I said he will take what is mine and declare it to you."

This is a key passage in Scripture about the work of the Holy Spirit. Christ has received all glory from the Father because of his perfect obedience. The Holy Spirit now takes from the Son and gives to us. Here we see the unity in the Trinity, the complete and perfect cooperation, and the one work of our salvation. And at the heart of it all is the atoning sacrifice of Christ, our Lord.

There is freedom

Then the apostle adds "and where the Spirit of the Lord is, there is freedom." We may rightly say that here is the true and deep glory of the dispensation of the Spirit. The Spirit was always present, working and renewing, guiding and leading, but now that the work of atonement has been completed and the Spirit has been fully poured out on Pentecost, we may truly share in his abundant presence. This Spirit does a mighty work, for he grants us freedom. This freedom is the glory of the new dispensation. Never was this freedom so evident as now in the dispensation of the Spirit.

Note carefully that Paul does not say: where the Spirit of the Lord is, there *will be* (perhaps) freedom, but he writes: there *is* freedom. This freedom is not a pious wish, but a reality which is experienced. This freedom is a wonder and every day again we are amazed at it.

What is freedom?

What is this "freedom" of which Paul writes here? For many people freedom is being able to do what they want to do or doing nothing, if they choose. *Freedom's just another word for nothing else to do.* But that is not the freedom of which the Bible speaks.

We must again compare it with the old dispensation. The people of Israel did not really have the "freedom" to behold the full beauty and glory of God. They did not have free access to God. Access to God was always via the priests and the sacrifices through the rules and regulations of the law

that in fact condemned them. Were the Israelites ever really free from their many obligations and restrictions? Was it not a covenant that with its emphasis on works actually functioned to enslave them?

But that situation has now drastically and definitely changed. Now the final and full sacrifice has been made for our sins. We are free from sin and guilt. The outpouring of the Spirit is also proof of this freedom. Where the Spirit of the Lord is, there is freedom. This means freedom from the bondage and the curse of the law. It is freedom from the need to atone constantly for sin. It is freedom also from the power of Satan and sin and the condemnation that results from sin.

We should not interpret or understand the Biblical word freedom in a modern political sense. Freedom is always first of all freedom from sin and death through Jesus Christ.

Freedom only in Christ

The Spirit makes us free. It may be better to say: the Holy Spirit places and confirms us in the freedom which we have in Christ. The Spirit shows us the vast expanse of the true riches of the Scriptures. The Spirit gives us an open and broad perspective on the mercies of God in Christ. The way to heaven is open for us through the atoning work of Christ, and we may freely travel it and have the boldness and the confidence to come before God in prayer and with praise.

The glory of the new dispensation of the Spirit is precisely the freedom to associate with God as his children through Christ. We are not slaves of sin anymore but servants of Christ. We are no longer doomed to do Satan's bidding, but liberated to follow Christ's commandments. In Christ we have freedom to breathe, freedom to live, and freedom to relax. No more does the burden of our sins oppress us and weigh us down. No more are we guided by people who do not understand the riches of the Scriptures. No more do we see everything as through a veil. But we may look upon God in Christ as he truly is.

Freedom is a big word. Many people do not understand it at all. Freedom is deliverance from the bondage of sin and death, being restored fully after Christ's image as sons and daughters of the highest God. The old dispensation already saw glimpses of this glory. It shone from Moses' face. Therein God's children saw how close God had come to his people. But in the new dispensation we may see in Christ through the Spirit even more clearly the glory of God. And one day we will stand in it completely.

Christian freedom

We should remember that Paul writes these words about the Spirit and freedom in the second letter to the Corinthians. The Corinthians prided themselves on their so-called Christian freedom. They felt that everything was lawful. The old restrictions of the Mosaic laws are gone, they said, and we are free. This is true, but the new freedom is not to be abused or misunderstood. It is the freedom from sin for service. It is a heartfelt commitment to Christ.

Where the Spirit of the Lord is, there is freedom. This has tremendous consequences. Where the Spirit of the Lord is, people do not want to sin anymore. There people want to keep the commandment of love. There people are really being changed into new people according to the demands of the new dispensation.

Where the Spirit of the Lord is, people still fall into sins. That saddens and grieves them. Yet they do not live in these sins, but instead repent from them and start anew. For where the Spirit is, there is freedom. The Spirit again makes us free. Christian freedom is never received as a license to sin.

The Spirit is given to confirm and establish our freedom in Christ. He does so by binding us to Christ and leading us into a deeper and fuller understanding of the riches of the Scriptures. Where this happens, people can really say: I am free from the burden of sin and guilt, from the curse of the law. I am free to serve God again thankfully as his child.

Do not abuse Christian freedom

We should never abuse this freedom or misunderstand it. If the glory of salvation was never more evident than it is today in the new dispensation, the same holds true for sanctification. Holiness and piety must now be evident as never before. Now we have to live, more than the Israel of old, as free people.

We may never use this freedom as a cover-up or an excuse for sin. Instead we should grow in the experience and expression of this freedom. We must show that we are really free from the ways of sin and death. It must be clear from our lives that we are led by a true and deep knowledge of the Word of God. We must be free from apostasy, immorality, and selfishness. We must go back time and again back to Christ who has set us free. Constantly we must seek the Spirit, who alone preserves us in the freedom of Christ and renews us in God's service.

This freedom is the glory of the dispensation of the Spirit. It is the new reality and norm since Pentecost. There are no reasons anymore whatsoever to lead a life of slavery to sin and death. There never were any excuses, but now there certainly are none at all. Whoever now sins willfully and constantly does not only deny the very heart of the new covenant but also tarnishes its glory in the Spirit of Christ.

It is sad that many have the Bible, as the Jews have the Scriptures of old, but do not understand it. It has no effect on them. Their eyes are dim and it's like they are looking through a veil. They have not really turned to Christ, and therefore not truly received the Spirit. They do not experience the freedom.

But we may say and know: I am free from all my sins and guilt, from the curse of death and free as a child of God. I may experience this in Christ through the Spirit. This freedom is the most exhilarating thing there is in life. It is the glory of the new dispensation that we can say: we are free.

The challenge of life is not to become free, but to *remain* free. Let us praise God that the Holy Spirit has been poured out, for there lays the guarantee that we shall remain free until we behold the full glory of God and taste the perfect freedom of the new earth.

XVI

Sealed with the Holy Spirit

And you also were included in Christ when you heard the word of truth, the gospel of your salvation. Having believed, you were marked in him with a seal, the promised Holy Spirit who is a deposit guaranteeing our inheritance until the redemption of those who are God's possession – to the praise of his glory.

(EPHESIANS 1:13, 14)

In this section we focus on an important passage in Ephesians 1 that speaks about the Holy Spirit. It says there in verse 13: you were marked in him [Christ] with a seal, the promised Holy Spirit. The Holy Spirit does not simply give a seal, but he is himself the seal of Christ.

There are those who have seen this "sealing" with the Spirit as one of the steps or demands in the process of becoming a truly committed Christian. The sealing is then understood as the ultimate and undisputable proof that one is really a child of God. Unfortunately not every Christian has this experience or reaches this height of grace. Those "sealed" are truly Christians par excellence, and they also are the most effective witnesses of Christ.

Some follow a specific order here. There is, first, the need for conviction of sin. Second, there must be repentance. This is followed by regeneration. Fourth, faith is received. Then we are justified (Step 5), and, sixth, adoption as God's children follows. In this scheme of things, the seventh and final step and the crowning touch is the sealing with the Holy Spirit, sometimes seen also as the baptism with the Spirit. When one is thus sealed, the possibility exists that one can perform miracles and wonders. We are here right in the very heart of Pentecostalism.

Sealing not for everyone?

In this line of thinking, apparently not everyone receives this sealing. Some would have us believe that you can be a Christian without it, but not as effective a Christian as you could be or even should be. While not essential to salvation, this sealing is seen as being the indisputable proof of salvation. Some defend the position that this sealing is something which happens after conversion and that we therefore can be a Christian without it. It's better to have it, but we don't really need the sealing to be saved.

Someone may ask whether all the above is important or whether it is just another useless theological debate. I think it is important. If God gives to all believers this sealing with the Holy Spirit, we should know about it. We must understand exactly what it is and how we are to use it.

I am convinced that this "sealing" is indeed something which *all* believers receive. It is not a bonus for some, but a blessing for all.

In Ephesians 1:3 Paul praises God who has blessed us with *every spiritual blessing in Christ*. God gives different gifts to different people, but we all have the same blessings in Christ. Every spiritual blessing in Christ is ours. It would follow that this also includes the sealing with the Holy Spirit. Besides, when Paul mentions this "sealing" he continues in the plural, addressing all the believers, and he makes no distinctions. The miracle is really that not only Jews are being saved but that also Gentiles are "included in Christ" when they hear the Gospel and believe it.

Therefore we consider what this sealing with the Holy Spirit is. All believers are marked with a seal, the promised Holy Spirit. We will see when this sealing takes place, what this sealing implies, and why this sealing is needed.

When sealed?

When does this sealing with the Spirit take place? In verse 13 Paul writes: and you also (the Ephesian believers, of which the majority were from the Gentiles) were included in Christ, *when you heard the word of truth*, the gospel of your salvation. In this letter Paul more than once refers to the great mystery or miracle that the heathen are no longer excluded from the *covenants* of promise (2:12), but have been brought near in Christ. The word "covenants" here refers to the covenant made of old with its various dispensations.[16]

---

[16] See my publication *The Covenant of Love,* Premier Publishing, Winnipeg, p 35 ff, "How Many Covenants Are There?"

When the Ephesians heard the gospel, they were called to faith. They responded positively to the gospel, for we read, "Having *believed*, you were marked in him with a seal, the promised Holy Spirit." Note the expression: having believed. Some translate: *after* having believed, you were marked in him... This is the rendering of the RSV and the KJV. Then it is easy to conclude that the sealing took place *after* the Ephesian Christians came to faith, even as a separate matter. The order would be: they came to faith (regeneration must play a role here somehow) and after that in due course this was confirmed or augmented by the *sealing* with the Spirit.

The element of time here is rather important for it casts a certain light on this "sealing." Is it something the believers receive at the moment they come to faith or is it something that stands completely loose from faith as a totally different experience? Can we be believers, and not yet be sealed with the Spirit? Is this some kind of added blessing or higher level than other Christians receive? You will understand that Pentecostal evangelicals tend to go in this direction.

Simultaneous

The expression "having believed," as rendered by the NIV, is here indeed the proper translation. The NIV does not see this sealing as taking place at a later time, but in accordance with the original language understands the coming to faith and being marked with a seal as events that take place simultaneously. When we believe, we are immediately marked with a seal, namely, the Holy Spirit. This marking with a seal, then, pertains to *all* believers and not just to some in the church.

I hope that you appreciate the importance of this. Otherwise we get different classes of believers in the church. Some are merely believers, while others have above and beyond faith also been marked with a special seal, namely the Holy Spirit. The Spirit then functions more in the lives of some believers than in that of others. But Paul does not write in this way. All believers upon coming to faith are also marked with a seal, the Holy Spirit. This mark sets them apart from this world and gives them a lawful place among God's people.

It would be wrong, therefore, to ask a believer if he has also been sealed with the mark, the promised Spirit, because that mark *is given with faith*, comes along with faith, and even authenticates this faith. The fact that a mark or seal is given when we come to faith lies fully in the line of biblical thinking. When do we receive a mark or seal? This happens always when we become part of something or when we join a certain fellowship. The

mark or seal then confirms that we are indeed truly members with all the rights and all the obligations of membership.

Apply this to the church of Christ: when do we become members? This occurs when we come to faith. At that very same time also we receive the mark or seal of that membership, which is the Holy Spirit.

Full access in Christ

This begs another question. Was the Holy Spirit not active in us before we came to faith? He certainly was at work, for how could we come to faith without the Holy Spirit? But when we believe, we receive *full access* with all the saints to the presence and blessing of the Holy Spirit as he is poured out over the church. As we join the church of Christ, we are set apart from the world, and the distinguishing mark or seal is the Holy Spirit himself. He has put his claim on us and set his mark upon us. He now dwells in us and makes us more and more into living members of Christ.

What the Bible tells us here is that you cannot be a true Christian and not have the Holy Spirit. When you truly believe in Christ, you are marked with a seal, namely the Holy Spirit. This does not come later or earlier. It comes with faith. It is given the moment we become by faith members of the holy catholic church.

When we come to faith in Christ our Savior, and, as Paul writes, are included in him, we receive all this with Christ. It says even: you were marked *in him* with a seal. We did not merit this seal. We cannot earn this seal of approval by climbing higher and closer to God. When we are included in Christ by faith we are marked *in him* with a seal. The seal does not come by itself or separate from Christ, but the seal comes with Christ, and we receive the Spirit only in Jesus Christ. When it comes to the sealing with the Spirit, we must be very humble.

The promised Holy Spirit

Paul also writes here of the *promised* Holy Spirit. This is covenantal language. We did not earn this Spirit, just as we did not merit salvation in Christ, but the Spirit has been *promised* to all believers. And when God deals with believers, he also deals in these believers with their children, their generations. For that is the structure and the way of his covenant. We received the Spirit because the promise of God is that the Spirit is given to all who believe in Christ. God keeps his promises.

We must keep together what God has put together. We may never see the Holy Spirit as a kind of addendum, a bonus given only to certain believers who are worthy of this, but the Spirit is given to all, and works in and through all who truly believe. The first question is not: how do I know for sure that have I received the Holy Spirit but the question is: do I believe in the Lord Jesus Christ? For if I believe in him, I have received also in him the seal of God, which is the Holy Spirit.

A mark of authentication

This becomes even more important when we consider what this being marked with a seal implies. I wrote earlier that a seal is a mark of authentication. It means that something is the real thing. It means also that something is legitimate, true, and not a false imitation. This seal gives us an *identity*.

This may not be as evident to us today as it was in the days of the apostle Paul. When one sent a letter in those days, the envelope or scroll was sealed with wax, and on this wax a signet ring was pressed to leave behind a clear and visible mark. The one who received the letter could know from the unbroken seal that the letter was authentic. No one had tampered with it and no one had changed the contents. The sealed letter is perfectly valid and carries the authority of the one who sent it. It bears a mark of authenticity.

The seal and baptism

The question is now how we are to envision this marking with a seal. It has to be an internal thing which we do not as such see from the outside. Still, I think that we must lay a close connection between the seal of Christ, the Holy Spirit, and the water of *baptism*. If there is any event which symbolizes the receiving of the Spirit, it is holy baptism, and if there is any substance with speaks of cleansing and renewal, it is the water of baptism.

When people came to faith and were admitted as members of the church, they were baptized. Holy Baptism is the sign and seal of admission to the church. This baptism is a "sign" that we from now on belong to Christ and his people, and it also functions as a "seal" that we are truly in every way a child of God in Jesus Christ. The seal of which Paul writes here is then shown and presented in the water of baptism. We also note how baptism speaks to us of our inheritance (see the next verse). The *Form for*

Baptism says that we are heirs of the kingdom of God and of his covenant (*Book of Praise*, page 585).

Other passages about sealing

Also elsewhere the New Testament speaks of this matter of sealing. I'll mention only a few passages. It is remarkable that *circumcision* is called in Romans 4 a sign and a *seal* of the righteousness of faith. Like baptism circumcision marked one's admission to the people of God. We read in Ephesians 4:30, "And do not grieve the Holy Spirit with whom you were sealed for the day of redemption." All believers are sealed, the Holy Spirit dwells in them, and therefore they must watch not to grieve this Spirit.

Perhaps the most significant use of the word seal is found in Revelation 7. In this chapter we first read about four angels standing at the four corners of the earth, holding back the four winds of the earth to prevent great damage from being done on the earth. Apparently the day of final judgment and total destruction has not yet come at this point. Why not? Verse 2: I saw another angel coming up from the east, having the seal of the living God. He calls out with a loud voice: do not harm the earth, *until we put a seal on the foreheads of the servants of our God*. I have italicized the key words. And then John *hears* the number of the sealed, 144,000 from all the tribes of Israel.

The seal is the mark of the living God. It shows that we belong to him. Notice that this seal is placed on the *forehead* so that it is immediately visible. You look at a person and immediately see this seal,. So you know right away that he belongs to the living God.

What is this seal mentioned in Revelation 7? Is it the same as in Ephesians 1 and 4? It cannot be much different.

The seal in Revelation 7 has a three-fold purpose. It protects against tampering. Those sealed cannot be destroyed. Second, it indicates ownership. It points to a relationship of love as we find in the Song of Songs (8:6): set me as a seal upon your heart. Those who are sealed belong to the one whose seal they bear. Third, a seal certifies a genuine character: it is true and irrevocable.

We see this three-fold sense also in baptism. The Father assures that he will take care of us, and protect us. The Son assures us that he has bought us with his own blood, and we belong to him. Finally, the Holy Spirit assures us that he will work in us so that we persevere in the Lord's service.

Outright reference to baptism?

I do not say that this sealing in Revelation 7 is an outright reference to baptism. But we cannot escape some sense of a connection here. The sealing is most likely symbolic, just as baptism is symbolic. The message is that the final judgment will not come until all God's children have been called and sealed. Then the end is here.

In the final period of history, holy baptism functions as a clear sign and seal, as we read in Matthew 28. So baptism is called in the *Belgic Confession* a "mark and emblem of Christ" (Article 34). Lord's Day 27 of the *Heidelberg Catechism* (about baptism) does refer us to Revelation 7, especially to the fact that this multitude of the sealed "have washed their robes and made them white in the blood of the lamb." The sealing in Revelation 7 is therefore not to be seen loose from the sealing mentioned in Ephesians 1 and 4.

I want to mention yet that in Ezekiel 9 we also read about a "seal" or distinguishing mark. There a man with a "writing kit is supposed to go through Jerusalem and make a mark on the foreheads of all "who grieve and lament over the detestable things that are done in [Jerusalem]." We may also think of the blood that was placed on the doorframes of the homes of the Israelites when the angel of death went through all of Egypt (Ex 12:7). The people of God are distinguished from those of this world by a mark that God sees and knows, so that they may escape the great judgment. They bear the seal of Christ, and the seal they bear is ultimately the Spirit of Christ himself. The seal has wondrous implications of redemption, renewal, and certainty.

Eschatological thrust

We truly need this seal, because the days are evil, as Paul writes in Ephesians 5. There is for Christians always the danger that they do not persevere, fall away, and maybe even come to deny the Lord Jesus. Will we make it across the finish line? Will we be able to run the race, to complete the course, and to receive the crown of glory? (2 Tim 4:7).

It is remarkable when we read of this sealing with the Spirit that there is always an eschatological thrust, which means, the Spirit is always focused on our perseverance and we look towards the *future*. Notice how in verse 14 the Holy Spirit is called a *deposit guaranteeing our inheritance*. I touched already on the word inheritance, being heirs of God's kingdom and covenant. The Spirit is called a "deposit" of this inheritance.

It may seem a bit strange at first that the Holy Spirit is called a deposit. A deposit is only a dead substance, while the Spirit is a living and active Person. How are we to understand this word deposit?

In Lord's Day 18 of the *Heidelberg Catechism* (about the ascension of Christ) we can read that the Spirit is sent as a "counter-pledge" by whose power we seek the things that are above. The word *counter-pledge* comes from the rendition of the RSV. The original word is the word deposit and the reference is to 2 Corinthians 1:22, where we read something similar as in the present text: God (Christ) set his seal of ownership on us, and put his Spirit in our hearts as a deposit, guaranteeing what is to come. We have assurance in heaven. Christ's flesh in heaven is a pledge that we will also go there. And then the Spirit is called a counter-pledge, a deposit, and our assurance on earth. He directs us heaven-ward to the great inheritance that we have in Christ. A deposit is an installment which guarantees that the rest will come also, maybe later, but it will come.

The Spirit reassures us

We all know what a deposit is. Sometimes when we purchase something, we do not pay the full price until it is delivered. But we do give a "deposit," let's say 10% of the price. This deposit has a two-fold purpose: it assures the seller that the remainder will be paid upon delivery, and it gives the buyer a firm right to the matter purchased. Both the seller and the buyer are assured that the transaction will be completed in time. It's like both having a guarantee.

The Holy Spirit was poured out over the church and dwells in the church precisely for this reason to assure us all that we will receive the inheritance that Christ has earned for us and has promised us. The Holy Spirit keeps our faith and hope alive. He directs us forward so that we do not doubt the inheritance itself and persevere in the hope that we will receive it.

The Spirit has come, and he stays. But one day Jesus Christ will return and he will put an end to all sin and death. He will bring full redemption. That is the focus of the passage: until the redemption of those who are God's possession. The Spirit stays with us and is our seal until the whole work of redemption is completed and Christ has come again. The Spirit reassures us until Jesus Christ has come back.

God's possession

Notice that this passage speaks about the redemption of those who are God's *possession*. Those who believe and who already now have the sealing with the Holy Spirit belong to God as his possession and shall always belong to him. Whoever is sealed with the Spirit, will receive the inheritance of Christ.

We need to have this assurance in our lives, as church and as individuals. There are so many things that can bother us and even hinder our assurance. Am I really God's child? Will I persevere to the end? Can I handle my responsibilities as a Christian? Will I receive the inheritance? We are so weak that we cannot stand for a moment, and our arch-enemies do not cease to attack us. But we are marked with a seal. The devil knows that we are God's possession. He cannot decisively influence our lives, for the Spirit of God keeps us. The seal indicates that we are private property. The sign says: out of bounds, no trespassing. The Spirit assures us that the inheritance in Christ cannot be taken away or lost. We may believe that even in our darkest hour God will finish what he started (Psalm 138).

The mark of the beast

Those who belong to Satan, to the beast, also have a "mark" (Revelation 13) either on their right hand or forehead. There is no in-between phase or state. You either bear the mark of the beast or the mark of Christ. You either face glory with Christ or desolation with the devil.

May it be so then that the Holy Spirit always directs us forward to the day of Christ when we may receive in full the inheritance that is assured. And all this is not because we are worthy of it. The text ends with these words: to the praise of [God's] glory! God is to be praised and will be praised for this wonderful work of redemption. He receives from all believers the glory and the honor, now and forever.

We are saved by the Son. We are sealed by the Spirit. We are heirs of the kingdom and the covenant. Let us live then to the glory of the Father. So the triune God is praised by us all.

XVII

Filled with the Holy Spirit

*Do not get drunk on wine which leads to debauchery.
Instead be filled with the Spirit.*

(EPHESIANS 5:18)

At first glance the above passage may be somewhat surprising if not confusing. Why is it necessary to specify that we be filled with the Holy Spirit? This question is important because Paul has in this letter to the Ephesians already stated that the saints there *have* received the Spirit. See chapter 1:13: having believed, you were marked in him with a seal, the promised Holy Spirit. We looked at this passage in the previous chapter. The Spirit had already come upon the Ephesians when the Gospel was first preached to them and they came to faith.

Also later in the same letter Paul refers again (4:30) to the fact that the Ephesian Christians "were sealed for the day of redemption" by the Spirit of God. "Sealed by the Spirit" means at least that the Holy Spirit had come over them and dwelt in them.

The Ephesians were no strangers to the Holy Spirit. In Acts 19 we read how the Holy Spirit came powerfully on the believers there and how many extraordinary miracles were performed by Paul. Some of the believers in Ephesus who had even practiced sorcery publicly burned their valuable scrolls on devil worship. We know that there arose a great disturbance in Ephesus because of the powerful effect of the work of the Holy Spirit. The craftsmen who made silver shrines and other objects of heathen worship saw their profits threatened, and a well-planned riot resulted.

In Ephesus, then, the church knew all about the power and the work of the Holy Spirit. Paul calls the church there " a dwelling in which God lives *by his Spirit*" (2:22). Why would he write to such a church that they must "be filled with the Spirit"? Were they not already filled? Is this not unnecessary? Is it not so that once filled, we are always filled?

Constant filling?

Must we see this passage in a different light, namely that *after* we have received the Holy Spirit, we still need to be *filled* with the Holy Spirit on a regular basis? Let's go one step farther. Is it so that we should not rely as believers on a one-time experience of being filled (let's say when we are born again) and that we cannot rely only on whatever may have happened in the past, but must time and again be filled with the Holy Spirit in each and every new situation or issue that comes our way? Is being filled with the Spirit a unique event or does it happen time and again?

How do we then experience this "being filled"? How does it happen? What does it lead to? I think we need to examine this passage carefully in the light of Scripture so that we may know what it means to walk by the Spirit of God.

One thing is indisputably certain here in this passage. All explainers which I consulted agree that the present tense of the verb to fill means that this filling takes place on a *constant* basis, not just once in our lives but many times, as the situation demands it.

One Reformed explainer translates as follows: *go on* being filled with the Spirit! Some focus on the moment when they first received the Spirit and even think that they have then achieved a certain status, but Paul exhorts the church which is sealed with the promised Holy Spirit to go on being filled with the Spirit. We are once sealed but repeatedly filled. The Lord Jesus calls us constantly to be filled with the Holy Spirit.

We will note three elements: how this being filled with the Spirit is prescribed, how this being filled with the Spirit is prevented, and how this being filled with the Spirit is presented.

Not an option

When we focus on the main words in the text, "be filled with the Spirit," we should note that this is not an option which we might consider, but it is a prescription or a command. It is written in the imperative sense. That's why I wrote in an earlier paragraph that the Lord Jesus *calls us* to be filled. Having received the Holy Spirit by faith as members of Christ's church, we must from then on also be *filled* with the Spirit.

How are we to understand this? Surely Paul does not mean that Pentecost must constantly be repeated. Pentecost and the outpouring of the Holy Spirit are a one-time event which marked a new phase in the history of redemption, and which therefore is not repeated. There are a few in-

stances in which the reality of Pentecost is confirmed (in Jerusalem after the first threats of persecution, in Samaria, and also in the house of Cornelius). Pentecost-like manifestations occur when we see a major transition, when the circle of the Spirit's work is widened from Jerusalem, to Judea, to Samaria and to the ends of the earth, but Pentecost, as such, is not repeated. The Spirit is poured out once and abides with the church.[17]

Therefore we must understand this being filled (also in the context of the letter itself) as the believers coming increasingly under the influence and power of the Holy Spirit and so under the dominion of Christ. It means that Christ shall rule over us more and more. "Filling" is not just done by the Holy Spirit, or by the Spirit loose from the other work of God as a separate item, but this being filled is always to be seen in connection with the redeeming and renewing work of Christ.

Filling and fullness

Let us turn back for a moment to Ephesians 1:22 and 23. There we find the verb to fill for the first time in this letter. It says: and God placed all things under his [Christ's] feet, and appointed him to be head over everything for the church, which is his body, *the fullness of him who fills everything in every way*!

The church is called the "fullness of Christ." What does that mean? He fills the church with all his merited blessings. This means that our Lord Jesus Christ, who is in heaven, takes form and becomes visible on earth in his body, the church. If we want to see Christ at work, we must look at his church which is his body. It means the church has everything from Jesus Christ. The church has all its gifts, blessings, and resources from the Lord Jesus Christ. He fills his church in every way. In every need and situation, Jesus Christ provides for his church. He fills this church individually and together as a body.

How does the Lord Jesus do this? He does this through the wondrous presence and powerful work of the Holy Spirit who has been poured out over the church. In chapter 2 Paul calls this church a holy temple in the Lord, and he then states (2:22), "And in him you are being built together to become a dwelling in which God lives *by his Spirit*." God is at work in the church through Jesus Christ by the presence of the Holy Spirit.

---

17 See my publication *Celebrating Salvation*, Premier, Winnipeg, 1997, pp 251-259.

Draining empty

The expression "be filled with the Spirit" means, then, that more and more by the presence and power of the Holy Spirit we let our lives be governed by Jesus Christ, the head of the body. The Holy Spirit must gain decisive influence in and total dominion over our lives. For Christ rules us by His Spirit and Word. The Spirit has been received by faith, and he dwells in the hearts of the believers, but he must now also more and more govern us, lead us, and, indeed, fill us. The verb to fill means to fill to the brim, even to overflowing, so that we are completely filled, and there is no empty space left over.

This matter of being filled with the Spirit is an apostolic prescription. It is something that must happen and to which we also must give ourselves, on which we must focus, and about which we must be concerned. In this light we understand that this filling is an ongoing process that never stops. It does not stop because the Spirit cannot achieve this fullness, but because we always drain empty. Therefore the tense is in the present: be constantly filled with the Holy Spirit.

We drain empty. That is the consequence of our sinful and mortal nature. There are many problems in life that we have to tackle and the struggle takes so much out of us. We can become wearied and tired of fighting the same battle every day. It is hard to battle the same stubborn sins, to oppose constant weaknesses, and to face growing responsibilities. Sometimes all this can become too much for us, and we feel we can hardly keep our life together and continue living as God's children.

Filled every day again

We should not say: I have the Holy Spirit, now I am filled, and I can travel on this full tank for the rest of my life. The truth is that we need to be filled *every day again*, our whole life through. As the challenges of life come to us day by day, so the daily filling with the Spirit is required to meet all these challenges. In this way Christ reveals and shows his dominion over us as our Savior and Lord.

We should not be surprised at this daily filling, but rather be amazed at Christ's love for us. For every day we truly need the complete help of the Holy Spirit. We need God's grace to fill us and Christ's love to sustain us daily, or we will go under in the cesspool of this life. This world of darkness is like a strong suction mechanism or a huge vacuum-cleaner, that threatens

to swallow us, and if we are not constantly filled with the Spirit, how could we ever stand against this incessant attraction of the world?

Be filled. The verb means that we are to be focused and involved in this matter. Christ does the filling, but we need to realize *that* we must be filled, and *how* we must be filled. We may not stand idly by as if this does not spur us into action. In the church of Christ, you may not be a spiritual couch-potato, for then you will not last in the spiritual warfare that is going on. We must rise to meet the challenges of life in the strength of the Holy Spirit.

Sharp contrast

Someone may ask: how do I tap into this daily filling with the Holy Spirit? How does one receive access to this blessing, to these riches, and to these wondrous gifts? Let us first see how the apostle tells us what we should *not* do: do not get drunk on wine, which leads to debauchery. Then: *instead* be filled with the Spirit. There is a sharp contrast here. We have to be filled not with spirits but with the Spirit.

It is remarkable that Paul in this connection mentions drunkenness. Perhaps you remember how on Pentecost the people of Jerusalem thought that the disciples were drunk. Spiritual ecstasy should not be confused with drunken euphoria. Ephesus was a leading, commercial city in Asia which was devoted to the cult of Diana or Artemis, and therefore also of Bacchus, the god of wine and frolic. It was not uncommon for pagan worshipers to go to the heathen temples and there become utterly drunk, cavorting with shrine prostitutes.

Paul does not write that we may not drink wine, but that we may not get *drunk* on wine. Drunkenness is a state in which one is no longer in control of his thoughts, words, and actions. Drunkenness leads to "extravagant behavior, exaggerated self-confidence, and loss of self-control," as Donald Macleod writes on this text. One is totally dominated by the alcohol.

Consider the contrast. Either the Holy Spirit is in complete control of you, or you are under the control of alcohol. The one cannot go with the other. Drunkenness rules out the Holy Spirit. The Holy Spirit rules out drunkenness. You cannot be filled with both, only with one of these. I am not sure if we all understand the implications here.

Drown the sorrows?

Does this mean that the Gentiles in Ephesus were always drunk? Paul is not suggesting this at all, but when it came to their heathen religion

and their way of dealing with the pressures and challenges of life, many Gentiles sought escape in wine and spirits. Those Ephesian Christians who still associated with Gentiles were always placing themselves in a situation of extreme temptation to drown the sorrows and join the party. We may as well in our time include all substances that change or control our moods and feelings. There is much alcohol and drug abuse, even the use of illegal drugs.

Our modern society needs this way of escape because it is so empty. People are drained. Many people live with pain and sorrow and they need alcohol and drugs to escape the harsh reality of life and to make the burdens seem lighter. But it is a false sense of euphoria that follows, for soon the world comes crashing down and the sad reality is even more painful.

We are to be filled with the Holy Spirit. This is not a way of escape but a way to tackle life and its problems in the strength of the Lord Jesus Christ. We put on the armor of faith (Ephesians 6), and we fight the good fight. The Spirit fills us time and again to meet the challenges of life, to bear the pain, to overcome the disappointments, to weather the storms, and to carry the burdens. If we learn in our youth to escape reality in a worldly manner through alcohol and drugs, it will often affect us throughout our life. We may become addicted in due time or at least think that these things offer a way out.

When the Holy Spirit has no solid grip on our lives; we drift in and out of fellowship with the Lord, and one day we may drift out altogether. Christ therefore pleads here with all not to go the way of alcohol and drugs, for it is grieving to the Spirit, and much wine will quench the Spirit.

Debauchery

It says here that being drunk with wine leads to *debauchery*. What is debauchery? The Greek has a word that means something like "unsalvageable." It denotes a behavior so disgusting that it has no redeeming feature whatsoever. People are totally out of control and are doing things they would otherwise not think of doing. All inhibitions are gone and the floodgates are loose. Everything is scattered all over the place.

Debauchery is a word that especially denotes extremely sensual activity leading to a complete loss of sexual control. How often is not alcohol a factor when there are date-rape and other sexual assaults? The one thing leads to another, and behavior becomes gross and deviant. It can happen to anyone, no matter of what status, learning, or age. In fact the age is becoming younger all the time, and when debauchery happens, it is disgraceful,

ruinous, and often victimizing. Paul writes earlier in this chapter: it is shameful even to *mention* what the disobedient do in secret. Some things are so disgraceful; they can not be mentioned by decent folks.

Do not ever say: it cannot happen to me, I am in control, don't worry. Before we know it, we have been swept away, sucked in, and have become debased. Let us all heed the biblical warning: let him who thinks to stand, take heed lest he fall (1 Cor 10:12). It is better to be safe with the Spirit than sorry with Satan.

Worldly escapism

The world needs these things to escape. We, too, can fall into the trap of worldly escapism. But we are to be filled with the Holy Spirit. He controls us, but he always leaves our senses intact. He never blows our mind apart, but does guide it to see the real beauty of life and creation. Our spiritual act of worship is reasonable, and not irrational (Romans 12:1-3). The Spirit fills us but never impairs us. He governs us but never enslaves us. He gives no hallucinations, but grants illuminations. He leads us always on a path of which we know it is the right path.

Before we examine how this being filled with the Spirit becomes evident and is presented, we should realize how it is prevented. Not that alcoholic drink and sexual extravagance are the only dangers in life. There are many other dangers as well. But none, perhaps, affect our sanity and soul so deeply as these. Here we can deeply wound our consciences to the point that we loose the sense of God's grace. Let it not happen to you, for it embitters life.

How are we filled with the Spirit?

There is still the question how this being filled with the Holy Spirit is presented. How does Scripture indicate this filling as happening? How are we filled by the Spirit on a constant, daily basis?

Paul does not specify in our text how this being filled takes place, so we must be careful not to speculate. But in the last verses, he does point us in the right direction: speak with one another with psalms, hymns, and spiritual songs. Sing and make music in your heart to the Lord, always giving thanks to God the Father for everything, in the name of our Lord Jesus Christ.

I am not going to get into a debate about the possible difference between psalms, hymns, and spiritual songs. In my understanding that debate

is a senseless controversy, for all these songs are glorifying to God. Paul here directs us not only to the worship services of the church but also to the fellowship that we have with one another at many other times. I find it remarkable that *singing and music* are mentioned so prominently. Who was it that said: when the saints sing their songs of praise, the demons trembling flee?

I once heard the expression that music is a facilitator of the Holy Spirit. I am not sure about that expression. I wonder if the Spirit really needs a facilitator, a means by which he enters more easily into our hearts. The Spirit may not need it then, I thought, but we might. Why else would the Bible itself contain so many psalms, hymns, and spiritual songs? We need to pour out our heart before the Lord also in song and praise. God has surrounded himself in heaven with choirs of angels; do you think he does not love to hear us sing? Is it not for us a way to be filled with the Spirit?

We used to do a lot more singing in our families than we do today. Music today is more for entertainment than participation. Some churches have instituted a ministry of music, even with a "director" of sorts, (many psalms are dedicated to the director of music) and we tend to dismiss such extravagant things, but we can indeed praise God and minister unto one another with song and music.

How can I be filled with the Spirit?

I find it rather striking that one of the biggest consumer industries in our society is the music industry. Modern, popular music of all sorts is bought by everyone. If we do not know what to give someone, we can always buy a CD. How many CD's fall outside the category of psalms, hymns, and spiritual songs? Is it strange that things often go together? Rock concerts are hot spots for booze and drugs. The devil knows what he is doing. The most potent combination is booze, drugs, and rock. Then you can forget about self-control.

How can I be filled with the Spirit? Go there, be there, where Christ rules. We should go where he imparts his gifts and blessings, where his Word is opened, where his praise is sung, and where people have spiritual music in their hearts. It says: sing and make music in your *heart* to the Lord. That's the core of it all: the Spirit of Christ who dwells in our hearts.

To be filled with the Spirit, the following is required. The items I mention now in the line of Ephesians 5:19 and 20 are nothing special in themselves, just simple things which together change our entire life. If we search for the spectacular, we will overlook the obvious. First, let there be

constant *prayer*. God will give his Holy Spirit only to those who constantly ask him, we confess in Lord's Day 45 of the *Heidelberg Catechism*.. Let's put that into practice more and more. Pray daily for the filling with the Spirit.

Secondly, let *us open the Word* on a daily basis, read it, and also meditate on it personally. No one can do this for us or take this from us. I know that many Christians do not personally read Scripture or meditate on it. This will be very detrimental to the church in and over time.

Thirdly, we must be active participants in the communion of saints. Seek the fellowship of the believers: speak with one another, encourage one another, sing and make music together, as it says here. The more we enjoy the company of believers, the less we will seek the company of this world.

And, finally, always give thanks. Paul does not add this as an afterthought, but as an essential ingredient for being filled with the Spirit. We may receive a lot from the Lord, also many spiritual gifts, but if we stop giving thanks, realizing how blessed we are, the flow of spiritual gifts dries up. The Spirit does not give to those who do not desire his gifts, appreciate them, and show gratitude for them.

One of the marks of the secular society is lack of gratitude. Many people today have so much, but they are not satisfied or happy. Let us not fall into the mentality of today where instant satisfaction is demanded but gratitude is hardly expressed, where people take or grab, and do not receive with thankfulness.

Caring and sharing

Gratitude is a mark of the Christian, and it leads to caring and sharing. It also means that *humility* is present. It says: always give thanks *in the name of the Lord Jesus Christ*. Now we are back at the beginning: Christ who fills everything in every way. We always give thanks in the Name of the Lord Jesus. All good things come from him and through him.

We do not deserve these blessings, especially not being filled with the Spirit. We cannot demand it of God. We cannot command the Spirit to come in, not even by forceful decisions of our will. We can take only when Jesus gives. Take only what he gives. But he gives much, and it is all undeserved from our side. He has earned it for us by his death on the cross, and he alone imparts it to us by the Holy Spirit.

So we give thanks *in his name*. In order to give thanks, we have to learn to count. Count our blessings, that is. There are those who do not see the

blessings of Christ, and have never really learned to count. They have learned no spiritual arithmetic, but only manage earthly inventories.

A praising, thankful, and humble person, who is a living part of the body, the church which is the fullness of Christ, is also filled with the Spirit, time and again, to face this life with courage and to await eternal glory.

XVIII

Grieving the Holy Spirit

And do not grieve the Holy Spirit of God, with whom you were sealed for the day of redemption.

(EPHESIANS 4:30)

When we celebrate the Lord's Supper, we remember particularly the one sacrifice of Christ and the gift of life which we receive because of it. Perhaps it is good to remind ourselves that the greatest gift we receive through that perfect sacrifice is the presence and indwelling of the Holy Spirit.

I think here of an important statement in the *Form for the Celebration of the Lord's Supper*: "For by His death He has removed the cause of our eternal hunger and misery, which is sin, and obtained for us the life-giving Spirit. By this Spirit, Who dwells in Christ as the Head and in us as His members, we have true communion with Him and share in all His riches, life eternal, righteousness, and glory" (*Book of Praise*, page 598).

The Form for the Celebration of the Lord's Supper directs us here to the events of Pentecost which followed Golgotha. Pentecost is the reality in which we live today. Because Christ died we may experience every day the power of the life-giving Spirit.

I wrote that this is a reality. I refer you to what Paul wrote in Ephesians 5:30, the words which are part of the passage presently receiving our attention: "(do not grieve the Holy Spirit) *in whom you were sealed for the day of redemption*." Paul does not ask the Ephesians *if* they were sealed with the Spirit, but reminds them *that* they were sealed with him. It is a grand reality. On the basis of that reality he dares to exhort them.

Sealed with the Holy Spirit

In an earlier section, I dealt extensively with the expression to be "sealed with the Holy Spirit." We considered what it means to be sealed with the Holy Spirit.

Let me now for the sake of understanding better the matter of grieving the Spirit, use a simple example. When a crime has been committed, the police seal off the area. Have you ever seen the yellow ribbon, which states: "Police line, do not cross"? That area is under the special jurisdiction and protection of the police.

So it is with us. We are a "sealed-off area," so to speak. God has put a protective boundary around us which indicates that we belong to him and are in his special care. The Holy Spirit is the one who exercises this divine authority in our lives and gives us the protection and security we need.

Whenever you see that yellow tape ("Police line, do not cross"), think of the protective power of the Holy Spirit, which surrounds you like a wall. The text even says: "We have been sealed for the day of redemption," which means that we are under God's protection until the great day of Christ's return. Is this not a tremendous comfort? Whatever happens, we will not be removed from the care and protection of the life-giving Spirit.

Living within protective confines

But this means that we from our side shall reckon with the presence and power of the Spirit. We shall live within the protective confines which Christ has obtained for us on the cross.

When we realize this we begin to understand the exhortation of the Apostle Paul in Ephesians 4 that we may not *grieve* the Holy Spirit. In 1 Thessalonians 5 we are told that we must not *quench* him. That is an even more serious matter, which we will consider in the next chapter. Now we concentrate on the warning that we must not grieve the Spirit. The Apostle Paul exhorts us not to grieve the Holy Spirit in whom we were sealed for the day of redemption.

The exhortations not to "grieve" and not to "quench" the Holy Spirit each stand in their own context, and if we are to understand them well we have to examine them in these contexts. I mention them together for a moment, because they are related in that they refer to common sins against the Holy Spirit.

Sins against the Holy Spirit

When I use the expression "sins against the Holy Spirit," we should not take this to refer to *the* sin against the Holy Spirit, or the unpardonable sin, as it is often called. You know that our Lord warned against this unpardonable sin in the following words (Matt 12:31, 32): "...every sin

and blasphemy will be forgiven men, but the blasphemy against the Spirit will not be forgiven. Anyone... who speaks against the Holy Spirit will not be forgiven, either in this age or in the age to come."

In the present text Paul obviously does not mean that specific sin, or else he would not speak of being "sealed for the day of redemption." In neither instance (Ephesians and Thessalonians) does Paul's admonition carry the weight of a penalty of eternal death.

I will come back to the matter of the sin against the Holy Spirit. For the sake of clarity, let me now put it this way: the sin against the Holy Spirit which is called blaspheming the Spirit is committed only by unbelievers (even if they are in the church, though not a part of it) who haughtily reject the Word of God. They are not bothered by this sin either, but are quite adamant in their rejection of God. There is deep truth in the saying that people who worry about having committed the sin against the Holy Spirit are precisely the ones who have not committed it. Those who have committed it, don't really care. That belongs to the nature of the sin. I'll deal with this sin further in a next chapter.

The sin which the Apostle Paul mentions here (and in 1 Thessalonians, do not quench the Spirit) is committed by *believers* who have strayed from the way and become embroiled in evil. These are serious sins, indeed, but there is a way back. Otherwise the exhortation of the Apostle would make no sense. I therefore conclude that Paul speaks in both cases about sins which Christians commit, against which they must be on guard, from which they must repent, but also from which they can by Christ's grace return.

God is not without emotion

Having said this, we ask ourselves the question, "What can the Apostle possibly mean with the expressions grieving and quenching the Spirit? Is this not a human way of speaking about God? How can God, the Holy Spirit, experience grief? How are we to interpret this grieving of God? And if the *grieving* is perhaps possible, can the Spirit really be *quenched*? Do we not believe and confess that the Holy Spirit's power is invincible, irresistible, and therefore basically unquenchable? Who can ever extinguish the fire of the Spirit? We will deal with that aspect further in the next chapter, but now already we ask in general: does this kind of language really do justice to the Holy Spirit?

Let us look more closely at the first expression, "And do not grieve the Holy Spirit of God." Obviously the Spirit of God can be grieved, touched in his heart and in his very existence. God is not without emotions. He is not

a God who acts mechanically but he is deeply involved with his creatures and he has strong personal feelings. How else could the LORD say in his law, for example, "The LORD your God is a jealous God"? Is not jealousy an expression of one of the most powerful feelings and emotions? And would it not be this divine jealousy which leads to the experience of grief?

Grief is a love word

It should strike us that the apostle uses the verb to grieve. Someone who grieves over another can do so only because he loves that person. I read somewhere that grief is a 'love' word. If you do not love someone, you do not grieve when that person does evil things or encounters problems. You may take note of someone's falling, but there is no grief, no personal feeling involved. You only grieve when a loved one falls.

Think here of the relationship between parents and children. When children do not follow the way of the Lord, this causes *grief* to the parents, because they love their children deeply. Others do not experience the same feeling. Think of David, who grieved publicly over his son Absalom, "Oh my son Absalom; Absalom, my son, would that I had died in your place!" (2 Samuel 18:33)

The fact that the Holy Spirit can grieve is related to the fact that he is the Spirit of love. In Romans 15:39 Paul speaks of this love of the Spirit. Like the Father and the Son, he loves God's children. That is the reason why he is grieved when we turn away from the Lord. We may get angry at someone whom we do not love, and even be hurt by him, but we can only grieve about someone when deep love is involved.

The Spirit is the Spirit of love

This is a comforting element in our text. The Spirit is the Spirit of love. In God's unfathomable love he seeks us, dwells in us, works in us, and is grieved when we do not respond to him or reject his work. God loves us not just when we do good, but also when we do evil, except that then his love is mixed with grief, pain, sorrow, and anguish. I think here also of our Lord Jesus who wept and grieved over Jerusalem, saying, "O Jerusalem, Jerusalem... how often have I tried to gather you as a hen gathers her chicks...." ((Luke 13:34, 35).

When the Apostle Paul here speaks of grieving the Spirit, he does not mention something new. Already in the Old Testament, the LORD made it clear via Isaiah that despite all God's grace and love evident in Israel's re-

demption, "they rebelled and grieved his Holy Spirit" (Isaiah 63:10). It was a source of sorrow and deep disappointment to God that Israel responded to his love by rebellion and idolatry. The most painful love is unrequited love. God was touched in his very being and heart, deeply affected, and brought to grieve over his people.

A specific context

When Paul here speaks of grieving the Spirit of God, he sets this in a specific context. How can the Ephesians grieve the Holy Spirit? When we pick up the context from verse 25 on we notice that there are some very specific sins by which the Spirit is grieved. Verse 25: falsehood, not speaking the truth. Verses 26 and 27: unbridled, unresolved anger. Verse 28: stealing instead of working. Verse 29: foul language instead of edifying talk. And this is summarized in the verses 31 and 32: bitterness, wrath, anger, clamour, slander, and malice, instead of kindness, tender heartedness, and willingness to forgive. We are reminded here of the Ten Commandments. Therefore I conclude that grieving the Spirit of God occurs when we deliberately transgress the law of God.

All these things point to one essential matter: our heart has not been changed but is self-directed and hostile to God and the neighbour. The Spirit is constantly working in us, but if we are directed to ourselves and do not live in holiness, that same Spirit is deeply grieved. He is hurt because these sins go completely against his very nature.

The Holy Spirit is the Spirit of *truth* (John 14:7). He cannot accept anything that is deceitful or hypocritical. He is the Spirit of *faith* (2 Cor 4:13). He cannot stand doubt, distrust, and anxiety among God's children. He is the Spirit of *grace* (Heb 10:29), and therefore whatever in us is hard, bitter, malicious, unforgiving and unloving grieves him deeply. The Spirit is the Spirit of *holiness* (Rom 1:4), and that is why anything vile, unclean, or dirty – also in our language – wounds him deeply.

The Holy Spirit seeks to renew and sanctify our life, and to change us completely. But if we tolerate in our lives whatever is deceitful, degrading, impure, and malicious, he is deeply grieved because he is opposed in his wondrous work of love.

Therefore this command: do not grieve the Holy Spirit of God who has sealed us for the day of redemption. But instead we are to yield to his work. Listen to his Word and do it. Break with those sins which grieve the Holy Spirit. Do this consciously and fervently. It means that we have to change our thinking and attitude. We must recognize Spirit-grieving sin,

confess it, and break with it. Is repentance not a matter of deliberate and conscious change?

The Spirit is especially grieved by these sins because in doing them we deny the love of the Father and spurn the grace of the Son. We make a mockery of the cross. This is one thing that the Sprit of God cannot accept. It touches him to the core of his very existence.

Turning away

What does the Holy Spirit do when he is grieved in this way? What do we do when we are grieved at someone's sinful actions? First, of course, we admonish, gently but firmly in love. But ultimately we turn away. We turn against such a person. We draw back and leave that person to his own designs.

Does the Holy Spirit act differently? Isaiah already spoke of this to Israel. He says: "They grieved his Holy Spirit. So he turned to be their enemy and he himself fought against them" (Isaiah 63:10). The grieving Spirit becomes a chastising Spirit who is no longer with us but against us.

Isaiah also said that this turning away was temporary. God in his grace "remembered the days of old, of Moses his servant." God recalled his covenant of grace and he did not cast Israel off forever. But in the meantime, what discipline resulted, what suffering for Israel – deportation and exile –, and how many died. Only a remnant returned. When the Spirit of God is grieved and turns against God's people, there are many casualties and there are very dark days.

The result of our grieving the Holy Spirit is that he turns away from us, even against us, and brings us into great trials. It can lead to great spiritual distress for us. The *Canons of Dort* speak about this in a deeply moving way (Chapter V, Art. 5). When we fall into serious and atrocious sins, we confess there, we "greatly offend God, incur deadly guilt, grieve the Holy Spirit, suspend the exercise of faith, wound [our] consciences, and sometimes for a while lose the sense of God's favour...."

Do you know what happens when we nurture and harbour a sin and so grieve the Holy Spirit? Consider what David confesses in Psalm 32 (*Book of Praise*):

"When I kept silent, sinful ways condoning,
I pined away through my incessant groaning.
Thy hand weighed down on me in my deceit;
My strength was sapped as by the summer's heat."

David and Bathsheba (Psalm 32)

David had greatly grieved the Spirit of God in his sin with Bathsheba and Uriah. But at first he did not repent. He tried to cover it up and pretended that it never happened. In the meantime, however, the Spirit of God put him in a spiritual vacuum. David began to pine away, and that means simply that he became a physical and emotional wreck. "My strength was sapped as by the summer's heat."

Hot and humid weather can make us feel tired and listless. David entered literally into a deep depression: "Thy hand weighed down on me...." God pressed down on him. God was no longer with him, but against him.

The result is that David experienced what we confess in the Canons of Dort: he lost the sense of God's favour. He experienced the Spirit of God turning away from him. That is why later, when he has repented, he exclaims, "Let nought me from thy Holy Spirit sever!" (Ps 51:4, *Book of Praise*). The worst thing that ever happened to him was that the Holy Spirit withdrew from him, that he was severed and cut off from the Holy Spirit, and he begs God: O Lord, do not ever let this happen again!

We see the depth of God's grace in that the Spirit of God only for a while turned against David. The Canons of Dort say it so beautifully: we sometimes for a while lose the sense of God's favour, "until [we] return to the right way through sincere repentance, and God's fatherly face again shines upon [us]." What we read in this text in Ephesians 4 was true for David: he was *sealed* by the Spirit for the day of redemption. God restored to him a sense of grace and new life. But at what cost! How deep did David have to bend before the Lord lifted him up.

The miracle of salvation

Do you know why it was possible for the Holy Spirit to take David up again in his comforting grace? Do you know why we can be sealed for the day of redemption? This is true only because of the great Son of David, Jesus Christ. He had to experience fully what it means to lose the sense of God's favour. When every one had left him in those dark hours before Golgotha, also the Holy Spirit withdrew from him and he was cast into the anguish of hell.

God took away from him the comforting presence of the Holy Spirit, so that he cried out in the greatest despair, "My God, my God, why have you forsaken me?" (Ps 22:1) He had never grieved the Holy Spirit, but had always lived in full obedience and yet he was forsaken of God for our sake.

There lies the great miracle of salvation. Christ bore for us the wrath of God, and underwent total desolation and loneliness so that he might obtain for us the life-giving Spirit. So we may know in all our weaknesses and failing that the Spirit will not leave us, not even in great sin. The light of God's grace will again shine upon us. We have been sealed by the Holy Spirit for the day of victory.

Do not despise God's grace

But if that is true, we must not despise God's grace in Christ. We must strive all the more never to grieve the Holy Spirit. It must be also our song: "Let nought me from thy Holy Spirit sever." For without the Spirit there is no joy. We may outwardly pretend that all is well, but inwardly we are deeply miserable and wretched. We make life very difficult for ourselves and for others around us.

Many difficulties in life – if not most of them – stem from this fact that we are nurturing sin and are grieving the Spirit of God. We are stubborn and foolish. We make it needlessly difficult for ourselves and cause despair in our life and grief to God. Why do we not begin with believing in childlike faith that we have been sealed by the Holy Spirit for the day of redemption? It is said here to us: you have been sealed. We must consciously build on that reality in a life of obedience. Then God will certainly grant us time and again the sense of his favour.

It is already terrible when we grieve each other. It is awful when husband and wife cause each other grief or when children cause grief to their parents. In these situations we must resort sometimes to strong discipline.

But it is worse when we grieve the Holy Spirit. If the Spirit turns against us, life becomes empty and meaningless. But when he is with us, we experience the peace that transcends understanding (cf. Phil 4:7). Then we learn the beauty of truth. We do not let the sun go down on our anger. We rejoice in our daily work. We who have received grace can be gracious to others. We will experience in our lives the wonderful, comforting, and renewing power of the Spirit of Jesus Christ. Then he surrounds us like a wall and lifts us up in all the trials of life to experience his salvation.

XIX

Quenching the Holy Spirit

Do not put out the Spirit's fire;
do not treat prophecies with contempt.
Test everything. Hold on to the good.

(1 THESSALONIANS 5:19-21)

In the previous chapter we considered the apostolic admonition contained in the letter to the Ephesians (5:30) about not grieving the Holy Spirit. We learned that the Holy Spirit can indeed be grieved. Our God is not an unaffected, emotionless God, but he has personal feelings that can be deeply wounded.

We also saw that this grieving of the Spirit is not to be equated with the unpardonable sin against the Holy Spirit. Grieving the Spirit is done by believers, by Christians who are not watchful but careless and so incur God's wrath and censure. We all have times in our life when we grieve the Holy Spirit and cause much distress for ourselves.

Quenching the Spirit?

In this section we look at a related text, which is often quoted in combination with the one discussed earlier "do not *quench* the Holy Spirit." Here we might raise an eyebrow. Is it not surprising that the Bible speaks of *quenching* the Spirit? Grieving the Spirit is one thing, but is it really possible to quench the Holy Spirit?

How can anyone quench God? Which human being has the ability to quench the Holy Spirit of whom we also confess that he is sovereign, almighty, and invincible? The very idea that the Spirit can be "put out," as it were, does not fit with our understanding of insuperable grace. Is it not an Arminian thought that a person can quench the Holy Spirit? Arminian theology teaches that human beings have the freedom (and so the power) either to give in to the Spirit or to block him out.

Of course, strictly speaking, no one can quench the Holy Spirit as a person in the Holy Trinity. God remains at all times sovereign and almighty. This must be kept in mind for a proper understanding of the text. But that is not the point of our present exercise.

Paul is also not speaking of the hidden, *inward* working of the Spirit in our hearts; the supernatural, mysterious, inexpressible work of regeneration or conversion, as the Canons of Dort formulate it (III/IV, Art. 12). He is not saying at all that we have in ourselves the power definitively to resist the Holy Spirit and that God's grace can be overcome by our sins.

The public work of the Holy Spirit

Paul is speaking of something different in this passage. He is referring to the *public* work of the Holy Spirit *in the congregation,* especially in the worship services. This is what we learn when we examine this text in its context. We discover that the apostle warns the church not to quench the Spirit. We also learn how the activity of the Holy Spirit is quenched in the congregation and how this activity is fostered in the congregation.

The apostle Paul is speaking in this chapter about the manner in which the congregation is encouraged and edified. See verse 11: Therefore, encourage one another and build one another up. There is within the congregation the calling to all the members to encourage and edify. This belongs to the office of all believers.

At the same time we note that in the verses 12 to 15 the apostle in connection with this edification mentions especially the work of the office bearers. The office bearers are to be received by the congregation and esteemed highly in love because of their work (verse 13). It is particularly the task of the office bearers to work for the edification of the church. Are they not Christ's gift to the congregation, as Paul writes in Ephesians 4, and instruments of the Holy Spirit?

The focus of all this is the life and demeanour of the congregation. In the verses 16 to 22, the apostle zeroes in on the worship services. He speaks of rejoicing, prayer, thanksgiving, and prophesying, and these are typically matters which take place in the worship services of the church. In these services the congregation is encouraged and built up in the faith.

A very specific admonition

In this context of congregational life and worship the apostle warns against the quenching of the Holy Spirit. This is not an isolated admonition

for each and every situation, but a very specific admonition which applies particularly to the gathering of the congregation in worship to praise God and to hear his Word.

This makes clear that the quenching of the Spirit first of all has to do with our attendance of and attitude in the worship services of the church. Notice how the apostle immediately connects the quenching of the Holy Spirit with the despising of prophesy. It is clear that this prophesying was done mainly in the worship services. The issue at stake is, then, that the quenching of the Holy Spirit happens when people despise prophecy, the Word of God, wherever is publicly and properly proclaimed.

A manner of speaking: putting out the fire

We recognize that the apostle Paul uses the word "quenching" in a figurative sense. One cannot literally quench the Spirit. But in a manner of speaking, you can. Most likely the verb "to quench" is chosen in connection with the fact that the Holy Spirit is often associated with fire.

Let me give you a few examples. John the Baptist prophesied of Jesus as follows: "He will baptize you with the Holy Spirit and with fire" (Matt 3:11). On the day of Pentecost, when the Spirit is poured out, there appeared tongues as of fire (Acts 2:3). So also Paul can use another interesting way of speaking (in his letter to the Romans): be *aglow* with the Spirit. The Holy Spirit in a manner of speaking sets us on fire and makes us glow like burning embers or shining lamps.

Now the point in this text is: just as you can quench a fire, so you can also quench the Spirit. This does not mean that we have the ability to expel the Holy Spirit completely. But we certainly can resist him and severely hinder the progress of his work.

How does one put out a fire?

I asked myself the question in how many different ways one can put out a fire. I came to the conclusion that there are really only two effective ways.

One method is to take away the fuel supply. It says in Proverbs: by lack of wood the fire goes out (26:20). If we cut the fuel line between God and us, we are no longer burning with zeal and aglow in the Spirit. To put it concretely, the fire goes out if we do not diligently use the *means of grace*.

The other method is to extinguish the fire by outward means. Throw water on it, smother it with a blanket or cast a shovel full of dirt on it, and

the fire goes out. The fire of faith goes out if we persist in wilful sin, and in doing so despise the Word of God.

We do not know how serious the matter was among the Thessalonians. Paul would not have warned if there was no real danger. It seems clear that there were those who *despised prophesying*, and by doing so quenched the Holy Spirit. Such people render the work of the Spirit unfruitful in their own lives and perhaps in that of others.

Despising prophecy

They do this, as it says literally, by regarding prophesying as nothing. To despise means to put aside as worthless. Apparently that was the attitude of some members of the congregation. They did nothing but criticise prophecy and downgrade prophets. They did so most likely because they did not like the contents of the prophecy and wanted to continue in a wicked lifestyle.

We know from 1 Corinthians that prophesying was one of the gifts of the Holy Spirit. Prophesying at that time was either the giving of new revelation or a clear interpretation of what had already been revealed. By this prophesying the Holy Spirit himself led the church further into the riches of the truth. When we keep this in mind, we understand the close connection between the commands: do not quench the Spirit, and do not despise prophesying. If you want to put out the fire of the Holy Spirit, you achieve this by shutting the mouths of the prophets. When the prophets speak no more – or when their words are rendered ineffective – the Holy Spirit does not work, for he works with the power of the Word of God.

Despising of Word and sacraments

Today we do not have prophesying in the same sense as in apostolic times. The revelation of God has now been completed and concluded. Prophecy has been replaced by preaching. Preaching is the normative proclamation of the gospel in the church, and it is made visible by and confirmed in the sacraments. These are the means of grace which the Holy Spirit uses today to edify us and encourage us in the faith.

A remarkable thing is that deformation and apostasy almost always begin with a despising of the preaching and the sacraments. We listen to the preacher, but we do not hear the Word of God. We are not using the sacraments, or we are using them improperly. We close our ears and eyes to the means of grace given in the church. Then slowly but surely the fire goes out.

For it is by means of Word and sacrament that the Spirit comes to us, and if we block off these ways, we quench the Spirit indeed.

If the Spirit is quenched, we lose sight of Christ's great work of salvation. Sin is then no longer something that should be avoided. We begin to accustom ourselves to various forms of evil. We do not hang on to what is good, but we widen our horizon to include what is forbidden. Satan gains ground at our expense.

Our personal life

What holds true for the worship services, also applies to our personal life. How do we quench the Spirit? We do so by not allowing God to work in us by his Word, by becoming lax with respect to prayer, by not consciously leading a life of faith before God every day again, and by blocking out the comfort and the encouragement of the Word as preached on Sunday.

Every Sunday in worship we are assured again of God's love toward us in Christ. We need to live in the fellowship of the life-giving Spirit. Therefore it is good that we hear this admonition: do not quench the Spirit. Let the Spirit's activity continue in our lives from day to day. Instead of quenching this activity, we must *foster* it. You have to keep a fire burning. There's a song that has a line like this: put another log on the fire. We do so by *heeding* the prophecy instead of despising it.

Test everything

It is quite remarkable that right after the admonition not to quench the Spirit by despising prophesying, we read that we ought to test everything. A Christian puts everything to the test of the Word of God, and if something does not measure up he rejects it.

There are explainers who relate the verb to test first to prophesying. Prophesying should not be despised, but tested. When you hear the prophecy – in our case the preaching – don't neglect it, but test it.

Prophesying, we saw, is the revealing or explaining of God's counsel of redemption. This prophesying was done by people who were fallible in themselves. Today the preaching is performed by weak, limited, and sinful men. That might lead us to despise it. We could say that the preaching is only what the minister thinks; it is certainly not what God says. But that is a wrong and misleading manner of getting away from under the preaching of the Word. We are to *test* the prophesying by preachers in the church.

Weigh what is said

How does one test prophesying? The apostle Paul in this connection explained to the Corinthians how they should deal with the gift of prophesying in their time. He said (1 Cor 12:29-31), "Let two or three prophets speak, and let the others weigh what is said. If a revelation is made to another sitting by, let the first be silent. For you can all prophesy one by one, so that all may learn and be encouraged."

In the apostolic time not all prophets were true prophets. The work of prophets had to be properly scrutinized. People may claim to bring the word of God, but this is not always the case. Weighing is needed.

The same is true of preaching; perhaps even more so now since there is no new revelation coming. The minister simply explains the Word of God, as best he can, but the hearers must actively weigh what is said. The verb to weigh here is equivalent to the verb to consider carefully. Weigh it to see if it is scriptural. Weigh it to see if it is applicable. Weigh it with respect to its truth and meaning for your life.

The very fact that preaching must be weighed or tested means that it is not perfect. Impure elements can very easily creep into a sermon. Wrong explanations can be given. One-sided applications can be made.

There is no rule in the Lord's churches that you have to believe something simply because the minister or any other office bearer says so. We are bound only to the Word of God, and when the preachers proclaim the true Word of the Lord, we cannot get away from its power. We have the calling to weigh what is said, and to apply the normative preaching of the Gospel to our lives.

This does not mean that we should sit in church critically to see if we can catch the preacher on an error or can discover some inconsistency. There must be a basis of trust between preacher and congregation. It is not without reason that ministers must be well-tested by the churches and must subscribe to the pure doctrine of the Scriptures.

This does mean that every member must be actively involved with the Word that is preached. The Word should be a subject of further consideration and discussion at home in a positive-critical sense. The worst thing that can befall a church is that being neither hot nor cold it just lays the preaching aside and continues as if nothing had been said (cf. Rev 3:16). Watch how soon the Spirit is quenched in such a church. We always must be aware of this danger.

Don't neglect the Word. Do not despise prophesying, but weigh what is said. Listen carefully, and let the Word work in you. Open your mind and

your heart. Ponder what has been said. Seek further knowledge on the basis laid in the preaching.

Then you will develop the ability to discern everything in the light of the Scriptures. Then you can understand the connection: do not despise prophesying *but* test everything. Put everything to the test of God's Word. Let the light of God's Word shine on everything so that you see things in their true light. Develop a critical apparatus which is formed by the Holy Spirit.

Hold fast what is good

What is the purpose and the result of this proper testing of everything? "Hold fast what is good." We will learn to discern between what is good and evil, beneficial and destructive, and we will reject everything that leads us away from the service of God. You will "hold fast," that is, hang on to what is good.

Do you see how we must foster the activity of the Holy Spirit in our lives? We do so by receiving the Word, weighing it carefully, and applying it. Then the fire will not go out. We will grow in spiritual discernment to distinguish between what is good and evil. We do not drift away from God but grow ever closer to him. Jesus Christ more and more takes control of our lives and takes form in our lives.

We should not be amazed that we are told to foster the activity of the Holy Spirit. This does not mean that the Spirit's activity *depends* on ours. He remains sovereign and almighty. But it has pleased the Spirit of God to institute these simple means of grace. We are called and obliged to use these means. That is our responsibility as congregation and individual members. For we have been bought with the precious blood of the Lord and filled with his Spirit so that we may be aglow in faith.

The Lord Jesus Christ in his great love has poured out his Spirit over the church. With this Spirit we are sealed until the great day of redemption. It is confirmed to us by Word and sacrament. Therefore it is said to each one of us that we must yield to this Spirit, not grieve or quench him, but be on fire for God's glory

Foster the work of the Spirit by submitting to this blessed Word, and by opening your hearts and lives to the probing, restoring, uplifting, and healing power of the Spirit of God through the simple means of grace.

XX

The Sin against the Holy Spirit

And so I tell you, every sin and blasphemy will be forgiven men, but the blasphemy against the Spirit will not be forgiven.
Anyone who speaks a word against the Son of man will be forgiven, but anyone who speaks against the Holy Spirit will not be forgiven, either in this age or the age to come.

(MATTHEW 12:31, 32)

From time to time questions arise concerning what is called the sin against the Holy Spirit. Matthew writes here about the *blasphemy* against the Holy Spirit or *speaking* against the Holy Spirit. In the parallel texts we find that Mark writes about blaspheming the Holy Spirit, and adds that persons who do so are guilty of "eternal sin" (Mark 3:28). In Luke's version of the account, these specific words are not found (11:17-22).

In Hebrews 6:6 we read about the sin of apostasy (falling away), a sin from which it is impossible to be brought back to repentance. The apostle John refers to "sin that leads to death" (1 John 5:16) and he adds, "All wrongdoing is sin, and there is sin that does not lead to death (verse 17)."

From all the above, we might conclude that some sins are worse than other sins. One sin, the blaspheming of the Holy Spirit, is the most serious, for it leads to death, eternal death, and is unpardonable. In this line Romanist theology refers to pardonable and unpardonable sins, and we know of the list of the *seven* deadly sins. The churches of the Reformation have thrown this listing of seven deadly sins out, but there is still this evidence about one deadly sin: the blaspheming of the Holy Spirit.

Are all sins equal?

Are there gradations when it comes to sin? Are not all sins equal? If there is one sin that cannot be forgiven, what exactly is this sin? In my pastoral work I sometimes come across believers who think that they have committed the unpardonable sin, and it leads them to great fear and despair, because they have concluded that for them there is no salvation. If such persons are asked what it is exactly that they have done beyond other daily sins to merit eternal death, they often do not know. They just have an awful sinking feeling.

We tend to avoid speaking about this sin, because it is so serious in its consequences, and perhaps also because we cannot get a good grip on this sin. What exactly is it? Very seldom will you hear a minister in the preaching warn against this sin. It is not a sin that is easily mentioned, if at all, in pastoral visits. How many times have the office bearers (including the minister) warned against this sin in a particular case? Yet the Lord Jesus explicitly warns against it, and the apostles do so as well in their letters. How can we ignore it?

Undivided attention

One thing should be clear from the start. When the Lord Jesus mentions to the Pharisees the sin of blaspheming against the Holy Spirit, he does not intend to frighten his church. Do not be afraid. But he does want to have our undivided attention in this matter. This explains his emphatic speaking, verse 31: and so I tell you... That means for us also: listen carefully, not to be frightened, but to be exhorted and edified. Christ warns against this sin so that we do not commit it. It is also here the preaching of God's love that drives the Lord Jesus.

In love the Lord Jesus warns for blasphemy against the Spirit. We will see when this warning is made by the Lord, how this warning is meant by the Lord and why this warning is marked by the Lord.

No constant mentioning of this sin

It is important to note that the Lord Jesus did not constantly go about mentioning this sin and warning against it. The accounts of Matthew, Mark and Luke agree that it was done only once, and it was made in a specific confrontation with the Pharisees at a very crucial moment in his ministry. We want to note this very carefully, for it has decisive bearing on our understanding of the sin against the Spirit. I must restrict myself now to the account given by Matthew, because that gives us the immediate context for our text here.

The text begins with the words: "...and *so* I tell you..." Literally it says: and *therefore* I tell you. The Lord Jesus gives this warning as the conclusion of a process of thought about certain events. We will see how this came about.

Confrontation over the Sabbath

We read in chapter 12 how there was a confrontation with the Pharisees on the Sabbath about the healing of a man with a shriveled hand. The Pharisees had actually prompted the Lord, for they asked him: is it lawful to heal on the Sabbath? They were looking for a reason (that is, an official reason) to accuse Jesus and to indict him for wrongdoing. The Lord did not back away from this confrontation. The Lord Jesus did heal this man, and we read that then the die was cast, verse 14, "But the Pharisees went out and plotted how they might *kill* Jesus." The Jewish leaders have made up their minds and have chosen for a certain course: Jesus must be killed, because he is a breaker of the law.

Notice how the Lord Jesus himself does not yet want to have things pushed that far. In verse 15 it says: "Aware of this, Jesus withdrew from that place." It was not yet the time for the ultimate confrontation. But notice also how difficult, how impossible, really, it is for the Lord to escape the crowds. They follow him, and he continues to heal *all* their sick (verse 15). Many of these sick were possessed by demons. Christ sees himself confronted with the power of the evil one who with his demons tortures God's people.

It is not without reason that Matthew then refers us to a passage from Isaiah, specifically a messianic passage from Isaiah 42 that identifies the Messiah as one who is especially gifted with the Holy Spirit to bring salvation and relief to the afflicted.

In that passage two elements come to the fore about the Messiah which should be noted. First, the Messiah will be a man of great *humility*, who quietly goes his way, and does not cry out in the streets demanding attention and recognition. The Jewish exorcists engaged in such loud spectacles, but the Lord Jesus did not. Do not mistake this humility for weakness, for secondly, the Messiah will be especially endowed with the power of the Holy Spirit. He is humble but powerful. Satan and his demons must make way for the Holy Spirit. The battle is not only physical and earthly, but it is spiritual and heavenly. The Holy Spirit breaks the devil's power in the lives of God's children through the ministry of the Messiah.

Worst case scenario

In verse 22 we read about a man who is brought to the Lord, and this man has major problems, more than others who came to the Lord perhaps until now. He is not only possessed, but he was both blind and mute. The man could not see. The man could not talk. If he could hear, he could not interact with his environment. He had to be *brought to* the Lord. Note that verb. This man was locked up inside himself in a body that was also de-mon-possessed. Who can imagine the fear and terror in which this man lived? This man suffered from a horrible combination of physical handicap and mental illness. Everyone knew: there is no hope for this man. This combination of physical and spiritual problems surely would be too powerful even for the Lord Jesus.

What does the Lord do? It says simply in verse 22: he healed him so that he could both talk and see. Suddenly this man was completely healed. The evidence was there. People were simply astonished and it says in verse 23 that they began to ask, "Could this be the Son of David?" Is Jesus maybe the Messiah of whom Isaiah prophesied, the great King, the long-awaited Son of David?

Do you see how we have come now to a very critical moment? Now the question needs to be answered: is this Jesus the Messiah of God? Is the evidence not overwhelmingly clear that here the promised Servant of the LORD is manifest?

Damage control

The Pharisees who are still in the area hear about this question, and they sense that the crowd might be lost to their influence and be won by the Lord Jesus. They need to engage in damage control and quickly, too, otherwise this Jesus will soar to popularity. But how can they prove that Jesus is not the Son of David? How can they disclaim the evidence that is winning the crowd? They cannot deny that Jesus did mighty wonders and signs. The nature and content of these signs appear to be legitimately messianic. They cannot deny all this. What shall they say?

You either acclaim the Lord or you disclaim him. If what he did is not done by the Holy Spirit, that is, if what he did, does not show forth the power and glory of God, then there can be only one other explanation: it shows forth the power of the devil. Either God did it or the devil.

Beelzebub did it

They say: it is only by Beelzebub, the prince of demons that this fellow (note the disclaimer, "this fellow") drives out demons. The name "Beelzebub" was slang for Prince of Baal, or Lord Baal. By changing one letter, the name meant "lord of the flies," and then you may think of the flies that hang around the manure pile. It became the derisive name for the devil.

The devil, the lord of the flies, is behind all this. This man is not the Messiah but a scoundrel, a cheat, an imposter, and his so-called signs are counterfeit, misleading and false. The kingdom of light does not manifest itself in Jesus, but the prince of darkness and the realm of the devil. Cast out demons? Why, it takes a devil to know a devil!

The instant damage control leads to an outright warning: do not believe this man, do not trust this man, and do not follow this man, for he is in league with the devil. The Spirit of God is not manifest in him, but he shows forth the power of the devil.

The breaking point

This is the breaking point, the cutting edge. The Lord Jesus shows that the viewpoint of the Pharisees does not fit with *logic*. One cannot drive out Satan except by the power of God. Demons do not go around driving out other demons. That is simply absurd. Instead, it is the other way around. Only someone who is more powerful than the devil, a stronger person, who binds Satan, can exorcise demons. Logically the Pharisees' conclusion does not fit.

But even more: spiritually it does not fit. Only the Holy Spirit, who is God himself, has power over demons. Here the Holy Spirit is showing forth the glory of the kingdom of God. If that is the case, then indeed the Messiah has come. Then it is so: whoever is not with Christ is against him. Whoever does not gather with Christ scatters (verse 30). Now the Pharisees are blocking the way for people to come to faith and be saved. They place their own unbelief and hate for Jesus as a barrier between him and the people. Do not go to Jesus for salvation: he is a devil.

This is the context in which Christ warns for sin against the Holy Spirit. He does not say: you are blaspheming against me, the Son, or you are sinning against me. He says, this is blasphemy against the Spirit. You seek to prevent the Holy Spirit from doing his work, from leading people to faith and repentance, and from the only way in which they can be saved.

When you do this, you block off the way of salvation to others by discrediting the glory of God. You block the work of the Spirit in the ministry of the Messiah. This is the breaking point, the cardinal sin, the only sin that can not be forgiven. It is the sin of *apostasy* or deliberate unbelief in which the salvation of God, the working of the Holy Spirit, is denied as being manifest fully and completely in the ministry of the Messiah.

A critical moment

The Pharisees have come to the critical moment. They have to realize this. There is a point of no return. They have now arrived at that point. Therefore we have to understand exactly what this sin really is and how the Lord Jesus means it. It is a spiritual sin, and if the Pharisees do not yet know this, now is the time for them to take stock and to be very clear on what they are doing.

Often people get stuck with the fact that Jesus says in verse 32, "Anyone who speaks a word against the *Son of man* will be forgiven. But anyone who speaks against the *Holy Spirit* will not be forgiven...." Principally speaking what difference is there between the Son of man and the Holy Spirit? Are not both God? If you speak against the one do you not speak against the other also? Why does the Lord Jesus make this sharp contrast?

I think that we can understand this as follows. You can be misled in your thinking about the Son of Man, who came in a lowly state without evident heavenly glory. You might at a certain point make all kinds of wrong and hateful statements against the Lord Jesus. You do not yet know better. No one made it clear and evident to you that Jesus Christ is the Son of God, the only Mediator between God and men, and the promised Messiah. The rejection of Christ in this case is based on ignorance or incomplete information.

Ignorance or lack of information can be dealt with and rectified. Until now this was also the case with the Pharisees. Give them the benefit of the doubt. But calling the driving out of demons the work of Beelzebub is crass. They know better than that. What Jesus does is in the light of the Scriptures very clearly the work of the Holy Spirit. This man is anointed with the Spirit, as Isaiah prophesied about him: the Spirit of the LORD is upon me!

To call this work of redemption the devil's own handiwork is not just crass and defiant of logic and Scripture; it is a blaspheming against the Spirit. This also implies that the Pharisees know better. God expects more from them than this pitiful, shallow, and unbiblical manner of reasoning.

Cold-blooded opposition

Make no mistake about it; the sin against the Spirit is also a sin against the Son and the Father. It is a denial of the work of redemption which God does in Christ. Why is it called sin against the Spirit? Because it is a direct and cold-blooded opposition of the evidence provided by the Holy Spirit and a falling away from truth, for the Spirit is the Spirit of Truth. It is the sin of willful unbelief combined with an active, cold-blooded opposition of the truth.

The Pharisees should and do know better than to characterize Jesus' work as that of the devil. Christ here warns them that they have come to the breaking point. They stand before a line that once crossed cannot be crossed back again. Their unbelief will carry them right through to Pontius Pilate and Golgotha and even farther when they deny the testimony of the guards who saw the tomb being opened. They have made themselves so blind to the truth that they can not find it anymore, even though they are looking straight at it. Their unbelief will have an awful momentum; it will wash them right into hell.

The Lord's ultimatum

The Lord Jesus does not say here that the Pharisees have already committed this sin. Look for a moment at verse 33. The Lord Jesus speaks suddenly about a tree and its fruit. He says: make a tree good and its fruit will be good, or make a tree bad and its fruit will be bad, for a tree is recognized by its fruit. Here is the Lord's ultimatum. What is it now? Is the Lord Jesus a good tree with good fruit or is he bad tree with bad fruit. Look at the fruit to recognize the tree. Look at Christ's works: do they give evidence of the power of the devil or of the power of the Holy Spirit? Does not the Spirit of God alone rule over the demons of Satan?

You simply can not look at what Christ does and call this the work of the devil. That is a blaspheming of the Spirit. It is striking that blaspheming is always done in derision and anger, saying things about God that are untrue. Blaspheming is giving a false picture of God and misrepresenting his Word. "Speaking against" has the same effect: denying the obvious truth and so misleading others, keeping them from Christ, from faith in him, and from being saved through him. Apostasy is always a falling away from a known, proven truth despite being repeatedly warned and shown what the truth is. Our Lord here is drawing a line and saying: we stand here at a very critical point.

Hardening in unbelief

It has been said that the sin against the Holy Spirit can only be committed by those who grew up in the truth, who were taught the truth, and perhaps even at one point appeared to follow the truth. Were they ever really true believers? The point is not what they once perhaps were, but what they became: enemies of the Gospel of Christ and deniers of the grace of God, who boast in their own deeds.

This sin is not necessarily one that appears right away, or even fully at all, but it can not be hidden completely for always. It is the forming of and hardening in unbelief, and that unbelief will more and more also determine one's deeds or actions. Just as faith cannot be hidden or remain unfruitful, so unbelief also must appear. A bad tree does bring forth bad fruit, and is recognizable by this fruit.

It is remarkable that it is said of the antichrists: they went out from us (1 John 2:19). The fiercest enemies of the Gospel come up out of the church and they turn their backs to the very same Gospel with which they are fully acquainted. It is this process of ungodly growth that eventually brings you to the cutting edge and to the point of no return.

Hebrews 6

Let us turn at this point to Hebrews 6. There we have the same element of being acquainted with the Gospel but turning against it. It says in verse 4, "It is impossible for those who have once been enlightened, who have tasted the heavenly gift, who have *shared in the Holy Spirit* (please note that) who have tasted the goodness of the Word of God and the powers of the coming age, if they fall away, to be brought back to repentance...." It is remarkable that these words are used in the letter to the Hebrews, because this is *covenantal* language, and the Hebrews (Jewish Christians) knew all about the covenant of God.

The things mentioned in verse 4 are the blessings which God gives in his covenant of love and which we must accept and use in faith. Some have said that this passage in Hebrews 6 proves that we can never be sure of our *election*, because we can always still fall away. But this passage does not speak about God's decree of election. It speaks *about God's covenant way*: he enlightens us, lets us live in fellowship with him and his people, in which all the benefits of the covenant, even the guidance of the Holy Spirit, are seen and shared. But where apostasy prevails, there is also a growing denial of truth and a refusal to live accordingly. The context here in Hebrews

is clear: what do we do with the covenant blessings of the Lord? We should not hide behind election or the lack of it to justify or excuse ourselves, but we should respond to the covenant of God's love in Christ.

Just as the Lord Jesus used the notion of bearing fruit, so also does the writer to the Hebrews. The land that drinks in the rain often falling on it must produce a crop useful for those for whom it is farmed. Such land receives the blessing of God. Otherwise it is useless and will be burned. What are we doing with the rain that is poured out over us by the Holy Spirit through the Word of God? Do we react as faithful covenant people?

You cannot get around Jesus Christ

What is presented indeed as a sin against the Spirit ("they have shared in the Spirit") is in fact a "crucifying of the Son of God all over again and subjecting him to public disgrace." If we may say that we find in Hebrews 6 the same sin as the one for which the Lord warned the Pharisees, note again the element of something becoming visible and apparent. The Lord Jesus is subjected, it says, to *public* disgrace.

That's what the Pharisees said. They called Jesus' work devil's work. He does it by the power of Beelzebub. Jesus Christ was publicly disgraced by them, ultimately on the cross of Golgotha. He is an imposter Messiah, they said, and laughed. But he arose from the dead, and ascended into heaven. God gave him a Name above every name that at the Name of Jesus every knee should bow, in heaven, and on earth and under the earth, and every tongue confess that Jesus Christ is Lord to the glory of God the Father (Phil 2).

You can not get around Jesus Christ. He is a stone over which you fall and break your neck forever or he is a rock on which you build to all eternity. Especially no covenant children can get around Jesus Christ, for they are baptized in his name. No matter how much we sometimes try, we cannot remove that claim, that mark, and that calling. Jesus Christ will be the life or the death of every covenant child.

Everything in Christ?

The sin against the Holy Spirit has eternal consequences because it brings to the fore whether you seek all your salvation in Jesus Christ or not. There is only one way to be saved and that is by faith in Christ in the way of his covenant. The Lord marked that way, not just for the Pharisees, but for everyone, when he said: anyone who speaks against the Holy Spirit will

not be forgiven, either in this age or the age that is to come. As long as the world lasts, this line will cut through everything and everyone. This question will stand into all eternity: who do you say the Son of man is? Eternal salvation is found in the answer: you are the Christ, the Son of the living God (Matt 16:16).

Otherwise there is no forgiveness, not now as long as the world lasts, and not then when the new world dawns. There is no forgiveness ever because the only Way is Jesus Christ. I am the way and the truth and the life, he said (John 14:6).

It is an unthinkable thought. No forgiveness, I cannot bear it. But remember that the Lord Jesus Christ did not say this to make us afraid. In Hebrews 6 we also read: God is not unjust; he will not forget your work and the love you have shown to him as you have helped his people and continue to help them. In his love the Lord grants us the reward of grace for all the good work we do in his service. Let us always remember that. God is not unjust or forgetful.

Not afraid but true fear

Our Lord did not speak about this sin to make us afraid. He did mention it to promote in us the true fear of God. He said it to have us properly focused. He gave all. We must give all, no matter what, even if we have to crucify our own flesh.

For that is the consequence. Whoever confesses Jesus as the Christ, must take up his own cross, deny himself, and follow the Lord Jesus (Matt 16:24). Then you have to make sacrifices, not to be saved, but as evidence of the joyous reality that you are saved, as a tree that bears fruit worthy of the Lord.

Only those who refuse to do this, who will not break with their sins, and fight against their weaknesses, will finally find themselves on a way of sin against the Holy Spirit. But then you are committed to the devil and have become a sworn enemy of the cross. It does not happen overnight, but it does come. Jesus said at this occasion: whoever is not with me is against me, and he who does not gather with me, scatters. We should note that the name "devil" actually means *one who scatters*.

We do not speak often about this blaspheming, this speaking against the Spirit. That is fine with me. Who wants to be an alarmist? We must think positive. Let it be clear, then, that Jesus was thinking positive when he said this. He was thinking of you and me.

Therefore, let us be aware of what this sin is, lest we crucify the Son of God all over again. Jesus Christ drew a line and said: do not cross, for here you are faced with the work of the Holy Spirit, the only One who can bring to faith and keep you in the faith.

Let us adore God's grace that Christ has warned and does warn us for this sin, so that we may walk steadfastly on the path of eternal life. You know the road you are going on, and you also know where it will end. Make no mistake about it.

XXI

The Anointing with the Holy Spirit

But you have an anointing from the Holy One, and all of you know the truth.

(1 JOHN 2:20)

Every year on Pentecost Sunday we particularly remember the outpouring of the Holy Spirit over the church at Jerusalem. We do so, of course, many centuries after the fact. The outpouring itself is truly a one-time event, and we cannot and do not have to recapture the atmosphere of what happened then. What we must do is continue to understand the lasting significance of this historic outpouring for the church of the latter days, which includes us today.

Therefore it is good to look at what one of the eye-witnesses of the outpouring himself wrote of it many years later. I refer to the first letter of John from which the above-noted text was taken. It is generally accepted that John wrote this letter when he was very old. He wrote probably forty years after the events which took place on that day in Jerusalem.

Forty years is a long time. You can forget a lot in the course of four decades. But the aged John has not forgotten what took place in Jerusalem on that great day. When we study his letter, we find that the outpouring of the Spirit, and thus the presence and work of the Spirit in the churches, is for him a very real, central, and significant truth.

The only reason the members of the church can remain faithful is because the Holy Spirit dwells in their hearts. In chapter 4:1 we read these words, "By this we know that we abide in him and he in us, because he has

201

given us of his own Spirit." That is the meaning of Pentecost. He (Christ) has given us of his Spirit, and so he abides in us and we in him.

An anointing

In this letter John calls the giving of Christ's Spirit an *anointing*: you have been anointed by the Holy One (vs. 20); the anointing which you received from him abides in you (vs. 27). The church is what it is by anointing. That is one of the themes of this letter. John had every reason to direct the church of his time back to the day of Pentecost, for there had been a very sad development, which was of great concern to him. In the churches of Asia Minor false prophets had appeared and done their devastating work. John was known as a kind and gentle man ("the apostle of love," as some call him), but in this case he does not hesitate to call these false prophets *antichrists*.

He writes: you know that in the last hour (the) antichrist will come. Well, *many* antichrists have come. We certainly are in the latter days. Moreover, they did not come up out of the world, but out of the ranks of the church. And although they have left the church, their influence is still noticeable. John's point in this text is that the churches can remain faithful only because of and through the anointing with the Holy Spirit.

As time progresses and the influence of antichrists becomes increasingly apparent, only the anointing with the Spirit of Christ will protect us so that we can abide in him. Therefore in this passage the Apostle John reminds the churches of the comforting significance of the anointing with the Holy Spirit, poured out at Pentecost. We read about the abiding presence of this anointing and the abiding power of this anointing.

Profile of antichrists

I need not sketch elaborately what these false teachers, whom John calls antichrists, taught. Let me give a simple profile of the main heresy and the accompanying attitude. Doctrine and lifestyle are always inseparably connected.

These false teachers could not accept the apostolic message that Jesus (the man) is the Christ (the Son of God). How could God ever die on the cross? Therefore they separated the man Jesus from the Christ, and taught that when Jesus died, the Christ had already gone up to heaven. John, however, summarizes the apostolic teaching in chapter 4:15, where he writes: "Whoever confesses that Jesus is the Son of God, God abides in

him." Jesus is the Christ, the Son of God. Like practically every heresy, this one also attacks the central position of Christ and reduces his saving work.

These false teachers claimed that they had received their special knowledge through careful reasoning and meditation, and they stressed that the churches had to come to a higher knowledge than simply the apostolic doctrine. There was a greater anointing to be received. These antichrists looked down upon other members who did not possess that higher knowledge. They actually insisted that the churches be subject to their further and higher instruction. Part of this instruction was to advocate an easier, more tolerant attitude towards the world and its many attractive religious forms. The heretics taught that those with the proper higher knowledge could easily handle heathen practices.

All you needed was a special anointing.

Very sharp contrast

John's response is that the church members do not need this teaching. For the church is not in any way dependent on the deep insights and discoveries of learned men. Its members are dependent only upon the Holy Spirit, for they *have all been anointed* with the Holy One (vs. 20).

Please notice the very sharp contrasts here. In both verses (20 and 27) when John speaks about "anointing," he says, "*But* you have been anointed ...," and "...*but* the anointing which you receive abides in you." The false prophets say: you need more than what the apostles taught, but John says: no, you have no need whatsoever for any new knowledge or anointing, *for* the anointing by the Holy One enables you to discover and learn what is the Truth.

You have been anointed by the Holy One. Who is meant by the Holy One? It could refer to Christ. In verse 27, John writes: the anointing which you received *from him*, and that, too, could mean Christ. For Christ is the one who poured out his Spirit over the church. So, Christ has anointed you. And of course, the notion is clear; he has done so through the Holy Spirit.

The word "anointing" in Scripture often indicates the *abiding presence* and *enabling power* of the Spirit. I think of what we read in Psalm 133, where the high priest is anointed with oil which flows down his head, into his beard, and even onto his clothes. Christ has been anointed with the Spirit without measure. On the day of Pentecost, he caused his church to share in that anointing. The Spirit who fills Christ filled the church as

well. The anointing of the Head, Christ, has a trickle-down effect upon the body, the church.

When were the believers anointed?

When did this anointing of the believers take place? John does not mention Pentecost directly. But the way he formulates things leads us to think in that direction. He writes (vs. 20), "...but you have been anointed by the Holy One, and you all know." This translation is disputed, as you can see in the footnote of the NIV Study Bible. Some translate: and you know everything, or, and you know all things. I prefer to go with the RSV here: you have been anointed and you all know. Every one in the church has access to the same source. There is no difference in this respect between clergy and laity.

The fact that all members of the church share in the anointing with the Holy Spirit became clear on Pentecost. In Acts 2 we read about the believers *all* being together in one place. When the sound of the wind is heard, it says, it filled *all* the house where they were sitting. The tongues of fire settled one *each one* of them, and they were *all* filled with the Holy Spirit. The account of Pentecost, as we saw earlier also, stresses the word *all*: all members, each and everyone, were filled with the Spirit. John can remember it as if it had happened yesterday. The anointing affected *all* those who believed in Christ. And that is still true forty years later. John can write even to those who never lived in Jerusalem or experienced Pentecost: you have been anointed, and you *all* know. Do not let these false teachers lead you to believe that you do not know anything or do not know enough, or that not all of you know, for you have been anointed from above and you all know what is necessary to know.

Even if we follow the other translation, "you know everything," the meaning is not principally different. The false prophets said: you have no real, higher knowledge; you don't know enough. But John says: don't listen to them, you know all; which means that you know whatever you need to know for salvation, and this comes from the Holy Spirit with whom you were anointed.

The anointing is a fact

See verse 26: "I write this to you about those who would deceive you." Every time someone comes along and says: "You don't have enough knowledge, you have to listen to me, let me enlighten you," don't be intimidated.

For the anointing which you received from Christ abides in you. You have no need that anyone should teach you, for Christ's anointing is sufficient.

Notice the very positive way in which John writes here about the anointing. He does not come with all kinds of unsettling questions, such as "Have you really been anointed? Did you truly receive the Holy Spirit? Have you been born again?" I do not say that these questions are unimportant, but they are not the essence of Pentecost. The anointing is an accomplished, established fact: you *have* been anointed. This anointing is something which the believers have as a permanent possession and a lasting gift. You do not lose this gift, for John writes (verse 27), "...the anointing which you received from him *abides* in you." You have it and you keep it. It is here and it stays.

Therefore John can approach the churches as the anointed people of the Lord. The church is not a body of people that is yet to be anointed, but, as also Peter writes, it is a holy priesthood. We do not come to you asking you whether all kinds of spiritual happenings have occurred in your life, but we come to you to tell you that you are a part of the people which has been anointed by the Holy One. Therefore *you* have been anointed as well. Is that not the significance of Pentecost? Pentecost is not a feast for one day, but an event which affects the entire church of the latter days.

Pentecost: the abiding presence of the Spirit

Pentecost means that the Spirit of Christ is poured out over the church, and when he comes to dwell in the church he does so with an abiding presence. He can never be removed from the midst of the church. He makes that church into his temple and his dwelling place, causing it to grow and mature to the fullness of Christ Jesus. Whenever individual people come to faith and so take a responsible place in the church, it is because of the anointing in which they share together with all the members.

That is why Pentecost cannot be repeated. The Spirit is not poured out time and again. The outpouring took place only once. At Pentecost the New Testament church is anointed, and this anointing abides throughout the days of the last ages, becoming evident wherever people profess Jesus as the Christ, the Lord. This is an important theme.

When we remember Pentecost we celebrate the abiding presence of the anointing with the Holy One. We know that the Holy Spirit came that day to stay with the church, with all the members of the church, to lead and guide them, to comfort them in trials, to strengthen them in weakness, and to give them the knowledge of Jesus Christ. The question is not: is the

Holy Spirit here? He is always in the midst of God's people.. The question is: do I consciously live out of this reality and work with it?

Modern day charismatic claims

Modern-day charismatic evangelical and Pentecostal movements like to emphasize what others *lack*. They have a lot of criticism on what they call the established or main-stream churches. They say: come to us, we will show you the way to higher knowledge and to real spiritual experience. Come to us, for then you will discover true liberation and a deeper joy. What is often the liberating centre of their teaching? The focus is (almost) always on the free will of man. The stress is on our efforts to climb up higher through spiritual activity. Everyone loves a more hands-on type of religion. But in that system Christ is bound to recede into the background, despite all claims to the contrary.

Let John's reminder be a help to us in our time. Let us rejoice in our anointing and be grateful that we have this promise: his anointing abides in us. The Spirit who has come from above will not depart from us. He came not at our invitation, but by his sovereign pleasure, and he stays not because we want him to but because he has chosen to stay. This is something we also experience in times when we are in need of comfort. The Spirit strengthens and encourages us in a way that he alone knows.

> Praise the Spirit who will never
> Leave the Church by blood once bought,
> He will show His presence ever
> Fierce though be the foes' assault.
> Fear not, flock which He is keeping,
> Though encircled by the night.
> Child of God, recall His might.
> Would the Spirit then be sleeping?
> Would He not securely keep
> Those whom Christ bought as His sheep?" (Hymn 36:3, *Book of Praise*).

This is our joy today. We have been anointed and the anointing abides. When we trust in Christ, we experience in our own lives the abiding presence of this anointing and its power.

You all know

John makes clear what it means that the Spirit abides in the church and in us its members. To turn once again to verse 20, it says: you all *know*.

The verb that is used here means knowing with a deep certainty, with the heart. It is the knowledge of faith. We all know that we belong with body and soul, both in life and death, to our faithful Saviour Jesus Christ. This deep, essential knowledge is not restricted only to some members; it is the confession of the entire church.

This is our confidence in life. True faith, worked by the Spirit, is a sure knowledge and a firm confidence. Our knowledge being sure and our confidence firm, no one has to tell us anything new. We depend on no one except the Spirit of Christ, who time and again shows his power in our weakness.

The idea is continued in verse 27: you have no need that anyone should teach you. Faithful members of the church who have come to know the Scriptures and received God's promises do not need all kinds of people to instruct them further. They can distinguish between truth and lie. An anointed one can spot a heretic a mile away.

Special offices still needed

Now we should not misunderstand these words by taking them out of context. Some explain this text as meaning that the church does not require any teachers or office bearers, because the believers are all individually guided by the Holy Spirit. There is also the teaching of the Scriptures about the special offices in the church.

We must understand that when John writes, "you have no need that anyone should teach you," he is referring to the false teachers who claimed to have decisive new information. The word used for teach here means to impart *further* knowledge. The church does not need those so-called teachers for this. Further explanation may be given and deeper insights obtained, perhaps, but this does certainly not come from those who have departed from the apostolic doctrine and left the church.

John makes that quite clear (in verse 27), "...as his anointing teaches you about everything, and is true, and is no lie, just as it has taught you, abide in him." All teaching must begin with and be based solely on the *given* revelation. Christ himself by the Holy Spirit instructs his church through what has been revealed. And Christ's teaching is true. He does not lie. Therefore the apostolic doctrine is sure and true, and anyone who claims to have something more up-to-date or better is an impostor, and in fact an antichrist.

Christ himself by his Holy Spirit will guide and lead the church in the truth. Beyond him we do not need anything. That is the reality of Pentecost. And so by his instruction the enabling power of the anointing with the Spirit will become visible. Christ will time and again lead us back to

God's Word, to the apostolic doctrine which is true and trustworthy, and in this way he will bind us to himself and strengthen us in this life.

I want to stress once again that the words "His anointing teaches you about everything, and you have no need that anyone should teach you" do not mean that no office bearers are required in the church. The words "his anointing" do not mean some inward voice or internal testimony, but refer to the *power of the revealed Word* which is proclaimed in the church by tested office bearers who are faithful to the apostolic doctrine. That is what happened on Pentecost: Peter preached the Word of God which is a power unto salvation. That is how Paul speaks about office bearers: they are gifts of the ascended Christ to his church, granted on the day of Pentecost and thereafter (Eph 4).

Properly tested and tried

The Apostles received the mandate to teach. The same mandate was later given to elders, especially to those who were able to instruct (1 Tim 5:17). The important aspect here is that these teachers are men who have been properly tested and tried, trained in the truth of Scripture, and who can be trusted to guide the church in the apostolic doctrine. These men must have bound themselves to the apostolic Word and the true confession, and in this way they have been called by God and his church to preach the Word. They do not force themselves and their insights on the church, but are received and accepted in the church because of their adherence to the Word of God. Instead of giving any new or higher knowledge, they bring only the revealed Word of God.

The important point here is that the church, also the youth of the church in its formal catechetical instruction, must be taught by men who have been *called by* the churches for this work. These men have, in turn, been *taught by* the churches, and they do their work in accordance with their subscription to the Reformed confessions. That is why ministers are first examined at Classis meetings and their integrity is approved. The churches have not without reason posted a watch at the pulpit and in the catechism room.

It is not a good development when we start on a systematic basis to use material from those who are not bound to the creeds of the church, who may be correct in many matters but perhaps mistaken in some. Who knows? Once we give the impression that our own pastors are incapable, our resources

inadequate, and that we need stylish expertise from the outside, we are already in danger, for then we jeopardize the bond to the Word and the creeds. In this way in a subtle manner a different kind of teaching can creep into the churches, little by little, like leaven. It is best to stop that from the beginning.

Stick with Christ

We must realize that Christ's anointing teaches us about *everything*. We have the Word in its full riches. We have the fellowship in confession with the Catholic Church of the ages. We stand in the Scriptural tradition of the Reformation. Our office bearers have bound themselves by public vow and subscription to these teachings and creeds, and they are held accountable to that vow and subscription. In this way the Spirit today still guides us in all truth.

Even if we can in our studies learn from the discoveries and insights of others, we do not in our formal teaching turn outside the Reformed tradition for guidance or information. We would do so only to our detriment. We must continue to insist that all our office bearers approach the church and its youth with nothing but the Word of God and the Reformed confessions. Then they stay within the anointing received from Christ, and only then can they properly guide the church.

This is an important matter. The focus of this guidance is that we *abide in Christ*. These are the last words in the text, but they are not the least significant. The work of the Spirit is always to direct us to Christ. He is our only Saviour. He has completed and is perfecting the entire work of salvation. We belong to him and must abide in him. Stick with Christ. For then you are enabled to lead lives with purpose and joy. That is the abiding power of this anointing. The intent of all heresy, subtle or blatant, is always to wean us away from what we have in Christ, and once we let go of Christ as our only Savior, we have nothing.

What a comfort it is that we can still hear it in our time: but you have been anointed by the Holy One. As Paul writes to the Corinthians: you have been sealed by the Holy Spirit who binds us to Christ and directs us constantly back to him. That is what Pentecost really means. We are anointed as a royal priesthood and a people who know the truth and live it; who need no one to tell them what to believe or where to go for insight. This is not because they know it so well by themselves, but because they have been anointed, and Christ's anointing is true and sure.

These people live by the fullness of the apostolic doctrine, the one and only Gospel. We may sing about it:

> The Gospel of salvation
> God has to us revealed
> And we, the Word believing,
> Were with the Spirit sealed. (Hymn 37:2, *Book of Praise*))

Because this is so, we can in all things abide in Christ.

XXII

The Seven Spirits

Grace and peace to you from him who is, and who was, and who is to come, and from the seven Spirits before his throne...

(REVELATION 1:4)

The text printed above is a part of a salutation which John has written at the beginning of his letter, the book of Revelation, to send to the churches in Asia Minor. We do not always see the book of Revelation as a letter, but that is what it is. It is an important, final letter sent to all the churches regarding what must yet take place.

Perhaps you know that there are various kinds of interpretations of the book of Revelation. The book is largely *symbolic*, which means that various truths and realities, happenings and events are depicted with symbols and numbers that have a deeper meaning. It is not easy properly to explain symbolic writing, but, nevertheless, the basic line is quite clear. The book covers the last period of time, the great millennium, which started with Christ's ascension (and the subsequent outpouring of the Holy Spirit) and which ends with the return of the Lord on the clouds of heaven.

In this book we read of sequels of events, which each culminate in the great judgment that is coming. It's like seeing the same sequence over and over again, but always with a new element and greater gravity not seen before. Therefore the book does not give mere repetition, but a constant deepening of what we already know.

Two main lines in the book Revelation

There are two main lines that we must keep in mind as being corre-lated. First, this final period of time will bring out the utter sinfulness of mankind and prepare the world for eternal judgment. Second, this period of time will be used by the risen and exalted Christ fully to gather his church out of all tribes and nations. God's total and final judgment will come when the holy, Catholic Church is gathered.

It will be a tumultuous and difficult time for the churches. The age-old enmity between Satan and Christ will come to its greatest intensity. There will be many casualties. But the message of the letter is one of tri-umph and hope. Jesus Christ is victorious. Christ is King. He has ascend-ed into heaven and poured out his Spirit. This book has a sense of anticipa-tion and longing of the Spirit and the Bride: come Lord Jesus, Maranatha! The Bible does not end on a sour note but with sweet music.

The Triune God

The salutation already has this melody of victory. I can hear music. A salutation is an official greeting which sets the tone. In a salutation the au-thor presents himself and the readers are qualified: who they are in rela-tion to the author. In the line of this book about the Holy Spirit we will fo-cus on one element of this salutation namely, the part about the seven spirits. We learn here that the Lord Jesus gives us the assurance that the Holy Spirit will fill his church until he returns in glory. We learn about the Person of the Holy Spirit, the position of the Holy Spirit, and the power of the Holy Spirit.

We will focus later on the fact that this passage speaks of *seven* spir-its. First it is important that we understand that this salutation or greeting is given by the *Triune* God. We must see how the parts of the salutation re-late to each other or we will not understand the middle part about the sev-en spirits.. Let's first briefly investigate the context.

It is a Trinitarian salutation. It is a greeting in the Name of the one God, Father, Son, and Holy Spirit. Therefore all the riches and glory of the Triune God are contained in this salutation.

I mention also that almost all of the apostolic letters begin with a salutation. But not all include in the salutation specifically the Holy Spirit. It often says something like "Grace to you and peace from God our Father and the Lord Jesus Christ" (2 Cor 1:2). The Spirit is not mentioned.

Still, the Spirit is often *implied*, in the word "saints" or the verb "sanctified." When you read: to the saints [in whatever place], you understand that there can only be saints because of the Holy Spirit who was poured out. One can even say that the Spirit is not mentioned because he is already present in the church, and not like the Father and the Son in heaven. Salutations may differ in their exact form and still be truly Trinitarian.

A Trinitarian salutation

Here we find very clearly and strongly a Trinitarian salutation. The words "grace and peace" are typical of a Biblical salutation. Grace is the source and peace is the fruit of God's work of salvation. Then three Persons are mentioned. Please notice that there is here a three-fold usage of the preposition *from*. The grace and peace come *from* him who is, *from* the seven spirits, and *from* Jesus Christ.

This means that each of these persons mentioned is a distinct Person. They are not separate, but still distinct. From each of them comes the same grace and peace. The first person mentioned is the Father. The play on the name "I am" (Yahweh) indicates God as the *originating* Source of all things. The name "spirit" indicates God as the *dispensing* Source of all things. The name Jesus indicates God as the *meritorious* Source of all things. Father, Son, and Spirit are the only source of all life; life revealed, redeemed, and renewed. I read somewhere that this salutation is an excellent proof-text for the doctrine of the Holy Trinity and the personality of the Holy Spirit.

In any case, what becomes clear is that the Holy Spirit is a distinct Person in the Godhead. He is not, as some would explain, merely a power that goes forth from God, but he is truly God himself. As Lord's Day 20 of the *Heidelberg Catechism* says, "...He is, together with the Father and the Son, true and eternal God."

Spirits in the plural?

Now we have to deal with the fact that the word spirit here is in the plural: the seven spirits. The question that arises is simple: is there not one Holy Spirit? Surely there are not seven. Therefore you see in the NIV printing that the word spirits is not capitalized. The RSV also does not use a capital letter. Better not take any chances, I guess. The King James Version is somewhat bolder, it seems, for it has "the seven Spirits." I must confide that the KJV version did make me feel better.

If you feel that the plural form (spirits) does not allow you to think of the Holy Spirit, then you must come with a different explanation. The only one that may have some credibility is the suggestion that the spirits mentioned here are *angels*. Does the Bible not elsewhere speak of angels as "ministering spirits"? (Heb 1:14) The problem with that explanation is, however, that in the book of Revelation angels are always specifically mentioned by name or nature, and they perform very significant works. But nowhere in this book are they called "spirits." It would be strange to find the idea of "angels" in a context which clearly speaks of God, the Father and the Son. I must conclude that the word *spirits* is a reference to the Holy Spirit.

Seven spirits?

But are there really seven spirits? Is there not one Holy Spirit? It is true that there is only one Holy Spirit. The number seven in the book of Revelation is a very important number; found actually 52 times in this book, as the NIV notes in the introduction. In the first chapter, we read about seven churches, seven spirits, seven golden lamp stands, and seven stars. It is explained by the Lord what this means. Later in the book we read about seven seals, seven trumpets, seven thunders, seven signs, seven plagues, and seven golden bowls. There are more series of seven which we do not note specifically now.

The number seven is the number that indicates *God* in his fullness and perfection. It speaks of the great glory of God evident in the abundance and riches of his works. In this connection we note that the number of man is 6, even multiplied, 666 (Rev 13:18). That number never becomes 7, because man cannot become divine. The book of Revelation describes how all things must come to their fullness and maturity, and that the world in this way is prepared for the final and full judgment of God.

Therefore the expression "the seven spirits" means here the fullness of the Holy Spirit. John sees how in heaven the glory of the Holy Spirit is fully and completely evident. Symbolically this is presented in the number seven. It is a very intensive number: the glory of the Holy Spirit is evident before the throne of God, envelopes that throne, and emanates from it. It is not without reason that the number seven, used so often of God's actions, is applied also to God the Holy Spirit.

The number seven is of great significance here. The Holy Spirit is true and eternal God. He is in the centre of the heavens before the great throne. From there he fills and controls all things. Imagine the effect when this Spirit comes to live in and among us.

Before God's throne

Here is a sublime description of the same Holy Spirit who was poured out on Pentecost. This does not mean that nothing of the Spirit is left in heaven. Remember that he is and remains omnipresent. But it does mean that the Holy Spirit came to the earth with the same great intensity to complete there the work of the Triune God. The seven spirits (to follow the usage of Revelation 1) come to dwell among the seven golden lamp stands with the seven stars. The Holy Spirit comes to live among and in the churches to bind them together in Christ and to equip them in the last phase of history. This is the very heart of what we remember at Pentecost.

Now there is another aspect to which I direct your attention. It says that the seven spirits are *before* God's throne. Not on the throne, not beside it, not behind it, but before it. That is a fascinating detail which we should for a moment explore, because it tells us something about the *position* of the Holy Spirit. I do not mean a position assigned by any higher power, because there is none, but a position voluntarily and purposely taken in by the Holy Spirit in the one counsel of God.

Positions and places are important in the book of Revelation. In Revelation 5 we read how the Lord Jesus appears in heaven (the result of his ascension) and take a place at the right hand of him who sits on the throne. That is not a lesser position than on the throne, but it indicates having full executive power to carry out the counsel of God concerning our redemption.

The seven spirits are before the throne. Why are they located there? Questions have also been asked here about the order, not in rank, for there is none, but in mentioning. We read of Father, Spirit, and Son. Most often we find the order Father, Son and Holy Spirit. There are those who have attached great significance to this position of the Holy Spirit.

Being before the throne means that whatever comes to the throne must be first received and accepted by the Holy Spirit. He is between the throne and all living creatures. No one has access to the throne than through the Holy Spirit. The Holy Spirit determines and guides the traffic, as it were, around the throne. He will do this also when poured out over the church: guide and direct all to the throne up above.

Seven lamps blazing

One scholarly explainer made a comparison with the old temple or tabernacle. There is the holy of holies, where God the Father is. Then there is

the lamp stand that casts light on the curtain dividing the holy place from the most holy. I refer you to Revelation 4:5, where we again see the throne in heaven. It says, "From the throne came flashes of lightning, rumblings, and peals of thunder. *Before* the throne, seven lamps were blazing. These are the seven spirits of God." Symbolic language is sometimes a trifle confusing, for here the seven spirits are like seven lamps, blazing before the throne.

But it is not really as confusing as it seems. A lamp is not the same as lamp stand. The lamp stands are the churches. The lamp on those stands is the Holy Spirit. For he works in the churches and what comes forth from the churches is not our light, but the light of the Spirit. The church is called to hold up and hold open the Word of God by which the Spirit works. But it is the light of God alone that can enlighten dark hearts.

And then – to stick with our learned interpreter – when you come from the Holy of Holies, and through the Holy section, where the lamp stand is always burning, you come to the area where the *altar* is, where Christ's gave the true and final sacrifice. Hence the order here: Father, Spirit, and Son. This attempt is a nice construction, but I'd rather say: it is only in chapter 5 that the Son appears in heaven and takes his place on the throne, and therefore he is not presented yet as being in heaven in chapter 1. Let's not get ahead of things.

Directing people to the throne

The seven spirits are before the throne. They are in that sense an extension of the throne. They exercise the full power symbolized in the throne. The Holy Spirit regulates the heavenly traffic around the throne. He determines who comes before God and who does not. That very same function is also fulfilled by the Holy Spirit on earth after his outpouring on Pentecost. He directs people to the throne above, where God is, where now Jesus Christ is. They can enter only by his power, by the power of the Word. The way to the throne of God is still through the Holy Spirit. Only by the Spirit do we share in the grace of the Son and the love of the Father.

This brings us to reflect with the text on the power of the Holy Spirit. The Lord Jesus said, before he ascended, "To me is given all power in heaven and on earth." But that power is exercised on earth by the Holy Spirit. As in the beginning, when he hovered upon the face of the waters, so now also he exercises the power of God, manifest in power of Jesus Christ, over this world in true pastoral care.

Please note one more interesting detail. There are seven spirits before God's throne. In Revelation 5, where our Lord Jesus Christ is introduced as having entered heaven, it says in verse 6, "Then I saw a Lamb, looking as if it had been slain, standing in the center of the throne, encircled by the four living creatures and the elders. He had *seven horns and seven eyes* which are the *seven spirits* of God sent into all the earth." (Rev. 5:6) Seven horns mean omnipotence. Seven eyes denote omniscience. The omnipotence and omniscience of the Holy Spirit are also ascribed to Christ, who paid for us, and these will be used for our benefit.

The Holy Spirit is poured out on Pentecost. But he does not come as a lame duck. He comes with the omnipotence and omniscience of Jesus Christ to *complete* and finish the gathering of the holy Catholic Church. He comes to apply the reconciliation that Christ has achieved by his death and resurrection. He comes to show forth the glory of Christ, demonstrated in his ascension and heavenly splendor, and so the Father is glorified and praised ad infinitum.

Perhaps we do not always reckon enough with the presence and the power of the Holy Spirit, or we take it for granted, and then it doesn't affect us. We must take it, not for granted, but take it actively. We must live and walk by the Spirit, not gratifying the flesh but the Lord. These are Biblical directions. For this we must pray unceasingly. In the light of the foregoing, I may ask you this question, also implied in Lord's Day 45 of the *Heidelberg Catechism* about prayer, "Do you constantly and with heartfelt longing ask God for these gifts and thank him for them?" Because, it says in that Lord's Day, "God will give his grace and Holy Spirit only to those who constantly and with heartfelt longing ask and thank." We must be focused on the Spirit. Pray constantly in the Spirit. We must long for his grace. Beseech the Spirit not to leave us, but to continue in us and among us.

The Holy Spirit still determines the traffic: who shall enter and who shall not. He does this by applying to us the grace and love of the Father and the Son. He does this by granting us his fellowship. He now leads us to stand before the throne, and to stand there in Christ.

Nothing can stop him. We read about seven horns. All the power of the Lord is also in the Holy Spirit. No one can hide or pretend. We read about seven eyes. The Holy Spirit searches all things from the depths of God's counsel to the depth of our hearts. He is the other Advocate, the counselor, the conductor, and the connector, who binds us to God in Christ and binds God to us.

He is before the throne and now he is in the midst of the church. Open up. Experience increasingly how the Spirit leads you to the throne, where the Father is and where Christ, our Lord, is. Then you know what Pentecost really means.

✑he ✑pirit an∂ the ✑ride

The Spirit and the bride say, Come!
And let him who hears say: Come!
Whoever is thirsty, let him come;
and whoever wishes let him take
the free gift of the water of life.

(REVELATION 22:17)

With the outpouring of the Holy Spirit on de day of Pentecost, the last phase of history has really begun. We truly live in the last days, the time of the end of the ages. Christ has completed his work of redemption on earth, has ascended in glory, and now through the Holy Spirit is preparing all things, also his church, for the great day of his glorious *return*.

This final phase of history is elaborately described in the book of Revelation. I remind you of what I wrote in the previous chapter that there are in this final phase of history *two lines*: the world is being prepared for ultimate *judgment* and the church is being gathered for final *glory*. These two lines flow together in this way: only when the church has been fully gathered, will the Day of Judgment come. As the one is sure, so is the other.

In this time the Holy Spirit fulfills a very prominent and decisive task, especially in the life of the church and the lives of the believers. You find this already in the very beginning of the book of Revelation, in the seven letters to the churches in Asia Minor, where the constant refrain is heard: he who has an ear, let him hear what *the Spirit* says to the churches.

It is evident that in this last phase of history the church on earth stands under the special care and guidance of the Holy Spirit. The church and all its members will need this care, for we must go through what is called "the great tribulation" (Rev 7:14). When the world undergoes God's just judgments, the church will also be severely chastised and sorely persecuted.

The Spirit has come to stay

In the last chapter of the book Revelation we read of the final outcome of history: the promise of the return of the Lord Jesus Christ is confirmed. In this context again the Holy Spirit is expressly mentioned: He will never leave the church by blood once bought. As a matter of fact, we learn that the Holy Spirit keeps the expectation of the church alive that the great day of the Wedding Feast will come.

This brings us again to the significance of Pentecost, a matter that required our attention throughout this book. We know that on Pentecost the Spirit was poured out over the church. It is important to remember that this fact indicates the start of a new and final phase in world history. Pentecost means that the Spirit has come *to stay* with us until Christ returns. We are convinced by Scripture that Pentecost can not be repeated: it is an event that opens a whole new era, even *characterizes* that era as one of great spiritual activity. The Spirit has come to dwell *in* the church as the body of Christ and so to dwell in all its members. Pentecost marks the *permanent* indwelling of the Holy Spirit in the church and its members.

Because it is the *start* of a new era, it is accompanied by wondrous signs: a sound as of a mighty wind and tongues as of fire (Acts 2:1-4). Only at the beginning of this new phase are these special signs given. And while the signs are not repeated, we are nevertheless convinced that the new reality – the presence of the Spirit – is constant.

How will we persevere?

When we read in the book of Revelation about all the terrible things that will happen in this last phase of history, the judgments and trials, we can really wonder how we will be able to *persevere* in expecting the return of Christ. Our Lord in this last chapter may repeatedly state, "Behold, I am coming soon!" but it will not be easy for us to live in that expectation every day. We might even come to wonder if this promise is really true: things just seem to go as they go, from bad to worse, perhaps, but with little progress. The time of waiting may lead to feelings of hopelessness and despair.

In this last phase of history we will have our hands full, just managing to keep our heads above water, so to speak. Will what was evident at the *beginning* of the era of Pentecost last for the *duration* of that era, and even be still alive at the *end* of that era? Pentecost was a nice and enthusiastic beginning, but will the feeling last? Will the church persevere?

We know by experience that a good start is important, but also that in the course of time, we can lose sight of the beginning and get bogged down by the many woes and cares of life. Things never quite turn out the way we expected, do they? We know from Scripture that the apostasy of mankind and the accompanying delusion will be great, and that the love of many will grow cold, and what can then realistically be expected of the church and its members? We are all weak and mortal, and we are hardly able to withstand the many onslaughts of an enemy far more powerful and determined than we are.

The church is called the bride

The church is called "the bride." In Revelation 19:7, after the fall of Babylon is described, we read these triumphant words, "Let us rejoice and be glad and give him the glory, for the wedding of the Lamb has come and his bride has made herself ready!" The bride is ready, dressed in fine linen, bright and clean, prepared for the great feast. But how can we be sure that the bride will be ready? If the waiting for the wedding appears endless and the Bridegroom tarries, will the bride not lose heart?

Our Lord himself once spoke about the time between ascension and return as a time of mourning and *fasting* for the bride. In Matthew 9:14 and following we read that John the Baptist's disciples come to Jesus and ask him why his disciples do not fast. John's disciples fast, and even those of the Pharisees do, but those of Jesus do not. Fasting was a common religious practice in that time and the question is quite appropriate: why do Jesus' disciples not engage in it? He then said: how can the guests of the Bridegroom mourn when he is with them? The time will come when the bridegroom will be taken from them; *then they will fast.*" What does that mean other than that Christ himself recognized the great need and stress of the waiting bride in the last era?

Fasting, typically a practice belonging to the old covenant with its ceremonies, was prescribed in the law only on the day of atonement, and only after the exile was it extended to other times, but it had become in Jesus' days one of the many forms of *self*-righteousness, instead of a sincere expression of sorrow over sin. The Jews fasted left, right, and center, seeking thereby to achieve favor with God. But Jesus lets the disciples know that with the coming of Christ a *new era has come*, one of celebration and joy as of a *wedding feast.* You don't fast during a feast, do you? Later when the bridegroom is taken away, they will fast, and he means: really fast, mourn and grieve for all the right reasons, in longing for the return of the Groom.

A time of longing and yearning

My intention is not to discuss fasting as such. My point is to make clear that the time before the great marriage feast, the coming wedding, is described by Jesus as being in a sense comparable to a *fast*. It will be not a time of feasting but of fasting, not a time or rejoicing and celebration, but one of grieving and suffering, of great longing and yearning. We are now, as it were, a bride without a Bridegroom.

I fully realize that some explainers take this fasting to mean the time between Good Friday and Easter, and that element is certainly present, but we may also see it in a broader sense as denoting the time between the ascension and the return of Christ when we are as a bride without a Groom, waiting, longing, and yearning for the great Wedding Day.

How can we persevere in expecting the coming of the Lord? In this passage (as elsewhere in the book of Revelation) it is not without reason that the church is called a *bride*. It does not say: the Spirit and the *church* say: come, but the Spirit and the *bride* say: come! For the church is by definition a *bride*, some one who has received a promise or pledge and *knows* the great day is coming because the Bridegroom is trustworthy. A bride knows her bridegroom and she is prepared for the great day. Her life is characterized by readiness and expectation. She therefore does not cease to call out: come! Her only goal and purpose is that great day when her joy will be full.

Single focus and purpose

The bride says: come! She has a single focus. I do not know if you can find yourself in this profile. Is your only goal, focus, and purpose the coming of the Lord? Do we know the longing for the wedding and the yearning for the new heaven and earth? As intensely as it is voiced in our text, so weakly is it often experienced by us. Is it not so?

I once read a kind of poem that went something like this: come, Lord Jesus, come quickly, but not until... and you may fill in the rest. Christ has his focus; we have ours. Christ has his agenda but it is not always the same as our agenda, is it? We can not really be fully heaven-oriented, when we are still earth-bound, can we? How little does the return of Christ from day to day play a role in our lives? Sometimes we do not reckon with it at all, let alone ardently *expect* it or yearn for it. It sometimes takes great trial and much earthly difficulty to make us realize that this life here is not the purpose of our existence, and even then we easily forget.

The Spirit comes first

I am not trying to make anyone feel guilty about a possible lack of fervent yearning for the day of Christ. The text does not seek to make us feel guilty, either. Notice that it says: the *Spirit* and the bride say: come! The Spirit comes first here. The same Spirit who in the first chapters of the book Revelation spoke *to* the church now speaks *within* the church. The Holy Spirit is the one who is here the Motivator and he leads the church to echo the sentiment: come, Lord Jesus!

The bride does not and can not say this on her own. The bride can only say "Come" through the Holy Spirit. It is the Holy Spirit, therefore, who keeps the expectation of the church alive. The bride is and remains a yearning bride only because of the Holy Spirit within her; the Spirit who came from Christ and leads her to Christ. The yearning of the bride throughout the latter days, the last phase or era, is a direct work and fruit of the Holy Spirit.

As we saw, Pentecost marks a beginning. But the same Bible shows us that the joy and zeal, the longing and yearning of the beginning never end, because the Holy Spirit never ceases to work. The Spirit will keep the longing of the bride alive until the last day, from Pentecost on right through the great tribulation. The Spirit says, "Come," and therefore also the bride says, "Come." The Holy Spirit, now our Counselor and Comforter on earth, will lead the church time and again to the true prayer: come, Lord Jesus.

Freeze-frame or move forward?

Many would like to go back to Pentecost and relive it. But Pentecost by its very nature is the feast of the beginning that leads onward. The Spirit did not come to freeze-frame the church in a certain time or status, but came to move that church forward and onward to the great day, the wedding feast itself. The Spirit comes to dwell in the church but does so to propel that church forward throughout the last era until the day of the wedding feast comes.

At Pentecost, in Acts 2, we stand at the at the beginning of a great journey, but here in Revelation 22 we are shown what it is like towards the *end* of that journey. What is consistent is the longing and yearning of the bride for the Groom.

Much has changed since that first day in Jerusalem. The world and the church undergo constant change. But what does not change is the expectation of the bride for the coming of the Lord. If it has changed in any

way, it has only intensified. The farther we come in the history of this world, the more we see that our only real hope for decisive and lasting change lies in the coming in glory of the Lord Jesus Christ.

Great expectations

The Holy Spirit came to keep the expectation of Christ's return alive and vibrant, to make this a catholic, world-wide expectation. The permanent indwelling of the Spirit alone guarantees the functioning of that expectation.

Here I must add something extremely important. How does the Holy Spirit bring about this expectation and keep it alive? In the context of this chapter, John describes how he hears about the "words of the prophecy of this book." Verse 7: Behold, I am coming soon! Blessed is he who *keeps the words of the prophecy of this book*. Verse 9: the words of this book. Verse 10: do not seal up the words of the prophecy of this book. Verse 18: I warn everyone who hears the words of the prophecy of this book: if anyone adds to them, God will add to him the plagues described in this book. Verse 19: and if anyone takes words away from the book of this prophecy, God will take away from him his share in the tree of life and in the holy city....

The Spirit of the Word

There is a very strong connection, obviously, between the *work* of the Holy Spirit and the *words* of the prophecy of this book. The Holy Spirit is the Spirit of the *Word* of the prophecy of *this book*. This is not surprising, because Pentecost is the day when the *Word* of God began to be proclaimed in Jerusalem. The Holy Spirit works through the Word and the proclamation of that Word. It was only after Peter's *sermon* on Pentecost that the people asked: what shall we do?

It is important to note how the "word of prophecy" is here connected to a *book*. From the beginning in Revelation 1, John was expressly commanded to *write everything down in a scroll*, in a book.

Many commentators hold the view that in the verses 18 and 19 the expression "the words of the prophecy of this book" refers to the book of Revelation, and indeed it does directly. The Revelation to John is here recognized as the glorious and definite conclusion of the Word of God; nothing may be added, nothing may be taken away. But this being so, this warning has meaning for the *entire Scriptures* given by God.

The exhortation to adhere to the words of the prophecy of this book is also found earlier at other key moments in Scripture. In Deuteronomy 4:2,

where the *law* is repeated, it is said also, "Do not add to what I command you and do not subtract from it, but keep the command of the Lord your God that I give you." And in Proverbs 30 (a book in the Hebrew version towards the end of the Old Testament) it is also said: every word of God is flawless... do not add to his words or he will rebuke you and prove you a liar." So, indeed, this warning sounds familiar, functions strongly in the Old Testament, and comes out clearly at the conclusion of the New Testament: this is the full and final revelation of God. Do not add to it; do not subtract from it.

The Word of the Spirit

The point is now that the Holy Spirit *works* in the church with the full and complete *Word* of God. The power of the Word was evident already of old, and that is what will deeply characterize the last era as well in an unprecedented manner. The expectation of the church will be kept alive by the Holy Spirit through the working with the Word by the preaching of the Gospel.

The Spirit will guide the church and speak to the heart of the church by the *Word of God*, and this is what will nurture and deepen the expectation and the hope of God's people. The Spirit says through the Word: come Lord Jesus, that is the great goal, and the church says in response to the Word: come Lord Jesus, indeed that is the great goal.

The song of the bride, Come Lord Jesus, Maranatha! is the response of the church to the Word of God with which the Holy Spirit fills the church and the lives of all its members. Our Lord Jesus spoke of this himself even before he went to the cross, in that night of the Passover, John 16:13 and 14, "When he, the Spirit of truth, comes, he will guide you into all *Truth*." The Holy Spirit is the Spirit of truth, wisdom, and understanding, and he takes the Word of God and makes it known to us, applying it to our hearts and in our lives.

The main feature in the last ages

This means, then, also that in the last era, the time between Pentecost and the return of Christ, the main feature in the life of the church is the preaching of the Gospel, the teaching of the doctrine of Scripture, and an abiding in the revealed and written Truth.

It is so important to note this carefully. The last age is one of delusion and deceit (2 Thess 2:9-12). There will be many who will deny the Word of

God in the Scriptures and yet claim to bring truth and wisdom. There will be those who tell us that the Spirit cannot be limited to the Scriptures. People will come who suggest that preaching and teaching actually restrict the Holy Spirit. No formal doctrine or preaching is needed, but – they say – a spontaneous working of the Holy Spirit within the heart and soul is the essence of religion. But the whole dilemma is false. The Holy Spirit, sovereign and omnipotent God, who can never be restricted but does remain true to himself, will keep alive the expectation of Christ's return through the working of the Word, the power of the Gospel, that unique Word which speaks of life in Christ through grace.

The big question for the last age

The big question will be for this last era: what will you do with the Word of God? Pentecost brings that question everywhere to the fore: what are you doing with the Word of God? For you are the *hearers*, and it says specifically in this passage also: let him who *hears, say: come*! Hearing leads to longing and calling: come, Lord Jesus! This Word will go out as the water of life, and we are assured: whoever is thirsty, let him come; and whoever wishes let him take the *free gift* of the water of life. We need not earn salvation or realize it for ourselves, but we must simply take it by faith as God's free gift of grace.

As we come to the end of this book, we note once more that it has been Pentecost, and since then the Gospel of life in Christ has been proclaimed with a great promise: take freely; life is gift of grace from God in Christ. The Gospel is the Gospel of free and sovereign *grace* in Christ, and it is so: take it or leave it. But whoever *hears*, that means whoever listens and believes, will also speak the same words: Maranatha, come Lord Jesus! You cannot hear the Gospel and then not echo its longing and yearning for the day of glory.

As John comes to the end of this amazing and moving book in which the Lord Jesus outlines his final work of light in this dark world, his counsel of renewal, John may be assured and give assurance to all the churches that the bride will keep on longing for the day, no matter how long it takes, and the yearning will be deepened and intensified. For the Spirit will lead the bride in the call for the return of the Groom!

Preparing the Bride

Jesus Christ says: behold, I am coming soon! That means he is coming without any unnecessary delay. And the Spirit *and the Spirit-filled Bride* say: yes! Come Lord Jesus! God himself evokes the very response he seeks. The work of the Holy Spirit may in this sense be called a work of preparing the bride for the great wedding feast.

Then we understand that it can not just be a matter of *saying*: come! It must be a matter of *living*: come! Our whole life and lifestyle must show forth this longing for the day of Christ. What true bride will wait with longing for the one and only groom if she meanwhile consorts with all kinds of others? The church, as Christ himself so often stressed in the parables, must always be ready for the day. Each one of us must personally be ready for the day. You can not get ready after he has come; you must be ready while he is coming.

When you are waiting, it is not hard to lose your focus, to become distracted, and even to fall away. The best of brides are sometimes impatient for the great day and when it does not come as they want, may turn to others. One of the quickest ways to lose your focus is to shut out the Word, stop hearing the proclamation of the Gospel, and then other things will quickly fill the void. Stop listening and you will stop longing. You will seek fulfillment here and now, seemingly sweet, but always deadly. Only the Spirit can and will through the Word keep the hope strong, the expectation alive, and the lifestyle holy.

Never lose hope

One of the things which strongly characterizes our present society is the tendency to give up. People easily lose hope and expect nothing really to change anymore. With a certain despair also a sense of not-caring anymore sets in. Some give up quickly; others after a long struggle, but give up is what people tend to do.

Do you realize that someone who is part of this bride can never give up the struggle of faith? Giving up would be a denial of Pentecost and of the very power and work of the Holy Spirit. The bride can not be defeated because *the Spirit and the Bride* are inseparable. If you stay with the Word of God, believe it heartily, and act accordingly, much can go wrong, but you can not be defeated. You will always find the way and the strength to carry on in faith, sadder in yourself perhaps, but wiser in God. We can be bent, but not really broken, for the *Spirit* and the bride say: come.

This is what the final age really means: the Spirit preparing the bride for the great wedding feast. He alone can do it, right through the great tribulation of the latter days. There is only one of two ways: play the false harlot or live as a true bride. What will it be? If we did not have the Holy Spirit and his abiding presence, we would not be able to persevere. But now we can. He has come to stay and lead us to the great day when we shall be perfectly united with Christ. The Spirit is truly the Spirit of hope and perseverance, causing love and zeal to flourish there where all may fade and fail. He is himself the guarantee that we shall be forever free when Christ returns on His great day.

"O come, Lord Jesus, come," we pray.

Jeremiah:
6 ....p. 46
23: 23, 24 ....p. 35
31 ....p. 62

Ezekiel:
9 ....p. 159
37 ....p. 47, 48
39: 29 ....p. 36

Daniel:
2: 36-45 ....p. 18

Hosea:
1:2 ....p. 41

Joel:
....p. 88

Jonah:
1-4 ....p. 35

Matthew:
1: 20 ....p. 49
3: 10, 12 ....p. 55. 183
3: 14 ....p. 49
3: 16, 17 ....p. 49 ff.
4: 17 ....p. 61
5 ....p. 96
5: 9 ....p. 56
7: 11 ....p. 21
9: 14 ....p.221
10: 16 ....p. 55
11: 2, 3 ....p. 56
11: 28-30 ....p. 46
12: 31, 32 ....p.174, 189ff.
15: 9 ....p. 13
16: 16 ....p. 198
16: 24 ....p. 198
17: 5 ....p. 51
23: 29, 30 ....p. 108
24: 36-51 ....p. 9
27: 46................................. p. 57
28: 19 ....p. 74, 90

Mark:
3: 28 ....p. 189

Luke:
4: 19 ....p. 55
4: 21 ....p. 19
11:1 ....p. 136
11: 17-22 ....p. 189
13: 34, 35 ....p.176
23: 35 ....p. 54

John:
1: 3 ....p.22
1: 16 ....p. 57
1: 29-36 ....p. 64
1: 32 ....p. 51
3: 3-5 ....p. 59 ff.
3: 7 ....p. 59
3: 8 ....p.15
3: 16 ....p. 66
3: 34 ....p. 56
10: 7 ....p. 75
12: 28 ....p. 51
12: 31 ....p. 78
14: 6 ....p. 198
14: 7 ....p. 177
14: 16ff. ....p. 67ff.
14: 24 ....p. 17
14: 26 ....p. 25
15 ....p. 78
15: 26 ....p. 17, 57, 124
14: 30 ....p. 78
16: 3 ....p. 225
16: 7 ....p. 17
16: 13-15 ....p. 148

Acts:
1: 15 ....p. 97
2 ....p. 50. 56, 204
2: 1-4 ....p. 220
2: 3 ....p. 185
2: 4 ....p. 92
2: 7 ....p.70
2: 13 ....p 99
2: 17, 18 ....p. 87ff.
2: 20, 21 ....p. 95

'Come on,' he whispered under his breath, his eyes darting from Rouche to the men in the doorway and back again.

Rouche pushed himself off the wall. He could feel his shirt sticking to his skin and tried to tell himself that it was sweat rather than blood that had saturated the material. It felt as though he had a gaping hole in him. He could feel the breeze that snuck in with each revolution of the door, inside him, as if it were blowing straight through him. Unable to pinpoint any specific source of the pain, his brain told every last nerve in his body that it was burning.

He forced himself to stand up straight, and stepped round the corner into the corridor, walking purposefully towards the open doorway. The two men watched him carefully as he approached. Behind them, the audience looked to have taken their seats, and the hum of conversation was dying down.

The two men appeared to be brothers, both sharing the same sharp features and imposing way of being fat. Rouche approached the bigger of the two, in a psychological display that he had nothing to hide. He nodded curtly.

Eyeing him warily, the man directed him just inside the doorway, tactically positioning Rouche so that he could no longer see the other man behind him.

He gestured to Rouche's chest.

Gritting his teeth, Rouche unbuttoned his suit jacket, feeling the wounds ripping back open as he slid his arm out of the sleeve. He didn't need to look down to assess the damage; the expression on the man's face was enough.

His white shirt was now no more than a red-and-brown rag clinging to him, a bandage in need of changing. Suddenly, there was a large, rough hand over his mouth, the stink of nicotine-tainted skin, and a tree trunk of an arm locked round his throat.

'We've got a problem!' Edmunds told Baxter. 'They know something's wrong.'

'Are you sure?' she asked him, unable to hide the panic in her voice. 'If we're blown, we need to move in now.'

'I can't say for sure . . . I can't see them.'

Baxter's voice went distant for a moment:

'Prepare to breach,' she told someone in the background. Her voice then returned at full volume. 'It's your call, Edmunds.'

'Hey! Hey! Hey!' said a softly spoken man as he rushed over to the scene in the doorway.

Several members of the audience had noticed the disturbance and were watching avidly. Rouche was struggling in vain against the arm round his neck. His shirt had been torn open to reveal the word, rendered almost illegible from where it had bled over the lines, like a poorly coloured-in picture.

'What's going on?' the newcomer asked the two doormen.

He was in his late forties, and had an ironically kind face beneath his neat beard considering where they were.

'You told us to act on anything suspicious, Doc,' said the taller brother. 'His scars are fresh,' he explained unnecessarily.

The doctor gently pulled Rouche's shirt open and winced at the mess beneath. He met Rouche's eye and gestured for the other brother to let him speak.

Rouche gasped as the hand moved away from his mouth and the arm round his throat slackened a little.

'My, my, what a mess you have made of yourself,' the doctor said, calm but suspicious. He waited for an explanation.

'I cut them into myself every morning,' said Rouche. It was the best answer he'd been able to come up with.

The doctor looked undecided. 'Who invited you here today?' he asked Rouche.

'Doctor Green.'

The answer, although possibly true, had been of no use. The FBI had made Alexei Green one of the most famous people on the planet almost overnight. The man stroked his chin as he regarded Rouche:

'Kill him,' he said with a pained shrug.

Rouche's eyes grew wide as the arm tightened round his throat. He kicked out and pulled desperately at the asphyxiating appendage when something caught the doctor's attention:

'Stop!' he ordered. He took hold of Rouche's wrists and raised them out in front of him. 'May I?' he asked politely, as if Rouche had any choice.

He unbuttoned Rouche's cuffs and rolled the shirtsleeves back to reveal the jagged line of scar tissue torn into his forearms. The doctor delicately ran his fingers along the wrinkled and raised pink skin.

'Not so fresh,' he smiled at Rouche. 'What's your name?'

'Damien,' Rouche croaked.

'You need to learn to follow instructions, Damien,' he said, before addressing the two doormen: 'I think we can safely say that Damien is one of ours.'

Rouche was released from the chokehold and gasped for air, staggering two strides forward so that Edmunds would be able to see him in the open doorway.

'Excellent work,' the man told the two brothers. 'But I think you owe Damien here an apology, don't you?'

'Sorry,' said the taller man, staring at his toes like a chastised child.

The man who had restrained Rouche, however, turned to face the wall. He began punching it as hard as he possibly could.

'Whoa! Whoa!' said the doctor, taking hold of his damaged hands. 'Nobody's angry with you, Malcolm. I was only asking you to apologise to Damien. It's polite.'

The man couldn't meet his eye: 'Sorry.'

Rouche waved off the apology graciously, despite still being bent over struggling for breath, and seized the opportunity to remove the earpiece from his pocket.

'You take a moment,' said the doctor, resting a hand on Rouche's back. 'When you're ready, find yourself a seat.'

Still bent double, Rouche glimpsed Edmunds in the lobby, phone to his ear, as the heavy doors between them were pulled together and locked, sealing him inside.

The doctor walked away.

Forcing himself upright, Rouche re-dressed himself, quickly poking the two-way earpiece into place while taking his first proper look around the hall. In comparison to the depressing venue across the street, the room felt modern and light. He quickly counted the number of chairs in the back row and the number of rows standing between him and the stage to estimate the size of the audience. The stage itself stood perhaps five feet above the floor, with a large projector screen hanging down as a backdrop. The doctor who had permitted him entrance climbed the steps in the centre to join two other people whom Rouche did not recognise.

'I'm in,' he mumbled. 'Between thirty-five and fifty suspects.'

He spotted a vacant seat towards the end of a row and side-stepped his way through, facing the rear of the room. Just as he reached the chair, everybody around him got to their feet and he found himself staring into a sea of faces.

His first instinct was to run, even though he knew he had nowhere to go, but then they broke into rapturous applause.

Alexei Green had taken to the stage.

Rouche turned round to see the long-haired man waving to his adoring audience. To make his entrance a little more memorable, he had dressed in a sharp suit with a metallic-blue sheen and, perhaps more importantly, had projected behind him an enormous photograph of the Banker's suspended body set against the New York skyline.

Rouche joined the applause, conscious that he was somewhere within that photograph, one of the indistinguishable crowd of emergency-service personnel staring up at the corpse from the safety of the bridge.

'Obs on Green,' he almost had to shout over the cheers and intensifying applause as the image changed: a crumpled black truck replaced the Banker, its back end protruding from the entrance of the 33rd Precinct like the handle of a knife.

Rouche recalled seeing what was left of Officer Kennedy's body in the morgue, a good man by all accounts. He remembered the dirty rope still wrapped round his right wrist from where he had been bound to the bonnet before being driven through the wall of a building populated with his friends and colleagues.

Rouche clapped harder.

'All teams: move into position,' Chase ordered into his radio.

'Thirty-five to fifty people in the audience,' Baxter told him.

'Between three-five and five-zero perps,' Chase helpfully translated into American.

Baxter moved away from the mobile surveillance unit to resume her other conversation:

'Edmunds, evacuate the lobby. They're coming in.'

Edmunds looked around the crowded space in concern: 'Yeah . . . No problem.'

'Do you need any help?' she asked.

'No, I'll be all right. I've got Fi—'

Finlay shook his head, having joined Edmunds a few moments earlier.

'I've got things covered,' he corrected himself before hanging up.

'She'd only fret if she knew I was in here,' Finlay explained. 'Let's just get these people out and she need never know.'

Edmunds nodded. They split up and began shepherding people outside as quietly as they could through one set of doors as the armed officers rushed inside through another.

Rouche risked a glance around the room, expecting Chase and his men to be joining them imminently. There were three exits, one on either side of the stage and the large double doors through which he had entered. He had already warned Baxter that there were two makeshift security personnel on each exit, none of whom appeared to have heard the arrival of the tactical teams, who were undoubtedly mere inches away from them behind the wooden doors.

He returned his attention to Green as the psychiatrist jogged down the steps at the front of the stage to join his followers, his floppy hair held in place by the headset microphone. Rouche had to hand it to him – he was a charismatic and charming public speaker, exactly the sort of magnetic personality suited to inspire the impressionable.

'Our brothers and sisters have made us so, *so* proud,' he told the room passionately, his voice cracking.

He appeared to be set on meeting every eye in the audience as he roamed up and down the aisle. A woman at the end of a row wrapped her arms around him as he passed, falling out of her seat as she wept in delight. Rouche noticed one of the doormen moving in, but Green held up a hand to signal that he was fine. He stroked the woman's hair and then lifted her chin to speak directly to her.

'And we, in turn, are going to make them equally as proud.'

The room applauded the idea enthusiastically as he continued: 'And one very fortunate person, sitting in *this* room *right* now, just a little sooner than the rest of us,' smiled Green, finally able to detach himself from the woman.

Rouche used the comment as an excuse to take another look around the hall as the audience searched the faces of their neighbours for their unidentified champion. By the time Rouche turned back, Green was at the end of his row. Just two people sat between them. He was three metres away at most.

The police would breach at any second.

Rouche wondered whether he could reach him.

Green must have noticed him staring because he was looking right at him. His eyes flicked down to Rouche's soiled shirt, but he did not falter:

'Two days, my friends. Just two more days to wait!' he shouted, firing up his audience as he continued up the aisle, out of reach, to the sound of thunderous applause.

On seeing the looks of adoration on the faces around him, Rouche understood the necessity for this risky final meeting: these people worshipped Green. There was nothing they wouldn't do to earn his approval, even dying for him, and in return all they asked was that he love them back. They had *needed* to see him this one last time.

And now, they were entirely his to command.

'Do not breach. Do not breach,' Rouche mumbled, hoping that Baxter was still listening. Green voluntarily offering up his plans would be a far more reliable way of extracting them than the defiant silence or self-preserving half-truths of an interrogation. 'Repeat: do . . . not . . . breach,' he said again, raising his voice.

The tapping of rain against the skylights transformed into a sudden shower of hailstones to complement the applause.

'Each of you already know what is expected of you,' Green told the room, his tone now serious. 'But know this: when the eyes of the world fix on Piccadilly Circus and witness our glorious victory for themselves, when they carry their dead up out of the ground to be counted, *that* is when they will finally take notice. *That* is when they will finally understand . . . that we are not "damaged". We are not "afflicted". We are not "weak".'

Green shook his head dramatically before raising both of his arms up into the air:

'Together we . . . are . . . strong!'

The room was on its feet once more, the roar from the crowd deafening.

Chase and his handful of FBI agents were in position at the two sets of doors adjacent to the stage and therefore adjacent to Green. He was in the middle of a whispered argument with Baxter.

'For Christ's sake, Chase. Just give him a minute longer,' she said.

'Negative,' replied Chase, able to raise his voice a little as the applause continued inside the room. 'He's eyeballed Green. We're going in.'

'He said not to breach!'

'Goddamn it, Baxter! Keep this channel clear!' he snapped. 'We're going in. All teams. All teams. Breach! Breach! Breach!'

*

The ovation faltered as the three sets of double doors shook fiercely against their metal locks. It was Green who reacted first, backing away towards the stage, where his alarmed colleagues were getting to their feet. The fear on the faces of their leaders spread through the crowd like a contagion. Rouche started shoving his way out into the aisle as, behind him, the main doors yielded.

The crowd surged.

He was suddenly pinned against the wall as the people at the end of the rows were thrown into him, the audience moving as a single entity. Green had reached the stage by the time the exits either side of him finally burst open.

'FBI! Get down! Get down!'

Rouche was fighting desperately to break free of the crush as the crowd moved as one again, swelling towards this fresh opening. The wave of bodies crashed over the FBI agents, the audience not dispersing in all directions as expected but concentrating on a single point.

The crowd swallowed up two of the armed officers as the first shots were fired. But still they pushed on. Rouche could see Green, surrounded by his entourage, making a beeline for the open doors. Shoving someone over, Rouche managed to break free of the herd. He clambered over rows of seats, positive that the overwhelmed officers had not spotted Green heading towards them and were in no position to intervene even if they had.

There was the crack of a gunshot.

The man in front of Rouche dropped to the floor, leaving only open space between him and a panicking officer. The order to use deadly force had evidently been given once the police started losing control. He could see that the officer had not recognised him, that amid the chaos, and in his self-mutilated state, he appeared no more than another of Green's fanatical followers.

The officer took aim, the heavy gun clicking in anticipation.

Rouche froze. He opened his mouth to say something but knew he would never get the words out in time . . .

The assault rifle fired just as a swarm of people engulfed the officer, wasting the gunshot into empty air. The man was shoved onto the floor. Rouche was trying to reach him when a second wave of people, flowing into the path of least resistance, swept him up, trampling the floored man.

He was carried through the doors and into the corridor outside. The majority of the audience stampeded towards the lobby, but then Rouche spotted Green climbing through an emergency exit at the far end of the hallway.

The glass had been smashed. He climbed out through the jagged pane and into the service area at the back of the hotel. Beyond the Armed Response vehicle, Green was running towards the main road.

'Baxter!' Rouche shouted, pushing the earpiece hard against his skull. 'Green's outside. On foot towards Marble Arch.'

He was unable to decipher her distorted response.

He sprinted round the side of the building and onto the street, where people were huddling together beneath storefronts and doorways. The frozen raindrops felt excruciating as they struck his burning chest.

Rouche thought he'd lost him, but then Green tore across the road in front of the three grand archways, his coiffed long hair now dark strips stuck to his face.

'Oxford Street!' Rouche yelled as he rounded the corner, unsure whether Baxter was even still receiving his comms in the deteriorating weather.

Green was putting more and more distance between them as Rouche's body started to fail him, no longer able to ignore the damage to which he had subjected it. The hail felt more like ball bearings striking him, his painful breathing returning.

Green was confident enough to pause and watch as Rouche slowed to walking pace, every last drop of adrenaline spent. He scooped his hair out of his eyes, laughed and started walking away.

Rouche was on the verge of collapsing when Baxter's Audi sped past.

The car mounted the pavement metres ahead of Green and made contact with the wall of a building, cutting him off. Caught off guard, Green deliberated between the busy road on one side and the lingerie shop on the other when Rouche tackled him from behind, the metallic suit tearing as he dragged him to the ground.

Baxter rushed out of the car and contributed a knee to the back of Green's neck, pinning him to the pavement as she secured the handcuffs.

Utterly exhausted, Rouche rolled onto his back, the sleet easing into the first graceful snowflakes as he stared up into the blank sky. He was gasping for breath, holding his chest, and yet, for the first time in as long as he could remember, he actually felt peaceful.

'Rouche?' shouted Baxter. 'Rouche?'

He could hear her speaking to someone.

'Ambulance . . . 521 Oxford Street . . . Yeah, it's an Ann Summers shop . . . Police officer injured. Multiple deep lacerations, severe blood loss . . . Please hurry.' Her voice became louder. 'They're on their way, Rouche! We got him. We got him! It's over.'

He slowly turned his head to watch as she pulled Green up onto his knees, somehow managing a smile . . . but then his eyes grew wide.

'Rouche? Are you all right? What's wrong?' she asked as he started crawling back over to them. 'I don't think you should move. Rouche?'

He cried out in pain as he dragged himself across the freezing concrete. He reached up and ripped the rest of Green's saturated shirt open to reveal the familiar word scarred into his chest:

PUPPET

'Shit,' gasped Baxter as Rouche rolled onto his back again. 'Why would he . . . ? Oh shit!'

Green smiled up at her triumphantly.

'He was never the one holding the strings,' Rouche wheezed, his words turning to mist above him. 'We haven't stopped anything.'

CHAPTER 32

Sunday 20 December 2015

12.39 p.m.

Chase was furious.

His botched operation and subsequent failure to apprehend Green himself had, at least temporarily, countermanded the FBI's claim to the prisoner. Baxter was all too aware that this situation would be short-lived with her spineless commander throwing the fight in her corner. As such, she had arranged to interview Green the moment he arrived at Homicide and Serious Crime Command.

The rest of his followers had been distributed across a number of local stations based on a complex algorithm calculating current workload against predicted operational demand, written by a man in IT. A man who, as chance would have it, had been briefly mistaken for the Ragdoll killer and unjustly robbed of his lunch almost eighteen months earlier. The officers on duty were conducting interviews based on a set of questions that had been written and circulated by Chase.

Baxter had expected Green to delay proceedings by demanding a lawyer; however, to her surprise, he had made no such request, an ill-advised decision on which she intended to capitalise. With Rouche in hospital, she had reluctantly asked Saunders to join her. As much as she disliked the loud-mouthed detective constable, he was so vile that he had proven to be the unit's most effective investigative interviewer time and time again.

They made their way to the interview rooms, where the officer on guard opened the door to room 1. (Only new staff to the department ever used the pristine room 2.) Green sat patiently at the table in the centre of the room. He smiled at them pleasantly.

'You can wipe that shit-eating grin off your face for a start,' Saunders barked at him.

Baxter wasn't used to being the good cop.

For the first time ever, Saunders looked quite professional. He was still dressed in uniform from the operation and was holding a file full of paperwork in his hands, which he slammed down threateningly on the table as he took a seat. It was, of course, just a copy of *Men's Health* he'd tucked inside a plastic folder, but she thought it was a nice touch.

'If you think you've beaten us, you are sorely mistaken,' Green told them, tucking his hair behind his ears.

'Is that so?' asked Saunders. 'That's strange, because I thought we'd arrested all your bat-shit-crazy friends, all of whom are spilling their guts to our colleagues at this very mome—'

'How many?' Green interrupted.

'All of them.'

'How many precisely?'

Saunders faltered over the question.

Green smiled smugly and leaned back in his chair.

'So, including however many escaped your poorly executed raid this morning, plus all of those I instructed not to attend, I'd say that makes you . . . *fucked*.'

To buy himself a moment to think, Saunders picked up the file and flicked it open to appear as though he was checking something. It was, in fact, yet another article on how to achieve a six-pack in just six weeks, which in theory would have put the magazine out of business after a month and a half if any of them actually worked.

Feeling instantly fatter, he closed the file and turned to Baxter with a shrug.

'I suppose he's right,' said Saunders, before slapping himself on the forehead theatrically. 'Do you know what? I've done something really bloody stupid! I've already arranged to meet that woman on Tuesday. What was her name again?'

'Maria,' Baxter reminded him.

Green tensed.

'And you'll never guess where I've asked her to meet me.'

'Don't say Piccadilly Circus Underground Station!' Baxter shook her head in pantomime dismay.

'See,' said Saunders, turning back to Green, 'I figured, as your sister, she might recognise any ex-colleagues, friends, possibly even patients of yours. Legitimate request, I'm sure you'll agree. She'll be there all day.'

Green's change of mood was verification that the Tube station was indeed the intended target.

'She means nothing to me,' shrugged Green quite convincingly.

'Really?' asked Saunders. 'You know, I was the one who interviewed her the day we realised it was you.'

'One of *you* interviewed me,' said Green, speaking over him, meeting Baxter's eye. 'At the prison. That's right. An agent . . . Curtis, wasn't it? How's she doing these days?'

Baxter's back straightened. She clenched her fists.

Saunders swiftly continued: '*I* was the one who had to tell her what an evil piece of shit her brother really was. She didn't believe it at first. She defended you passionately. It was . . . *pathetic* watching her belief in you crumble like that.'

The comment landed.

Green glanced at him before returning his gaze to Baxter: 'You must have left her,' he said, watching her closely. 'If you're sitting here, to save yourself, you must have abandoned her in there.'

Baxter's eyes narrowed. Her breathing quickened.

Saunders was also watching her. Should she lash out at Green, the interview would be over, and he'd be protected by the Met's self-imposed red tape and army of crusading bureaucrats.

It had become a race to see who broke first.

'I know you're not like the rest of them,' said Saunders. 'You don't believe in any of this. You're doing this for a payday, aren't you?'

Their handsome suspect gave them nothing:

'From what little I know of knife wounds,' Green spoke over him, 'they very seldom kill instantly.'

Baxter's hands were trembling with anger, her jaw set.

'So what was it?' Saunders shouted. 'Money or their silence? Hang on. You're not some sort of paedo or something, are you?'

'I don't think she could have been dead when you left her. She wasn't, was she?' smirked Green, taunting Baxter.

She got to her feet.

Realising that his current angle wasn't working, Saunders changed tack:

'Who's Abby?' he asked. 'Sorry. I should have said, who *was* Abby?'

For no more than a split second, Green's eyes filled with emotion. He turned to address Baxter once more, but it was too late – Saunders had found his 'in' and was going for the jugular:

'Yeah, your sister mentioned her. She died, right? What would she think about all this? I wonder. Think Annie would be proud of you? Think Annie would—'

'Abby!' Green yelled at him. 'Her name is Abby!'

Saunders laughed:

'Honestly, mate, I couldn't give a toss. Oh, wait . . . Unless you killed her?' He leaned forward in interest. 'In which case, I'm all ears.'

'How fucking *dare* you,' spat Green, now a red-faced version of his former self, deep frown lines betraying his age. 'Fuck you . . . both of you. I am doing *all* of this *for* her.'

Baxter and Saunders shared the briefest of glances, knowing how significant that aggravated admission could be, but Saunders wasn't done yet:

'That's all well and good – doing this as some form of fucked-up tribute to Amy . . .'

'Abby!' Green screamed again, spraying the table in spittle as he fought against his restraints.

'. . . but do you *really* think anyone's gonna give a second thought to you or your dead bitch of a girlfriend after the bombs start going off?' Saunders laughed bitterly in Green's face. 'You're nothing, no more than a distraction, a warm-up act for the main event.'

Both Baxter and Saunders held their breath, aware that he had just played his hand.

Slowly, Green leaned as close to Saunders as his handcuffs would permit. When he finally spoke, it was in a whisper tainted with rage and hate:

'Come see me on Tuesday, you smug piece of shit, 'cos I promise you – you *are* going to remember her name: A-B-B-Y,' he counted the four letters out on his fingers before sitting back in his chair.

Baxter and Saunders turned to one another. Without a word, they got up and hurried out of the room.

They had what they needed.

'I'd like to see MI5 try to tell us there's no threat of another attack now,' scoffed Baxter as they marched across the office collecting up the team en route to the meeting room. 'And find out where we are on the deceased girlfriend.'

'We've got a serious problem,' announced a detective the moment Baxter stepped through the door.

'Oh, but things were just going so well!' She could never remember the manly young woman's name: Nichols? Nixon? *Knuckles?* She decided to play it safe: 'Go ahead, Detective.'

'We've finished eliminating suspects in custody versus the self-deleting phone messages . . .'

'Suicide texts!' Techie Steve's voice called from under a desk somewhere.

'Thirteen of Green's Puppets remain unaccounted for.'

'*Thirteen?*' Baxter winced.

'And . . .' the woman continued guiltily, 'of the Puppets processed so far, at least five of them have no prior history of mental illness and no record of ever visiting any psychiatrist, let alone one of *our* psychiatrists. It confirms that, as in New York, this thing is much bigger than just Green and his patients. We've only been focusing on a very small piece of the puzzle . . . Just thought you should know.'

Baxter made a sound: the combination of exhaustion, disappointment and concern manifesting itself as a concise, but pathetic, squeak.

The woman smiled apologetically and took a seat.

'Hey,' whispered Saunders. 'What did Knuckles want?'

It bloody *was* Knuckles!

'Just to piss on our fireworks,' sighed Baxter as she walked to the front of the room and brought the team up to speed.

Blake raised his hand.

'For Christ's sake, Blake,' she shouted. 'You're a grown-up. Speak!'

'Would Green really have confirmed how many bombs they're planning?'

'Makes sense – same as New York. Plus, Saunders got it out of him.'

'Oh,' nodded Blake, requiring no further explanation.

Chase looked blankly between them.

'He was provoked,' Blake explained.

'How's facial recognition going?' Baxter asked the room.

'The City Oasis have sent their footage across,' said one of the FBI tech team. 'We're comparing video between both hotels to ensure we haven't missed anyone.'

'And the three people on stage with Green?' she asked.

'One was shot and killed while trying to escape.'

Baxter huffed.

'She pulled a knife on me!' one of Chase's agents said defensively.

'Doctor Amber Ives,' the man continued. 'Another psychiatrist and bereavement counsellor. Numerous occasions for her to run into Green – seminars, mutual colleagues.' He checked his notes. 'A second, who was with Ives, did manage to escape.'

Everyone looked accusingly at the FBI agent:

'There were a *lot* of people!'

'And the third?' asked Baxter, losing patience.

'Is being transferred here right now. Says he wants to make a deal.'

'Well, that's progress,' said Baxter. 'But continue working on the assumption he's gonna give us shit all in the meantime.' She turned to Saunders. 'Really great work in there,' she complimented him, before addressing Chase: 'We're done with Green. You can fight with MI5 over him now.'

Baxter hesitated on the threshold of Rouche's private room in St Mary's Hospital as the snow fell heavily outside the window. For a split second, she was back inside the dark church watching the thin line appear across Curtis's throat, her memories lured back there by Green's taunts . . .

Rouche looked dead as he slept, his head hanging forward over his chest, where the weeping wounds bled through the bandages. His arms were positioned unnaturally, each linked to a drip bag on a pole, the trailing tubes snaking up and off the bed like wires holding him in place.

His eyes flickered open and he smiled wearily at her.

She shook the image and walked towards the bed, tossing him the family bag of Crunchie Rocks she'd picked up from the newsagent's in the foyer, a touching gesture, only ruined by the restricted movement in Rouche's medicine-fed arms and his resultant shriek as the projectile landed dead centre of his bloody bandages.

'Bollocks!' she gasped, rushing over to place them on the wheelie bedside-cupboard thing instead.

She picked up the remote control to turn down the Christmas movie, which she secretly recognised as *Harry Potter and the Half-Blood Prince*, the similarities between their situations dawning on her as Albus Dumbledore imparted a grave warning to his students that their enemy's greatest weapon was them themselves.

She hit the 'mute' button and sat beside Rouche.

'So when are they letting you out?' she asked.

'Tomorrow morning,' he told her. 'They've got to pump me full of antibiotics until then so that I – and I quote – "don't die". At least I can breathe again now.'

Baxter looked at him quizzically.

'I had a rib poking into my lung,' he explained. 'Since the prison.'

'Ah.' Baxter stared guiltily at the bandages wrapped round him.

'I'm gonna get some funny looks down the pool now,' joked Rouche.

'Maybe they can do something,' said Baxter. 'Skin grafts or something?'

'Yeah,' he said. 'Yeah, I'm pretty sure they can.'

He wasn't very convincing.

'There are those people who transform tattoos into other things,' she suggested hopefully. 'Get rid of exes' names and stuff.'

'Yeah,' nodded Rouche. 'They could make it say . . . Buppet?' He pulled a face.

'Puppies!' Baxter suggested, straight-faced, before they both burst out laughing at the absurd suggestion.

Rouche held his painful chest: 'So what did you get out of Green?'

Baxter filled him in on their interview with the pseudo-leader and what they had gleaned from the captured doctor, Yannis Hoffman, who had provided them with complete details of his patients, three of whom were among the thirteen Puppets still at large. A medical doctor specialising in cancer and palliative care, he had been recruited by Alexei Green directly, who he had believed to be the sole architect of the murders. Vitally, however, and earning himself the reduced prison sentence he'd been seeking, the doctor had confirmed an exact time for the attack: 5 p.m. Rush hour.

'And get this,' she added. 'Green's girlfriend was killed in the Norway terror attacks.'

If that revelation upset Rouche, he didn't show it: 'Motive?'

'Vulnerability,' Baxter corrected him.

'None of this was ever about the Ragdoll case?'

'Only to ensure that the entire world was watching,' said Baxter. 'Just a very clever distraction, using some very vulnerable people, to set off some very big bombs. They used the worst parts of us against us, made possible by our own craving for bloodlust. And people haven't been this excited since the Ragdoll murders.'

She'd clearly been thinking a lot since her interview with Green.

'It's genius,' she continued. 'I mean, who's watching their back for someone sneaking up on them when they're consumed with fighting one another? They made us kill ourselves.'

CHAPTER 33

Sunday 20 December 2015

6.03 p.m.

The snowflakes glittered as they fell through the headlight beams of Baxter's Audi. The car had picked up a fresh grating noise and been pulling to the right ever since taking a chunk out of the Oxford Street Superdrug earlier that afternoon. The first niggling doubts had set in regarding the likelihood of it passing its upcoming MOT.

Baxter switched off the engine. A sharp hiss of air escaped from under the bonnet, suggesting yet another fault to fix/cover up. Either that or the car was literally sighing in relief at completing this latest journey unscathed.

On spotting the group of sportswear-clad youths loitering at the entrance to the park (the morbidly obese one apparently wearing it ironically), she unplugged her sat nav and tucked it under the seat. Gloves on. Hat on. She grabbed a bag from the passenger seat and crunched along the path to Edmunds's maisonette.

She rang the doorbell. As she waited, she noticed a set of dead Christmas lights trailing down the brickwork that looked to have been severed in half. Down the street, a bottle smashed and laughter rang out over the quiet houses. She heard the sound of Leila crying before the hallway light came on and Tia struggled to unlock the front door one-handed.

'Merry Christmas!' smiled Baxter, making a real effort. She held up the bag of presents that she had collected from her flat on the way over. 'Merry Christmas, Leila,' she cooed, reaching out to stroke the baby, much as she would Echo, while using the same silly voice she adopted to call him for his dinner.

Tia tutted and then disappeared back down the hallway, leaving Baxter stood on the doorstep like an idiot.

'Alex!' she heard Tia call, the sound coming from round the side of the property. Leila was still crying. 'Alex!'

'Yeah?'

'Your girlfriend's at the door. I'll be upstairs,' she told him as Leila's cries faded away.

A few moments later, Edmunds came rushing down the hallway, brushing snowflakes out of his hair.

Baxter was almost positive that the socially acceptable way to handle situations such as this was to pretend that she had heard nothing and then to drop in passive-aggressive comments about Tia whenever the conversation permitted.

'Baxter!' smiled Edmunds. 'Why are you still out there? Come in.'

'What the *hell*'s her problem?' she blurted, unable to help herself.

He waved it off. 'Oh, she thinks you're a bad influence on me . . . and I missed a one-year-old's birthday party or something this morning . . . *and* there was something else too,' he said cryptically as he closed the front door behind her and walked through to the kitchen, where the open back door invited the night inside.

She handed him the bag of gifts, only to receive an even larger one in return.

'Drink?' he offered.

'No . . . I shouldn't stay,' she said, looking pointedly up at the ceiling, deciding to go down the passive-aggressive route anyway. 'I just came round to . . . I just had to . . . I . . .'

Edmunds recognised the telltale awkwardness that preceded Baxter bestowing a compliment or praise.

'. . . I just wanted to say . . . thank you.'

'You're welcome.'

'You were looking out for me . . . like usual . . .'

There was more? Edmunds was astounded.

'. . . and you were brilliant today . . . like usual.'

'*Actually*,' said Edmunds, 'I think it's *me* who needs to thank *you*. Today . . . this last fortnight really has made me realise just how much I miss this. *God*, I miss it: the danger, the excitement, the . . . *importance* of it all. Tia's pissed off with me, well, with us, because I *kinda* handed in my notice this afternoon.'

Baxter's face lit up: 'You're coming back!'

'I can't.'

She deflated.

'I need to have a life. I need to think about my family. But at the same time, I can't waste away behind a desk in Fraud any longer either.'

'So . . . ?'

'I want to show you something.'

Confused, Baxter followed him outside and across the wedge of snow illuminated by the kitchen light to the rickety shed.

'Da-naaaa!' sang Edmunds proudly, gesturing to the in no way 'da-naaaa-worthy' eyesore.

His enthusiasm dissipated with Baxter's underwhelming reaction.

'Bollocks,' he said, realising why the unveiling had not earned the anticipated response. He stooped down to pick up the home-made sign. 'Stupid bloody thing won't stay up,' he explained, hooking it back on to the wood. 'Da-naaaa!'

ALEX EDMUNDS – PRIVATE INVESTIGATOR

He opened the flimsy door, which almost dropped off its hinges, to reveal the office he'd set up within. Lit by the cosy glow of a desk lamp, his laptop sat atop the work surface beside a printer and a cordless phone. An oil heater in the corner warmed the tiny space. There was a coffee machine, a kettle, a hose hooked over a bucket to form a makeshift sink, and even a 'client seating area' (second stool).

'So what do you think?'

Baxter didn't answer right away, taking another long look around the shed.

'It's just temporary, of course,' Edmunds insisted when she failed to respond. 'Just while I get myself set up and . . . Are you crying?'

'No!' replied Baxter, her voice cracking. 'I just think . . . I think it's perfect.'

'Oh my God! You *are* crying!' said Edmunds, embracing her.

'I'm just so happy for you . . . and it's been such a hard couple of weeks,' she laughed, before bursting into tears.

Edmunds continued to hold her as she sobbed against his shoulder.

'Christ!' she said, her mascara smudged across her cheeks, laughing as she composed herself. 'I've snotted on you. I'm so sorry! I'm gross.'

'You're not gross,' Edmunds assured her.

It *was* a bit gross.

'Leila already dribbled food all over this top anyway,' he told her, pointing to it. In actual fact, he suspected that stain had also come from Baxter.

'"Means something more to him,"' she said, wiping her eyes, reading one of the half-formed ideas scrawled onto the sheets of paper that littered the wooden wall behind him.

'Yeah,' said Edmunds, ripping the sheet down to decipher his own handwriting. 'Puppet . . . Bait. Why carve *those* particular words into themselves and their victims?'

'A sign of loyalty?' suggested Baxter, still sniffing. 'A test?'

'I'm sure his disciples see it that way – a brand of unity, of being a part of something, but I can't help feeling that it means something else entirely to our . . . *Azazel*.' He used the name reluctantly. 'Something personal.'

He hesitated before continuing:

'Baxter, I don't think you are going to be able to stop whatever's coming.'

'Cheers for the confidence boost.'

'It's just . . .' He looked concerned. 'Look at the amount of work that must have gone into persuading Glenn Arnolds to stitch another man onto his back, building him gradually to that level of delusion, systematically substituting his meds like that – all tailored solely to that one person. This is beyond obsession . . . This is someone's sole purpose on this earth . . . and that terrifies me.'

Ten minutes and a cup of shed tea later, Baxter was on the doorstep, bag of presents in hand.

'Oh, I almost forgot,' said Edmunds. He rushed back down the hallway to fetch something. He returned with a white envelope, which he tucked into the top of the present bag. 'Last one, I'm afraid. Listen, Baxter—'

'Do myself a favour and don't open it?' she interrupted, knowing Edmunds was once again about to voice his opinion on them spying on Thomas.

He nodded.

'Merry Christmas,' she said, giving him a peck on the cheek before walking back out into the night.

Baxter returned to the house to find it empty. She had completely forgotten that Thomas was out at one of the numerous work dos scheduled over the festive season. She placed the bag of presents beneath the Christmas tree and two things slowly dawned on her: One, Thomas had purchased a tree. Two, thanks to everything going on, she hadn't actually bought him a single present yet.

With Echo asleep in the kitchen, Rouche spending the night in hospital, and Thomas no doubt getting pawed at by Linda 'the Cougar', she wished she had dropped in on Finlay after all. She hadn't wanted to intrude on his and Maggie's evening with the grandchildren so had thanked him for his help over the phone and arranged to pop round to see him after Christmas.

Suddenly feeling very alone, and resolute not to start thinking about the other people, the ones she had lost from her life over the past year and a half, she kicked off her boots and went upstairs to run herself a bath.

Baxter picked Rouche up from the entrance to St Mary's Hospital at 8.34 a.m. Still buzzing from the pain meds, he was irksomely cheerful company for a Monday-morning rush hour. As they escaped the queue for one junction just to join another for the next, she didn't have high hopes of them making their 9.30 a.m. meeting with MI5 T-Branch, who were, all of a sudden, taking the threat against national security very seriously indeed.

Rouche turned up the radio.

'. . . morning, the UK's terror threat level has been elevated to "Critical", meaning that the security agencies believe an attack on the country to be imminent.'

'About *bloody* time,' said Baxter. She looked over at Rouche and caught him smiling to himself. 'How has *any* of this given you reason to smile?' she asked him.

'Because there isn't going to be an attack. We're going to stop them.'

Baxter jumped a set of traffic lights:

'I like your optimism – PMA and all that – but—'

'It's not about optimism. It's about purpose,' he replied as the news bulletin moved on to the story that both Betfred and Ladbrokes had ceased taking bets on a white Christmas. 'I've spent years drifting aimlessly, wondering why I survived that day and my family didn't . . . Now I know . . .

'Just think about the innumerable decisions and chance events required to lead me out of that Underground station a victim of a terror attack a decade ago, only to find myself in the position to prevent one tomorrow. It's like history repeating itself, giving me a do-over. It's like I *finally* understand why I'm still here and, at last, I have a purpose.'

'Look, I'm glad you're feeling more upbeat and everything, but our priority is that Underground station and whatever these shits have planned for it. *We* need to handle it. We can't let them manipulate us like in New York. We can't pull resources from elsewhere in the city, no matter what happens down there, no matter what happens to us. The *diversion* is our responsibility. The bombs are the security services'. We're not going to be involved with that side of things . . . Sorry,' she added, feeling guilty for raining on his parade.

'Don't be,' smiled Rouche. 'You're right, but I just *know* that by playing our part tomorrow, we'll stop this from happening.'

Baxter forced a smile to humour him.

'We're getting ahead of ourselves,' she pointed out. 'We might still have one more murder to deal with before then. And if our stitched-together Gemini man is anything to go by, it's going to be absolutely horrific.'

'Unless we've already arrested that particular Puppet.'

'Because we're just *that* lucky,' scoffed Baxter bitterly.

The traffic started moving more freely. Rouche kept quiet while Baxter changed lane and overtook a procession of buses. The sporadic sweeps of the windscreen wipers had already compacted the beginnings of a snowman around the edges of the glass.

'We could . . .' Rouche hesitated, trying to form a more compelling argument. 'We could wait until five to five and then evacuate the station.'

'I wish we could,' said Baxter. 'But we can't.'

'But if we—'

'We can't. If we do that, we're risking them dispersing across the city again and then they could attack anywhere. At least this way, we know where they'll be and we'll be prepared.'

'We're using innocent people as *bait* . . . Why does that sound so familiar?' he asked. He didn't sound accusatory, only regretful.

'Yes, we are, but I don't see another option.'

'I wonder if someone said something similar about me and my family back in 2005.'

'Maybe they did,' Baxter said sadly.

She felt a little disgusted with herself for her callous assessment of the situation. She suspected that Rouche was going to struggle with their day of strategic meetings, regarding people's lives as no more than figures on a graph. Sacrifice one digit here, save two there.

She suspected that she was going to struggle with it too.

By 6.04 p.m. Baxter was exhausted. As expected, the day had consisted of back-to-back meetings. Security had been doubled on the London Underground and at all major attractions. The five largest A&E departments in the city were on standby to implement their Major Incident Protocols, while the London Ambulance Service had arranged additional cover through private providers.

The Puppet interviews had continued throughout the day without any major revelations. It had been futile to threaten or bargain with Green's fanatical followers when they had no interest whatsoever in self-preservation. Green himself had been in the hands of MI5 overnight, being subjected to whatever enhanced interrogation techniques they could throw at him; however, the lack of communication suggested that they were yet to break the psychiatrist.

The department had spent the entire day on tenterhooks but reports of a final grotesque murder somewhere within the city never came. As such, the uninterrupted hours had left Baxter feeling as well prepared as possible for the Puppets' final act.

It was a strange feeling, knowing what might happen, a betrayal to every soul she'd passed on the street not to warn them. She wanted to call everyone in her phonebook, shout from the rooftops that people should stay out of the city, but to do so would only be to delay the inevitable and to sacrifice their one advantage.

She spotted Rouche waiting to say good night as she filed some paperwork. By then she felt as though there was nothing more they could do to prepare. She packed up her bag and walked over to him.

'Come on,' she yawned. 'I'll give you a lift back. I need to pick up a couple of bits anyway.'

*

Baxter and Rouche had made it as far as Vincent Square before both their phones went off in unison. They shared an exhausted look, anticipating what was coming. Rouche put the call on speakerphone.

'Agent Rouche,' he answered. 'I'm with DCI Baxter.'

Baxter's phone immediately stopped buzzing in her bag.

'Apologies, Agent Rouche. I'm aware you've both left for the day,' started the woman on the phone.

'It's fine. Go ahead.'

'One of Doctor Hoffman's patients, an Isaac Johns, just used his credit card to pay for a taxi.'

'OK,' he said, presuming there was more to the story.

'I called the taxi firm and got put through to the driver. He said the man was very intense, told him that he was dead anyway, that he'd go out while he still had his dignity, in a way that people would remember. According to Hoffman's statement, Johns was recently diagnosed with an inoperable brain tumour. The driver had already called it in. A unit from Southwark has been dispatched.'

'Location?' asked Baxter as she switched on her sirens and manoeuvred out of the traffic.

'The Sky Garden,' replied the woman.

'In the Walkie-Talkie?' asked Baxter, using the building's nickname.

'That's the one. Apparently he was heading for the bar, which is on the thirty-fifth floor.'

The wheels spun against the slushy road as Baxter sped down Rochester Row, heading north.

'Stand them down,' she shouted over the noise, 'and back us up with an armed unit. We're seven minutes out.'

'All understood.'

'Have you got a description?' asked Rouche.

'Caucasian, "built like a brick shithouse", short hair, dark suit.'

Rouche hung up as the colours of the city flashed by. He took out his firearm and checked it:

'Here we go again.'

Baxter stifled a yawn: 'No rest for the wicked.'

CHAPTER 34

Monday 21 December 2015

6.29 p.m.

'Come on. Come on,' Baxter uttered under her breath as the LED numbers ascended towards their destination.

Rouche had already unholstered his service weapon, but doubted that this latest Puppet could have smuggled anything illicit through the airport-style security check on the ground floor.

31 . . . 32 . . . 33 . . . 34 . . .

The lift slowed to a gentle stop.

'Ready?' asked Rouche.

The doors parted; music and the soft hum of sophisticated conversation greeted them. They shared a pleasantly surprised shrug before Rouche quickly concealed his gun and they stepped into the cavernous space to join the smartly dressed queue waiting to be seated.

As moodily lit as the city sparkling in the background, the immense cage of steelwork was glowing pink, an enormous arch of glass and metal reaching fifteen metres overhead, greedily laying claim to a little more of the sky.

While they were waiting, they scanned the busy hall for anyone matching the description they'd been given, only to find that at least a third of the clientele were wearing dark suits and that a person's brick shithouse-ness was a difficult thing to judge while seated.

A smartly attired man gestured for them to step forward. A not-so-subtle look down over Baxter's practical winter outfit and then back up via Rouche's crumpled suit ended in a condescending smile.

'Good evening. You have a reservation?' he asked sceptically.

Rouche flashed the man his identification.

Baxter leaned in close to speak quietly:

'Detective Chief Inspector Baxter. Don't react!' she told him when he suddenly recognised her and looked around for a supervisor. 'I need you to check your list. Do you have a reservation for an Isaac Johns?'

A brief pause; then the man ran his finger down his clipboard of names: 'Johns . . . Johns . . . Johns . . .'

'Really think he'd use his real name?' Rouche asked her.

'He used his own credit card,' replied Baxter. 'He's got nothing to lose now. I don't think he cares.'

'Johns! Found him!' the man exclaimed. Several people looked in their direction.

'Again,' said Baxter patiently, 'don't react.'

'Sorry.'

'Which table? Don't turn round! Don't point!'

'Sorry. Beside the window. Right-hand side. Closest to the doors, as he requested.'

Baxter held the man's gaze as Rouche glanced across the room:

'Table's empty.'

'Did you see what he looked like?' she asked the man.

'He was . . . tall . . . and big, as in muscular. He was wearing a black suit and tie . . . like he was going to a funeral.'

Baxter and Rouche shared a look.

'OK,' she told him. 'I want you to carry on as normal. If you see him, I want you to walk over to us very, very slowly and whisper it in my ear. All right?'

He nodded.

'Start on the terrace?' she suggested to Rouche.

Unexpectedly, she linked arms with him. They walked through the bar under their camouflage of happy couple and out onto the terrace, the tip of the Shard sparkling white in the distance like a snow-capped mountain. As they strolled over to the metal railing, snowflakes blew around them from all directions before scattering over the twinkling metropolis below.

The only people braving the cold were a shivering couple toasting champagne glasses and some accommodating parents being led outside by their excited little girls. From the relative privacy of the dark terrace, the indoor space was lit in neon pink, allowing them to search the room of faces without attracting attention.

'Perhaps he went home,' said Rouche optimistically, but then he spotted their well-dressed assistant pacing around the room searching for them. 'Or perhaps not.'

They hurried inside and then followed the man's directions back past the lifts to the toilets. There, they were confronted with a row of identical cubicles, the shiny black doors promising a more pleasant setting than the last set they had occupied together.

Rouche took out his weapon: 'I'll go in. You keep watch.'

Baxter looked like she might hit him.

'We don't know for sure he's in there,' explained Rouche, glad he was armed. 'Plus, there might be more than one of them. I need you watching my back.'

'Fine,' Baxter huffed, slumping against the wall to stay out of the path of the harassed waiters struggling to cope with the demands of simultaneous Christmas parties.

Rouche made his way down the narrow corridor of partitioned bathrooms to find the first two standing empty.

'Someone's in here!' a woman's voice called from the third when he tried the door.

'Sorry!' he shouted over the sound of a hand-dryer as the next door along unlocked.

Fingers wrapped round the handle of the weapon inside his jacket, he relaxed when an elderly gentleman wobbled out, giving him a rosy-cheeked smile.

Rouche passed one more vacant cubicle before reaching the final black door, propped closed despite clearly being unlocked.

With his gun raised, he kicked the flimsy piece of wood open. The door swung back loudly into the side of the empty room.

Against the back wall stood the lid from the cistern; beside it, a rubber bag had been discarded, dripping water onto the floor. On the back of the door hung a large black suit jacket and tie. Rouche turned to leave, kicking something metallic across the floor. He walked over and picked up a brass 9-millimetre bullet.

'Shit,' he said to himself, rushing back out into the main room.

'He's not in th—' Rouche started, colliding with an overladen waiter, who dropped his tray of precariously balanced glasses across the floor. 'Sorry,' Rouche apologised, looking around for Baxter.

'Entirely my fault,' the young man responded politely, even though it entirely wasn't.

'Did you see a woman waiting out here?'

Then came the sound of chair legs scraping across the floor as people abandoned their tables.

Rouche hurried towards the uproar and shoved his way through the crowd moving away from the glass windows.

He paused.

He could see Baxter out in the dark. She was standing by the railing as her hair blew wildly in the wind. A few metres from her, huddled in the corner beside the glass, the young family were cowering, the father crouching defensively in front of his two daughters.

Weapon first, Rouche slowly stepped outside.

Free from the glare of the lights reflecting in the glass, he finally understood the situation; there was one other person out on the terrace with them, behind Baxter.

A muscular arm was holding her still, a small pistol pushed up under her chin.

In the other hand, a second weapon was pointed at the family in the corner.

'Rouche, I presume,' said an unfittingly high-pitched voice from behind Baxter, only a sliver of a face visible behind his human shield.

He pronounced it correctly, meaning that Baxter had either given up his name or, more likely, she had called out to him.

'Mind putting that down?' asked the man pleasantly, pulling the hammer back on the gun beneath Baxter's chin.

She gave a subtle shake of her head, but Rouche hesitantly lowered the weapon.

'Isaac Johns, *I* presume,' said Rouche, hoping that his calm tone was catching. 'You all right, Baxter?'

'She's fine,' Johns answered on her behalf.

'I leave you alone for one minute . . .' laughed Rouche, casually taking a step towards them.

'Hey! Hey! Hey!' yelled Johns, dragging Baxter backwards, losing Rouche the ground he'd just made up.

He was as imposing as his description had promised. Although Baxter's slender frame was insubstantial cover for the man's bulk, his vital organs, and therefore any hope of an instant kill, were safely out of sight.

'So what's the plan, Isaac?' asked Rouche, keen to get Johns talking. He had already registered the difference between this man and the other killers: he appeared calm and in control. He was *enjoying* his moment in the limelight.

'Well, it *was* to get our audience to decide which of them' – he gestured towards the huddled family – 'lives or dies. But then I spotted Detective Baxter here and simply couldn't help myself. So that responsibility has, regrettably, fallen to you.'

The man was momentarily distracted by his indoor audience. Rouche slowly raised his gun a couple of inches, just in case an opportunity presented itself.

'No!' yelled Johns, careful to keep Baxter between them. 'Tell those people if *anyone* leaves, I'll start shooting. *These* people have the right idea: get your phones out. It's OK. I *want* you to film this. I *want* the world to hear Rouche make his decision.'

Satisfied that enough cameras were about to capture his moment of triumph, Johns turned his attention back to Rouche.

'So which is it, Rouche? Who would you like me to kill, your colleague or a completely innocent family?'

Rouche looked anxiously at Baxter.

She gave him nothing.

With the barrel of the gun pressing into her chin, she couldn't move at all, let alone create an opportunity for him to take a clean shot. He then looked over at the family, recognising all too well the look of utter desperation on the father's face.

There were shouts from inside as the first armed team arrived.

'Stop!' Rouche called back to them. 'Don't come any closer!'

When one of the officers failed to obey the order, Johns fired a warning shot, which ricocheted off the wall close to the younger girl's head before cracking the glass barrier that separated them from the sky. The officers inside raised their hands and remained with the watching crowd.

In the quiet that followed, Rouche could hear the little girl's teeth chattering. She was only five or six, freezing to death while Johns protracted the ordeal under a pretence of hope.

There was no choice to be made. This was no game. He intended to kill them all, and Baxter knew it too.

After all the theatre, all the media-seducing horrors increasing in spectacle and ambition, there was still one simple, despicable act left in their arsenal, something worse than all the mutilated bodies put together – the public execution of an innocent child. They had already proven capable of it, having murdered the entire Bantham family behind closed doors. Rouche was confident that Johns wouldn't hesitate to pull the trigger.

The falling snow was hindering his vision. He was careful to keep his trigger finger moving before it could stiffen and slow in the cold.

'It's decision time!' Johns shouted to his audience. 'Speak up so that the world can hear you,' he instructed Rouche. 'Who do you want to die? Answer or I'll kill them all.'

Rouche remained silent.

Johns groaned in frustration: 'OK . . . Have it your way. Five seconds!'

Rouche met Baxter's eye. She had no way out.

'Four!'

He glanced at the family. The father was holding his hands over his younger daughter's eyes.

'Three!'

Rouche sensed the room of camera phones at his back.

He needed more time.

'Two!'

'Rouche . . .' said Baxter.

He looked at her desperately.

'One!'

'. . . I trust you,' she told him, closing her eyes.

She heard Rouche move, the crack of a gunshot, the air whistling past her ear, shattering glass and the muffled impact all at once. She felt the pressure release beneath her chin, the restricting arm fall away . . . the presence behind her vanish.

When she opened her eyes again, Rouche looked shaken, still standing with the weapon pointed directly at her. She watched a bloodstained snowflake dance in the air between them before it plunged over the edge of the building to join the rest of the crime scene five hundred feet below.

Her temple began to throb from where the bullet had grazed her as their backup ran out to join them. The traumatised parents were sobbing inconsolably in relief and shock, in desperate need of some words of reassurance, just somebody to tell them out loud that they were safe.

Rouche slowly lowered his weapon.

Without uttering a word to any of them, Baxter headed back inside, swiping a bottle of wine from one of the vacated tables as she passed, before sitting at the deserted bar to pour herself a generous glass.

CHAPTER 35

Monday 21 December 2015
11.20 p.m.

Rouche parked the Audi outside number 56, a powder-blue town-house set on an affluent side street, the designer wreaths adorning the doors more fashion statement than decoration. Outdoor Christmas lights pulsed in white and gold, content in the knowledge that there wasn't a single plastic Santa Claus in sight. Old-fashioned lamp-posts lined the street, stark black towers against the snow, like urban lighthouses warning of the hidden dangers concealed just below the surface. Their warm orange glow was charming but served as a reminder as to why the rest of the city had upgraded to uglier varieties that actually gave off some light.

Rouche trod in a puddle of slush as he stepped out of the car and slipped round to the passenger door. He pulled it open and Baxter dropped out. Half catching her, he dragged her across the pavement to the bottom of the steps that led up to the front door. Rouche could feel the wounds beneath his bandages stinging as he picked her up, ringing the doorbell with a carefully aimed swing of Baxter's feet.

An energy-sapping forty seconds later, he heard someone rushing down the stairs. The locks clicked and then a man, who had apparently been playing badminton in his pyjamas, peered round the door before throwing it wide open:

'Oh my *Christ*, she's dead!' gasped Thomas as he looked down at Baxter's limp body in his arms.

'Huh? No! God, no! She's just drunk,' explained Rouche, turning Baxter's top end towards Thomas as proof. Her head lolled forward, and her mouth hung open. Reasonably confident that she was still with them, he gave her a shake. She groaned. '*Very* drunk,' he added.

'Oh . . . right,' said Thomas, relieved and surprised in equal measure. 'God, I'm sorry. Do come in. I'm being extremely rude. Ummm . . . Shall we get her up to the bedroom, then?'

'Bathroom,' suggested Rouche, struggling to support her, suspecting that Thomas's use of the word 'we' meant that he wouldn't be taking her off his hands after all.

'Bathroom. Of course,' nodded Thomas, closing the front door behind them. 'It's upstairs.'

'Fantastic,' puffed Rouche, staggering across the hallway.

He was a little surprised by Thomas. He was certainly handsome in a wholesome catalogue-cardigan-model sort of way, but he'd been expecting someone . . . Now that he thought about it, Rouche had absolutely no idea what he'd been expecting.

He followed Thomas through the bedroom and into the en-suite bathroom, where he was finally able to deposit Baxter next to the toilet. Almost instantly, she reanimated and pulled herself up to the bowl. Rouche held her hair back for her as she was sick. Thomas, meanwhile, crouched on the other side of her with a glass of water.

'Thomas, by the way,' he introduced himself, habit making him offer out a hand that Rouche was clearly unable to take. 'Right. Sorry,' he said, taking his unshaken appendage back.

'Rouche.'

'Ah, you're Rouche,' he smiled, looking down in concern as Baxter slumped back onto the floor between them. 'I've never seen her like this before,' he admitted, flushing the toilet.

Rouche managed to hide his surprise both that Baxter had chosen to share her ongoing struggle with him but not with her boyfriend of eight months and that Thomas could possibly be that utterly unobservant.

It was Thomas's turn to grab a handful of Baxter's hair as she climbed back up the toilet.

'What happened?' he asked.

Rouche didn't feel it was his place to say. What Baxter chose to tell him was her business. He shrugged apologetically: 'Open case and all that.'

Thomas nodded, suggesting that Baxter had already used that line on him before. He changed the subject:

'You and Emily must be very close.'

'Who?'

Baxter raised a floppy hand.

'Oh, Baxter! I suppose we . . . Yeah,' said Rouche, realising just how much they had been through together during their short time on the case, a lifetime's worth of horrors. 'Yes,' he said decisively. 'She's very, very special.'

Baxter vomited loudly.

Rouche was back on hair-holding duty.

Once she was done, he got to his feet.

'It looks like you've got everything under control here,' Rouche told Thomas. 'I can show myself out.' Then he remembered something. 'I've got a . . . silly present for her out in the car.'

'You're more than welcome to put it under the tree with the others,' said Thomas. 'And, please, take the car tonight. I can drop her at work in the morning.'

Rouche nodded appreciatively and went to leave.

'Rouche.'

He turned back.

'She doesn't really tell me everything that's going on,' started Thomas, submitting his entry for Understatement of the Year. 'Just . . . you know, if you could . . . just . . . look after her.'

Rouche hesitated. He wouldn't make Thomas a promise he couldn't keep.

'One more day,' he said evasively before leaving the room.

*

Baxter woke up in Thomas's arms. The cold bathroom tiles pressed into her bare legs and she was instantly conscious of her scar even without looking at it. Her trousers were crumpled up in the corner, but she was still wearing her sweat-dampened shirt. They were both wrapped in a bath towel, and Thomas was wedged uncomfortably between the toilet and the wall.

'Shit,' she whispered, angry with herself.

She wriggled out of his hold and slowly stood up, swaying as she adjusted to the new altitude. Carefully, she headed downstairs.

The Christmas-tree lights were blinking, a lone source of light and warmth in the dark house. She crossed the room and slumped down in front of it, crossing her legs as she watched the colourful bulbs take turns to shine. After a few hypnotic minutes, she noticed the pretty angel peering down at her from the top of the tree. Lennox's 'reassuring' words about their fallen colleague returned to her like an unwelcome voice inside her head: 'I guess God just needed another angel.'

Baxter got to her feet, reached up and tossed the fragile ornament onto the sofa. Feeling better, she began sorting through the pile of presents to which she had not contributed.

She had adored Christmas when she was younger. But in recent years the degree of celebration had only extended as far as the usual five festive movies in December and perhaps crashing somebody else's Christmas dinner, on their insistence, should she get out of work in time.

She reached for the remote control and switched on the television, turning the volume down until it was barely more than a buzzing in the speakers. She was irrationally excited to find a Christmas-themed rerun of *Frasier*, and then, unable to keep the smile off her face, she started separating the presents into three piles. Most were for her, of course. Echo hadn't had a bad haul, but Thomas's was pathetic.

She picked up an unfamiliar and oddly shaped gift to read the tag:

Merry Xmas, Baxter. His name's Frankie.
Rouche x

Intrigued, fuelled by the excitement of her private mini-Christmas, and in need of an approximate price so as not to look tight/overly keen when reciprocating the gesture, she tore the wrapping paper open and looked down at the orange-hatted penguin in her hands, the same stuffed toy that she had admired back at Rouche's house . . . that had belonged to his daughter.

She stared at the gormless-looking bird. Her disbelief that Rouche would want her to have something of such importance was outweighed by a feeling of unease, a suspicion that he no longer felt he needed it, that whatever final test they were about to be confronted with, he did not expect to be coming back.

She placed Frankie on her crossed legs and pulled the large gift bag from Edmunds and Tia closer. She reached inside and found the blank white envelope sitting on top.

She had forgotten all about it.

She took it out and held it in her hands, just above Frankie, reminding her of her unfounded suspicions about Rouche, her initial irritation with Edmunds, her best friend, who pleaded with her every time not to take his illegal reports on Thomas. She pictured Thomas, be-towelled and more than likely stuck in the bathroom upstairs, where he had spent the night taking care of her.

She realised that she was smiling just at the thought of her bumbling boyfriend. She tore the envelope into several pieces, showered the rubbish over the tattered wrapping paper and continued dividing out their presents.

CHAPTER 36

Tuesday 22 December 2015

9.34 a.m.

Baxter followed the signs for the Bakerloo line, descending deeper beneath the city into Piccadilly Circus Underground Station. She had tied her hair up into a ponytail and plastered herself in the few items of colourful make-up that had been gifted to her over the years – most a not-so-subtle hint from her mother to 'stop looking like a vampire'. The disguise was effective enough, however, and she had barely recognised herself in the mirror after she'd finished.

She followed the crowds onto the platform. Halfway along, she spotted her destination and stopped outside a grey door adorned with the London Underground logo and a sign that read:

NO ENTRY – STAFF ONLY

She knocked, hoping she was in the right place and not trying to gain entry to a cleaning cupboard.

'Who is it?' a female voice called from inside.

Several people were within earshot, and she was not about to yell her name in front of them after going to the trouble of painting herself up like a clown.

She knocked again.

The door opened a cautious inch, but then Baxter shoved her way through into the darkened room. The woman quickly locked the door behind her, while the two other technical officers continued setting up the racks of monitors, radio base units, frequency boosters, computers and encrypted relay stations, converting the sparse office into a fully functional tactical command station.

Rouche was already there, sticking an assortment of maps up next to a list of radio call signs.

'Morning,' he greeted her.

He reached into his pocket and handed over her car keys, making no mention of the events precipitating the need to borrow them in the first place or of her alarmingly colourful new face.

'Thanks,' Baxter replied curtly, shoving them into her coat pocket. 'How long till we're all up and running?'

'Ten . . . fifteen minutes?' one of the people crawling around under the tables replied.

'We'll come back then, then,' she told the room ineloquently.

Rouche took the hint and followed her out onto the platform to speak in private.

By the time he'd returned to the flat the previous night, footage of the shooting had already spread to every major news channel in the world, immortalising him in grainy video as he saved Baxter's life. As a result, he had neglected to shave that morning, the dark shadow a notable change to the clean-cut agent's appearance. He had also combed back his quiff, exposing the greyer layers beneath, a look that actually suited him far better.

'You're a bit of a silver fox today, aren't you?' smiled Baxter as they strolled to the far end of the platform, passing a huge poster for Andrea's book.

'Thanks. And you . . . well, you . . .'

He was struggling.

'I look like a bingo nan,' said Baxter, unamused, amusing Rouche. 'The FBI have elected to grace us with their presence,' she said quietly. 'They wish to "assist in any way possible to bring to a close these atrocious acts of barbarism". Translation: they can't piss off back home without Green, but MI5 aren't done waterboarding him yet, so they might as well stick around and shoot somebody.'

'Yeah, I'd worked that much out myself,' said Rouche, a subtle nod towards the enormous ponytailed man standing a little further along the platform. 'Steven Seagal over there's been choosing a chocolate bar for nearly an hour now.'

'For Christ's sake.' huffed Baxter. 'Report from the night shift: two more Puppets were picked up overnight.'

'So . . . ten to go?'

'Ten to go,' she nodded.

'And our Azazel, whoever he may be,' added Rouche.

They stood silently for a moment as a train clattered to a stop.

Baxter used the interruption to compose what she wanted to say, although she didn't feel as though she could admit to opening his gift early and would probably have avoided the inevitably emotional conversation anyway.

'We're both gonna get through this,' she told him, watching the train departing to avoid his eye. 'We're *so* nearly there. I know you believe that today is some sort of test or something, but we can only do what we can do. Don't take any stupid risks or—'

'Do you know what I was thinking about last night?' Rouche interrupted. 'I never answered your question.'

She looked puzzled.

'How someone who's supposed to be intelligent and spends their life looking for evidence could ever believe in something as groundless and illogical as . . . "sky fairies", wasn't it?' he asked with a smile.

'I really don't want to get into this right now,' said Baxter, cringing at the memory of her vicious outburst on the plane.

'This is the *perfect* time to get into it.'

Another train decelerated into the station before a mass game of musical chairs played out over ten seconds of chaos, the losers' forfeit: hold a diseased pole or fall over the moment it sets off again.

'I was like you,' started Rouche. 'You know, before. I thought faith was just something for the weak – a delusion to help get them through their overwhelming lives . . .'

The way that Rouche had described it reminded her of how she had felt about counselling before it had saved her.

'. . . but then, when what happened . . . happened, I just couldn't even process the idea that I'd lost them for ever, that I'd never get to be with them again, to hold them, that my two girls and everything they were was just gone. They were too important, too special to just not exist anymore, you know?'

Baxter was struggling to hold it together, but Rouche seemed perfectly composed, just trying to articulate his thoughts:

'The second I thought about that, everything just sort of made sense: they weren't really gone. I could *feel* it, and now I've been led back down here today and . . . Am I making any sense at all?'

'I prayed this morning!' Baxter blurted, before putting her hand over her mouth as if she'd given up an embarrassing secret.

Rouche looked at her suspiciously.

'What? I don't even know if I did it right, but I thought, What if I'm wrong? What if there *is* someone or something out there and I don't? There's just too much at stake today not to, right?' Baxter's cheeks went bright red, but fortunately, the garish assortment of colours somewhat diminished the effect. 'Oh, shut up,' she snapped when she caught him smiling at her. She quickly moved on to her real point. 'While I'm making a complete fool of myself, I might as well tell you what I prayed for.'

'That we stop these sick bastards from—'

'Well, obviously! But I also prayed for you.'

'Me?'

'Yeah, you. I used my one and only prayer I'm ever going to make on *you*. I prayed that you'd make it through today with me.'

The unexpected revelation looked to have had the desired effect.

Whether Rouche's God wanted him to live or die that afternoon was out of their hands, but Baxter hoped he might now, at least, pause for a moment before actively inviting it.

*

'What time is it?' groaned Baxter, her head in her hands and lit by the bluish light of the monitors in the makeshift command unit.

'Ten past,' replied Rouche, keeping his eyes on the live camera feeds from all over the station.

'Ten past what?'

'Three.'

She sighed heavily:

'Where the hell are these shits?' she asked the room.

The heightened terror threat level had resulted in an interesting day in the capital. A man had been arrested attempting to smuggle a knife into the Tower of London; however, all signs were pointing towards stupidity rather than mass murder as the driving force behind his actions. There had been a bomb scare at an event in Kensington Olympia. That, too, had ended anticlimactically with an irate, but admittedly forgetful, exhibitor learning that his missing laptop had been subjected to a controlled explosion.

Baxter and her team of twelve had detained five people throughout the day due to suspicious behaviour. Although none had been involved with Green and his minions, it had highlighted the alarming number of weird people roaming the city at any given moment.

'Where are the MI5 guys?' Baxter asked. She didn't raise her head off the desk.

'Still in with the FBI on the Piccadilly line platform,' someone answered.

She made a non-specific noise in acknowledgement.

'Weirdo alert!' Rouche called out.

Baxter looked up excitedly. A man in a Santa hat, clearly concealing some sort of live animal inside his jacket, strolled past one of the cameras. She was just glad for something to do.

'Let's check it out.'

Back at New Scotland Yard, Constable Bethan Roth had been assigned the task of reviewing camera footage relating to the case but of too poor quality to be utilised by facial-recognition systems.

Over the week, she had compiled an entire album of fuzzy screen-shots, which, after being processed through image-enhancement programs, had led to the arrest of two more Puppets.

She had spent the day studying footage from the Sky Garden security cameras, watching the narrowly evaded disaster play out from every angle. The current black-and-white video was as mind-numbing to watch as the two hours of people passing in and out of shot as they visited the bathrooms.

She was reviewing a recording from the indoor bar area. Unable to see any of the action out on the terrace, she could only tell when Rouche had taken his shot by the reaction of the crowd. Several people turned away, others continued filming, phones extended, and one elderly lady fainted, taking her zombie-looking husband down with her.

She leaned forward to select the next video file when one of the monochrome figures in the background caught her attention. She rewound the footage and watched again as the crowd reacted accordingly to seeing a man killed in front of them.

Bethan kept her eyes fixed on the dark figure at the back.

Just as the fainting woman dropped out of frame, he turned away and walked calmly towards the exit. Everything about his demeanour, even the way that he walked, suggested a complete emotional detachment to what he had just witnessed.

Bethan zoomed in but couldn't find anything better than a pixelated circle where the man's face should have been.

She had an idea.

She loaded up the footage from outside the toilets again and continued from where she had stopped watching. After a few moments, the unidentified man rounded the corner and passed beneath the camera, making sure to keep his head lowered at all times.

'Bastard,' whispered Bethan, now positive that she was on to something.

She replayed the snippet of video in slow motion, wondering what the shiny circle on the ground could be. She zoomed in further: a tray surrounded by broken glass. She zoomed in further still until the reflective surface dominated the entire screen and started flicking through frame by frame, her eyes wide in anticipation.

A shadow spilled over the upturned tray; a few clicks later, the top of the man's shoe entered the frame. She continued clicking.

'Come on . . . Come on . . .' Bethan smiled. 'Got you!'

Framed in a circle of silver, a workable image of a middle-aged man's face.

'Boss! I need you over here!'

CHAPTER 37

Tuesday 22 December 2015

3.43 p.m.

Blake pulled up outside the property at the same moment as the Armed Response Unit. En route, he had been passed the information the team had cobbled together at short notice on their new prime suspect.

Lucas Theodor Keaton was the multi-millionaire owner of a telecoms company that had been bought out in the 1990s, providing him with a healthy payoff and a place on their board. From that time on, he had concentrated predominantly on his charity work and on helping start-up businesses.

Encouragingly, S-S Mobile, whose servers had contained the hidden messages, was a subsidiary of Keaton's original Smoke Signal Technologies. In addition, the depot that supplied all of the compromised mobile phones had links to this little-known parent company.

Keaton had a wife and two children, all deceased.

He and the two boys had been caught up in the 7/7 bombings. Although Keaton had escaped relatively unscathed, one of his sons had been killed outright. The other had succumbed to his injuries over a year and a half later, following which Keaton's wife had taken her own life by fatal overdose.

'Cheers for that,' Blake had said to his colleague on the other end of the line, now feeling suitably depressed.

'But it gets worse.'

'Worse than him losing his entire family?'

'His brother' – the constable back at New Scotland Yard clicked about on his computer – 'had taken his place attending a charity event back in 2001 over in the States . . .'

'Don't say it!'

'. . . September 11.'

'Jesus Christ!' Blake almost started to pity their prime suspect. 'How unlucky can one man be?'

'The brother had no business whatsoever at the World Trade Center. He was just walking past at the wrong time.'

'Reckon this Keaton bloke's cursed or something?'

'All that money and he's had the most miserable life imaginable. Goes to show, doesn't it?' was the constable's rhetorical farewell before hanging up.

With Saunders engaged with the operation at Piccadilly Circus, Vanita had sent Blake alone to accompany the team to Keaton's enormous Chelsea residence.

As the armed officers hurried up the steps to break through the front door, Blake sheltered out of the wind behind a postbox to light up a cigarette. Despite the prestigious postcode, the leafy street wasn't a particularly pleasant place to be: almost a third of the houses appeared to be undergoing major building works – lorries, vans and even a mini-crane were scattered among the sports cars in the resident parking bays. The noise was obtrusive.

'Mate!' Blake called to one of the passing construction workers, producing his identification. 'What's going on? Street falling in or something?' he asked, wondering whether it might be in some way relevant.

'This?' asked the rotund man, gesturing to the mess. 'Nah. With property prices at such a premium, every square inch you can stake a claim to counts. So some enterprising billionaire, becoming stir-crazy confined to his measly ten bedrooms, realised that directly beneath his basement, everything down to the Earth's core was wasted space that he could be utilising . . . and now they're all at it.'

Blake was a little surprised by the articulate response.

'Course, if I started digging through the floor of my place, I'd just end up in the kebab shop downstairs,' the man added with a sigh.

'Detective!' a member of the Armed Response Unit called from the doorway. 'All clear!'

Blake thanked the well-informed, kebab-scented man and hurried into the house. The entrance hall alone was larger than his entire Twickenham flat. A sweeping wooden staircase ascended from the mosaic floor, the other seven officers already lost within Keaton's sprawling home. Fresh flowers burst from expensive vases, and a large portrait of the family hung on the back wall.

'If you're in a hurry, I'd start on the third floor,' the team leader advised Blake with a knowing nod.

Blake started in the direction of the staircase.

'Sorry. I meant down,' the officer clarified, pointing towards the corner. 'The third floor down.'

Descending the stairs, Blake's phone made a quiet beep as he lost signal. There, just one level beneath the property's wholesome façade, the first signs of a tainted mind began to bleed through.

The room appeared to have been an office at some point in the past, but now the walls were suffocating beneath pictures of the happy family: another professionally commissioned portrait beside casual holiday snaps, hand-drawn sketches neighbouring their photographic counterparts, each and every one of them framed and hung with precision.

'Computer in the corner,' Blake told the officer, expecting it to be in the van by the time he resurfaced. 'Phone there . . . and this picture,' he said, choosing what looked like the most recent, based on the ages of the two boys – gapped-tooth smiles and matching haircuts.

They moved on, the temperature dropping as the stairs creaked underfoot, the stale air thickening in their lungs. To Blake, it felt as though they were sinking deeper into Keaton's subconscious . . .

This was where he slept.

A small camp bed stood unmade against the far wall, surrounded by what could only be described as a shrine. Items of jewellery, clothing, childish drawings and toys sat in ordered piles round the bed. Candles had melted into the wooden floor round the perimeter.

'Christ!' jumped Blake, only just noticing the depiction of the crucified Jesus hanging on the wall behind them: feet and wrists nailed to the wooden cross, hands dangling uselessly, a tangled crown of thorns tearing into his head: a violent inspiration for the atrocities of the previous few weeks.

Blake frowned and reluctantly took a step backwards into the room to read what had been scrawled in finger-paint either side of the Son of God:

WhEre tHe FuCK weRE yOu?

He almost tripped over the cushion on the floor as he took a photograph of the wall to include in his report.

'Moving on?' he suggested eagerly to the officer.

As the temperature dropped another couple of degrees, they negotiated the narrowing staircase to the property's lowest level.

They'd made it two steps into the room before Blake's heart sank.

Books, journals, folders, diagrams littered every conceivable surface – stacked several feet high or else adding to the paper floor underfoot – years of work, the harvest of an obsessive mind.

They had less than an hour.

Two other officers were already sorting through the mess, a recovered laptop bagged up and ready for transport.

'This pile contains just about every newspaper story on the Ragdoll murders,' one of them called across. 'On the desk is everything we've found so far relating to Alexei Green. This Keaton guy's completely obsessed with him from the looks of it – been collecting stuff on him for years.'

Blake moved over to the stack of articles and CDs, handwritten notes labelling Green's various interviews and talks at conferences.

He picked up a journal and flicked it open, the first page simply titled 'Session One', followed by what looked like a word-for-word transcript of Keaton's first meeting with the psychiatrist.

The lead officer was reading over his shoulder:

'Looks as though this Keaton was just another recruit, then.'

'But he can't be,' whispered Blake, looking again at the mind spilled out in ink around them.

There was a crash as one of the officers knocked a precarious stack of books across the floor. Very calmly, he leaned down to take a closer look at what he'd uncovered:

'Boss?'

'What?'

'Do ya wanna get the bomb squad boys down here?'

The team leader looked concerned: 'I don't know. Do I?'

'Doesn't look live . . . homemade, but still . . . yeah, I think so.'

'Shit . . . Everybody out!' he ordered.

'I'm staying,' Blake told him.

'Live or not, first sign of an explosive, I am to get everybody to safety.'

'If Keaton's our man—' Blake started.

'He's not!'

'But *if* he is, we *need* what's down here. Get your men out. Get these computers to the tech guys, and get the bomb squad here . . . *please*.'

The officer looked torn, but then collected up the recovered laptop and followed his men up the stairs, leaving Blake alone to wade through Keaton's thoughts.

He quickly picked the journal back up, opened it to Session One and skim-read the page. Aware of their time constraints, he skipped forward to Keaton's ninth session with the psychiatrist, rapidly losing hope that they had found their Azazel after all.

SESSION NINE

Thursday 1 July 2014
2.22 p.m.

'. . . and the world just carried on as if nothing had happened,' said Lucas, lost in his own thoughts. 'I have *nothing* left. I go home to an empty house, a mausoleum of everything they were, every night. I can't throw any of it away. It's all I have left of them, but I feel like I'm drowning in memories every time I step inside . . . I can still smell my wife's perfume . . . Are you all right?'

Green quickly got up from his seat to pour himself a glass of water.

'Yes. Fine . . . fine,' he said, but then his face scrunched up as he began to cry. 'I am *so* sorry. This is so unprofessional. I just need a moment.'

'Was it something I said?' asked Lucas in concern, watching Green compose himself.

Outside, it started to rain harder. It must have rained all day.

'Maybe this isn't such a good idea,' said Lucas, getting to his feet. 'All I seem to do is upset everyone.'

'It's not you, Lucas,' Green said quickly. 'It's me and my own issues.'

'Why?' Lucas asked innocently. 'Did . . . did you lose somebody too?'

'Let's just focus on you, shall we?'

'You can tell me.'

'No, I can't,' said Green firmly.

Lucas got up and started heading for the door.

'Lucas!'

'Everything you say is bullshit! I pour my heart out to you twice a week, but there's no trust here,' he told the psychiatrist, hurt.

'Lucas, wait! OK. OK. Yes!' said Green. 'You're right. I apolo-gise. We *do* have a trust, and yes, I *did* lose somebody very, very special to me.'

Keaton closed his eyes, exhaled in victorious relief and let his flicker of a smile fade before slowly returning to the sofa. He lingered, pausing to stand over Green as the cool and collected psychiatrist finally broke down.

He leaned down to address the troubled man, passing him a handful of the 'man-sized' tissues he kept on his desk:

'Please . . . tell me about *her*.'

Blake urgently flicked through the pages to find the final entry – Alexei Green and Lucas Keaton's eleventh session together.

SESSION ELEVEN

Thursday 10 July 2014
6.10 p.m.

'Why the *fuck* are we the ones who got punished?' asked Keaton, pacing around the room as Green listened. '*Still* being punished! We are good people – my family, your beautiful Abby were good people!'

He sighed heavily as he stared out of the window, the early evening sunshine warming his face:

'These Ragdoll murders,' Keaton started casually, 'you're following them, I presume?'

'Isn't everybody?' replied Green, utterly drained by the conversation. He hadn't managed a decent night's sleep in over a week.

'Can you name the victims? Actually, let's make it a challenge. Can you name them in order?'

'Why, Lucas?'

'Just . . . humour me.'

Green let out an exasperated groan:

'Fine. Well, there was Mayor Turnble, of course, and then Khalid's brother. Something Rana? . . . Vijay Rana. Jarred Garland, and the other day it was Andrew Ford . . . Again, why?'

'Immortalised – a backpedalling politician, the brother of a child-murdering serial killer, a greedy and opportunistic journalist, and finally, a disgusting, alcoholic specimen of human refuse. Their unworthy names etched into history simply because they died in an "entertaining" fashion.'

'I'm tired, Lucas. What's your point?'

'I have an admission to make,' announced Keaton without turning round. 'I did some research into the Oslo and Utøya attacks.'

'Why would you do that?' asked Green. 'I don't understand why you'd—'

'The news stories mainly,' Keaton continued, speaking over him as he dominated the conversation. '"Seventy-seven dead", "multiple casualties", "several victims". Want to know how many acknowledged Abby by name?'

Green didn't reply.

'None. Not *one* that I found even bothered to report that your fiancée had been taken from you.'

Green started to weep as Keaton walked back over to sit beside him:

'All those people out there got to carry on with their lives, while ours crumbled . . . and they couldn't even be bothered to learn their names!' shouted Keaton passionately, tears pouring down his cheeks. '*None* of them has suffered as we have . . . None of them.'

Keaton paused a moment to read Green's expression.

'I'm not much to look at, Alexei. I know that. I'm successful, but people don't listen when I speak . . . not really. And all the preparation and manipulation in the world isn't going to get them to do what I need them to do. I need them to surrender themselves to me . . . to *our* cause, entirely.'

'Puppets?' asked Green, glancing up, recalling their previous conversation on the futility of holding an inanimate object accountable for its actions.

'Puppets,' nodded Keaton encouragingly. 'I need someone who can inspire them, someone for them to look up to, someone to *lead* them . . . I need you.'

'What are you saying?' asked Green.

Keaton placed a hand on his shoulder:

'I'm saying, what if there was a way to make things right? A way to make these self-obsessed masses understand what happened to us. A way to ensure that every *fucking* person on this planet knows the names of my family, knows the face of your beautiful Abby and exactly what she meant to you.'

There was a long pause as Green absorbed what Keaton was saying to him.

Slowly, he placed his hand on top of his and turned to face him: 'I'd say tell me more.'

CHAPTER 38

Tuesday 22 December 2015

4.14 p.m.

Baxter received an urgent radio call requesting that she return to the command unit/Bob's break room. She was handed the phone on her arrival.

'Baxter,' she answered.

'It's Vanita. Just a courtesy call to bring you up to speed. About an hour ago, the Central Forensic Imaging Team pulled an image from the Sky Garden footage, which they have since matched to surveillance from New York.'

'Why am I only just hearing about this now?' asked Baxter.

'Because nothing beyond the boundaries of that station concerns you right now. Both MI5 and SO15 have all the details. As I said, just a courtesy call. So I sent Blake—'

'What did you send Blake for?' Baxter interrupted as Rouche entered the room. 'Hang on. I'm putting you on speaker.'

'I sent Blake to the address,' Vanita continued, 'and he's confirmed it: Lucas Theodor Keaton, forty-eight. I'm sending details over to you now. Prepare to be underwhelmed . . . Ladies and gentlemen, meet our Azazel.'

They crowded round the computer as one of the technical officers brought up the email. Keaton's forgettable face stared out from the screen, his sensibly styled hair receding from his temples at the rate one would expect of a man of his age.

'That's him?' asked Baxter.

'That's him. His company facilitated the hidden messages *and* supplied the mobile phones. Numerous flights to and from JFK this past year, building in frequency. He last flew back Tuesday night,' Vanita added, significantly.

The other phone went off. Rouche hastily answered it and commenced a whispered conversation.

'On Blake's recommendation, the security services are prioritising targets with religious connotations. Seems this Keaton might have some sort of spiritual agenda, which would certainly explain the New York church,' Vanita told her.

'OK,' Baxter replied distractedly.

'I'll let you get back to work,' said Vanita, hanging up.

Rouche tore a map from the wall and urgently traced his finger across the paper.

'What is it?' asked Baxter.

'Three of our missing Puppets have just flagged up within a quarter-mile of each other.'

'So they've dispatched armed units, right?'

'They have,' answered Rouche, tapping his finger on a location almost dead centre of the three sightings. 'They're heading to Baker Street Station. I'm going.'

'No,' said Baxter. 'They can handle it. I need you here with me.'

'I can get ahead of them.'

'We need to stick together!'

'Baxter,' he sighed, a rumbling underfoot as another train slowed along the northbound platform. 'Just trust me on this. That's where I need to be. It's three stops away. I'll be back in time.' He picked up his coat.

Baxter grabbed hold of a sleeve.

'You're not going!' she told him.

'I don't work for you,' he reminded her, letting go.

'Rouche!' she yelled after him, following him up the stairs towards the other platform.

He jumped into a carriage just as the doors slid shut, Baxter only moments behind.

'Rouche!' she shouted again as the train started moving off. On the other side of the glass, he waved apologetically. She threw his coat to the floor in frustration. 'Rouche! Shit!'

Baxter had instructed the technical officers to disseminate Keaton's details and photograph to the teams, while she read up on his tragic history and the accompanying documents from Blake. An un-cropped version of the family photo had been included, the smiling faces blissfully unaware of the misery to come.

'He's Rouche,' she mumbled to herself, shaking her head, or rather, he was what Rouche could have become.

The two men's stories were disarmingly similar, even down to the religious proclivity, and yet where Keaton had allowed his hate and sorrow to consume him, Rouche had poured all of that negative energy into helping people.

She smiled; maybe something more than coincidence had led him back there after all.

Rouche stepped out onto the platform at Baker Street. Photographs of the three suspects had been sent to him en route. He had his phone at the ready to refer to as he followed the black-and-yellow 'Way Out' signs above ground.

'Baxter, are you still reading me?'

'I am.'

She didn't sound happy with him.

'I've just arrived at Baker Street, heading up to intercept the targets at the main entrance. I'll deal with CFIT directly but will keep you updated.'

'Great.'

He jogged up the left side of the escalator, swiped through a

ticket barrier and allowed the current of commuters to wash him
out onto the pavement.

The mouth of the station was a chaotic free-for-all, with a *Big
Issue* seller, Wham!-singing busker and sorry-looking homeless
man with an even sorrier-looking dog all vying for space in the
busy entranceway.

Rouche made it across to the wall bordering the congested road
and changed channel on his radio, his earpiece picking up the tail
end of a transmission to the FBI unit.

'Rouche here. I'm in position at the entrance. Did I miss
anything?'

'Suspect Brookes has been apprehended,' a female voice
informed him.

'Nine to go,' he whispered to himself.

He scrolled through the photos on his phone to see which of the
faces he could now forget. He looked up at the endless parade of
people approaching from either direction, their features obscured
beneath hats, hoods and umbrellas, as the woman continued:

'Armed units still one minute out. Remaining suspects arriving
at your location imminently.'

Rouche scanned the faces as they passed through sporadic
patches of light. And then he recognised one of them.

'Obs on the fatter one,' he announced.

'Richard Oldham,' his earpiece corrected him.

Rouche wrapped his fingers round the handle of his weapon:

'Moving in to intercept.'

He paused for a split second, waiting for a gap in the human
traffic, when he spotted a second familiar face coming from the
opposite direction.

'Shit! Obs on the other one now as well,' said Rouche. He
glanced between the two men on an apparent collision course.
'How far out's my backup?'

'Forty-five seconds.'

'If I move on one of them, I lose the other,' he said, now barely
having to turn his head to keep sight of them both.

'Forty seconds.'

It was clear that the two men had never met. They came within a couple of metres of each other without so much as a second look before shuffling through the station's entrance.

'I'm following them in,' he informed CFIT as he pushed through the herd walking dirty slush over the yellowed floor, struggling to keep the two men in sight as they veered left.

'Heading down to the Bakerloo line towards Piccadilly,' Rouche updated them. He quickened his pace as he descended the escalator. 'Train's coming!'

The people around him had heard it too. The sound of hurried footsteps surrounded him as the doors of the train slid open, releasing scores of people against the current. He shoved his way through them just as the doors were closing but was relieved to find both men still stood on the platform.

'Targets not on train,' he mumbled as people began filling every conceivable space along the platform. 'Be advised: one suspect is carrying a large rucksack.'

He was curious as to why both men had deliberately delayed their journey. Just then he noticed a dishevelled woman sitting on one of the benches, who had also made no effort to board the train.

'Tell my backup to hold out of sight,' said Rouche, attracting a strange look from the Japanese tourist standing next to him. 'Have you got a visual on a female, forties, blue jacket, black jeans, sat far end of the platform?'

'Wait one,' replied the CFIT officer in his ear.

As he waited, the woman picked up her plastic carrier bag and got up to stand at the edge of the platform. He glanced behind him to see that both suspects were displaying similar intentions of boarding the next train.

'They're about to get on a train. Tell the team to move in.'

No sooner had Rouche said it than a swarm of armed officers had surrounded the two men and pinned them to the ground. When he looked back at the blue-jacketed woman, she was walking away towards the very end of the platform.

The train came clattering in as one member of the team gently unzipped the heavy rucksack that their suspect had been carrying.

Rouche was straining to see over the crowds.

He checked his watch: 4.54 p.m.

He needed to get back to Baxter.

Unable to reach the rear of the train in time, he stepped up into the wall of people congregated in the nearest set of double doors, which juddered and reopened twice before eventually closing behind him. Ignoring their very British tuts and eye rolls, he pushed through the crowd to the less populated belly of the carriage.

'What was in the bag?' he asked the CFIT officer in his ear.

After a brief pause, she replied: 'Explosives of some sort . . . It's been made safe . . . Disposal unit's two minutes out.'

He momentarily switched channel on his radio:

'Baxter, I'm on my way back to you.'

'Whatever.'

'Seven to go . . . *and* we've just obtained one of four,' he told her carefully, unable to say any more in the packed carriage.

'Might be two of four in a minute,' she replied. 'Apparently the MI5 guys came tearing out of here a few moments ago. Just get back here.'

He switched his radio once more to catch the end of a transmission: '. . . a suspect.' There was a pause. 'Agent Rouche, did you copy last?'

'Negative. Repeat, please.'

'Confirmed: the woman in the blue jacket *is* another suspect.'

'Received,' replied Rouche, weaving through the wall of commuters.

He reached the end of the carriage and peered through to the next, hoping to spot the woman, but was unable to see a thing beyond the people pressed up against the other door.

'The next station is . . . Regent's Park. Exit here for . . .' an automated voice announced.

Everyone leaned in unison as the train decelerated. Dense crowds rolled past the windows as they came to an abrupt stop.

Rouche stumbled out onto the platform and fought through the throngs of people to climb aboard the rearmost carriage.

'Excuse me. 'Scuse me . . . Sorry,' he muttered as he squeezed between them.

He glanced up at the Tube map as he moved through the train; just one station stood between them and Piccadilly Circus.

He checked his watch again: 4.57 p.m.

'Sorry . . . Excuse me.' He was halfway through the carriage when he spotted the familiar blue jacket. The scruffy woman was sat with her hands placed protectively over the carrier bag in her lap. 'Obs on target.'

'Where are you, Rouche?' Baxter whispered under her breath as she watched a constant stream of people pour onto the already flooded platform.

The orange numbers on the display above counted up the seconds towards 5 p.m.

'Team 3: radio check,' she barked confidently into the radio, despite her heart galloping in her chest.

'Reading you loud and clear. Over.'

There was a bang from somewhere within the crowd.

'Team 3 on me!' Baxter ordered as she hurried towards the disturbance.

A flustered businessman was holding a split bag as he attempted to collect up his Christmas shopping before any more fragile items could get stamped into the ground.

She sighed in relief, her nerves already shot to pieces:

'False alarm. Stand down.'

On her way back to her post, she received an update from one of her constables: an explosive device, matching those used in Times Square, had been recovered from a homeless shelter in Clapham, the bag's owner having been one of those arrested overnight.

Two of four.

Rouche was just five paces from the seated woman when his ear filled with distortion and the CFIT officer's voice returned.

'Agent Rouche, be advised: one additional suspect believed to have boarded your train at the last station. Backup en route.'

'Send details,' Rouche replied, before shoving his way through to the woman in the blue jacket.

He dragged her out of her seat and pushed her face first onto the floor, restraining her arms behind her back. Some of the appalled passengers attempted to intervene.

'It's OK! It's OK! I'm CIA,' Rouche told them, producing his identification. 'And you're under arrest,' he shouted down at the squirming woman.

The Good Samaritans retreated back to their seats, sharing their fellow passengers' thinking that it was probably best to move as far away as was possible in the packed space.

Rouche had managed to handcuff one of the struggling woman's hands by the time the train pulled into Oxford Circus. Keeping one eye on his prisoner, he scanned the crowds scrolling past for any sign of his backup. Dozens of people alighted, but they were instantly replaced with more, filling the carriage in front and behind him.

He snapped the second handcuff closed and patted the woman down before dragging the plastic carrier bag out from beneath her. Keeping one hand pressed against her back, he reached in and removed the tarnished meat cleaver from inside. He was about to place it on the floor beside him when he realised how many children were among the frightened faces watching him.

'It's OK. I'm with the CIA,' he repeated for the sake of the newcomers. He deliberated for a moment and then gestured to the muscular man who had just taken a seat behind him. 'Can I borrow you?'

'Me?' the man asked uncertainly. He scratched at his beard as if he were still getting accustomed to it and then got to his feet.

Rouche placed his service weapon on the floor while he rewrapped the meat cleaver in the bag and held it out to him: 'I need you to hold this for me,' Rouche told him.

348   HANGMAN

His helper looked uneasy.

'Just hold on to it and make sure you don't touch what's inside.'

The bearded man tentatively took it from him and sat down next to them, holding the green plastic bag in his lap just as the woman had done.

As the doors slid closed once more, Rouche spotted two armed officers running out onto the platform too late.

The train started to pull away.

'Agent Rouche! Agent Rouche!' the voice called in his earpiece, louder than before . . . panicking.

'I've just secured the woman. I'm about to start looking for—'

'Agent Rouche! Three more suspects just boarded your train! Repeat: *three* additional suspects.'

'Copy that,' said Rouche slowly, looking up at the carriage full of faces. 'I need you to get a message to DCI Baxter immediately: the train is the target, not the station.'

He felt his phone buzzing frantically in his jacket pocket as they sent through the details.

'The train is the target,' he repeated, reaching for his weapon.

Unbeknown to Rouche, a clean-shaven image of the muscular man had just downloaded onto his phone.

Unbeknown to Rouche, the man had got to his feet to stand over him.

Unbeknown to Rouche, it was the tarnished meat cleaver that cut the first powerful blow through him.

CHAPTER 39

Tuesday 22 December 2015

5 p.m.

'Get these people out!' Baxter yelled over the pre-recorded emergency announcement.

She had reacted immediately to Rouche's relayed message; however, the sheer numbers bottlenecking up the stairway had brought the evacuation to a complete standstill as the orange display continued counting above their heads: 17:00:34

'DCI Baxter,' a voice buzzed urgently in her ear. 'I still can't get hold of Agent Rouche.'

'Just keep trying,' she replied as she grabbed the arm of a passing member of staff. 'We need to close the station! You *have* to stop people coming in.'

The man nodded and hurried away as Baxter's radio went off again.

'What?' she shouted in frustration.

'Apologies. I'm patching you through to a DI Lewis with the Imaging Team.'

'Now?!' asked Baxter as the automated male voice announced the imminent arrival of the train.

'We've just spotted Lucas Keaton on a CCTV feed from five minutes ago. Trying to get you updated information now.'

'That's good news . . . Where?'

'He's there . . . at the station . . . He's down there with you!'

Baxter looked in concern at the heaving crowd, trying to picture the photograph she'd shared with her team.

'Description?' she requested.

'Wearing a dark jacket, dark jumper.'

Everyone was wearing a dark jacket with a dark jumper.

She went to push the transmit button to relay this latest development when a piercing squeal of feedback tore through her ear. Instinctively ripping the earpiece out, she noticed her colleagues react in similar ways, sharing anxious looks as the transmission broadcast snippets of distant screaming, warped and distorted, a mutilated choir of voices.

'Rouche?' she murmured, but only static clicks answered her. 'Rouche, can you hear me?'

There was a rumble on the tracks.

Baxter turned her back on the crowd and stared into the dark mouth of the tunnel, the horrific noises still emitting from the earpiece in her hand a chilling prelude to an unknown horror.

Slowly, she moved to the edge of the platform. A delicate spiderweb above her began to quiver in anticipation.

A clattering emanated from the darkness, a galloping sound, vibrations underfoot of a monster advancing. The warm breeze preceding it was stale and laced with metal like blood-tainted breath, and then two bright eyes pierced the gloom as the train rushed towards them.

Baxter's long hair was blown across her face as the first smeared window flashed by, a dirty crimson veil concealing what lay within.

There were screams as people started to panic, climbing over one another in a desperate bid for escape, blocking the stairway down towards the Piccadilly line platforms as well. Nightmarish images flashed by, scenes from inside the brightly lit carriages lingering longer as the train slowed: people running for the doors, bodies pressed up against the glass, a face crying for help, blood-covered hands reaching skyward for a god that was never coming for them.

Baxter realised that the tiny speaker she was holding had gone quiet and tentatively placed it back in her ear as a set of double doors came to a stop in front of her. Beyond the smudged windows, the carriage lights flickered intermittently behind cracked casings. She could no longer hear the noise of the stampeding crowd behind her, only the set of cheerful beeps assuring that this was just a stop like any other.

The metal doors slid apart . . .

As hundreds of panicking passengers burst free of the train only to find themselves still trapped, a body slumped out onto the platform at Baxter's feet; the glazed look in the man's eyes confirmed that he was beyond saving. An electrical popping accompanied the failing lights as she stepped up into the carriage, struggling to comprehend the devastation.

There were gunshots somewhere further along the platform and then the hollow thud of bare feet running towards her.

Spinning round, Baxter held her arms out defensively, by pure luck catching the woman's hand as she slashed at her. They dropped to the carriage floor, the tip of the stained knife slicing through her lip on impact.

The feral woman was on top of her, her shirt hanging open to reveal the scarring beneath as she pushed her entire weight down onto the knife. Baxter cried out as she struggled to hold the woman at bay, her arms trembling with the effort.

The knife inched closer, scraping across Baxter's front teeth when she turned her head away from it. Recalling Rouche's advice at the prison, she reached up blindly and tore at one of her attacker's eyes.

The woman shrieked and recoiled as Baxter kicked out at her and scrambled backwards. Her attacker thrashed around like an injured animal for a moment before rushing at Baxter once more.

Two, much closer, gunshots sounded as a pair of gaping wounds disfigured the scar-tissue tattoo that adorned the woman's chest. She released the knife in her hand, dropped gently to her knees and then slumped forward onto the floor.

'You OK, boss?'

Baxter nodded and got to her feet, holding a hand over her throbbing lip.

'Rouche!' she called, checking faces as she stepped between the injured.

'DCI Baxter,' said a voice in her ear.

'Rouche!'

'DCI Baxter!' the voice demanded.

She held a finger to her ear:

'Go ahead,' she answered as she continued the search.

Two more gunshots were fired nearby.

She winced, having missed the transmission: 'Go again.'

'DCI Baxter, we've lost sight of Lucas Keaton.'

Rouche gasped for air.

Pinned to the floor of the rearmost carriage, he could feel his own warm blood trickling down his neck from the deep wound in his shoulder. He was trapped beneath the dead weight of his muscular attacker, whom he had shot five times in order to cease the indiscriminate massacre. He had been immobilised by the excruciating pain in his chest where the panic-stricken people he'd managed to save had trampled him in their desperation to escape. Something was grating inside him every time he took a breath.

He could feel heavy footsteps resonating through the floor.

'Clear!' someone shouted.

The footsteps moved closer.

Rouche tried to call out, an inaudible gasp all he could muster . . . He tried again.

He heard the boots step right over him and start moving away.

'Please!' Every time he exhaled, he had to fight even harder to force the air back into his lungs.

'Hey . . . Hello. It's OK. Take my hand,' he heard one of the voices say. 'You close your eyes for me, all right?'

'We've got someone trapped under here!' another shouted. 'I need some help!'

Rouche filled with hope and couldn't understand what was happening when the voice then announced: 'OK. I've got her. I've got her. Let's go.'

He listened to the footsteps change pitch as they reached the solid platform floor, leaving him alone with the dead once more.

'Baxter!' he tried to call out, barely able to hear his own whispered cry for help.

His breathing was becoming shallower, his muscles fatiguing beneath the weight pressing down on him as he surrendered to the realisation that he was going to bleed out onto the dirty vinyl floor long before anybody found him.

He had failed.

Baxter ran back out onto the platform and stared into the sea of people fighting their way above ground. Fear had spread through the crowd like fire catching, every individual blinded by self-preservation, each and every one consumed by panic, all oblivious to the detrimental effect that their actions were having . . . all but one.

As a group of people stumbled forward, Baxter spotted a face on the far side, eyes not pointed upwards towards safety like the others but watching the train, watching them, as they searched for survivors.

Their eyes met across the crush.

It was Keaton.

She hadn't recognised him from the photograph but from the key-shaped wound torn across his right cheek from where she had, unknowingly, confronted him at Phillip East's Brooklyn hideout.

She opened her mouth to broadcast his location.

And then he was gone, swallowed up by the surging crowd.

'Team 3: continue the search,' Baxter's voice ordered through Rouche's earpiece, dragging him back to consciousness. 'Teams 1 and 2: your target is Lucas Keaton. Man the exits. We can't let him leave the station.'

The name was like a shot of adrenaline to Rouche's failing body, muting the pain enough for him to slowly pull his pinned arm out from underneath the heavy man and wrap his fingers round the brown pole protruding from the carriage floor. Feeling his chest ripping and cracking under the strain, he gritted his teeth and dragged himself free, kicking the bearded man's limp body off him as he took an agonising but euphoric breath.

The handcuffed woman on the floor had not survived the evacuation stampede.

Rouche reached for his service weapon and staggered to his feet, panting from the exertion required to achieve so little.

He allowed himself a nod skywards.

He hadn't failed.

He was precisely where he needed to be.

CHAPTER 40

Tuesday 22 December 2015
5.04 p.m.

'Police! Move!' yelled Baxter, as the heaving throng inched gradually towards the blocked stairway. She scanned the crowd for Keaton. After a moment, she spotted him. He was already at the foot of the stairs, glancing back anxiously, looking for her.

As he began his scramble above ground, she could see that he was holding something.

'Eyes on Keaton!' she shouted into her radio. 'Bakerloo stairway, heading up. Be advised: suspect has something in his hand. Treat as a trigger until we confirm otherwise.'

A gap opened up in front of her. She pushed through, gaining several metres in just a couple of seconds.

'Disarm by any means necessary.'

'Baxter, can you hear me?' wheezed Rouche as he ascended the emergency stairwell at the far end of the platform, his damaged microphone screeching back at him uselessly.

He was still able to hear the rest of the team's transmissions as he joined the hordes rushing towards fresh air. Holding his wounded shoulder, he struggled against the current, searching for where the endless river of people was emerging from.

There was a loud crackle of distortion in his ear.

A moment later, he spotted a dark shape on the ground up ahead. Flickering between hurrying legs, he could make out the shape of a body-armoured officer lying face down at the top of the escalators.

'Shit!' He looked back at the sea of people disappearing through exits all around him.

With slightly more space to manoeuvre, the evacuees were now moving at walking pace towards the waiting night.

They were running out of time.

He ran blindly into the crowd, barging a route through the crush as he searched in desperation for Keaton.

'Officer down! Officer down! Top of the Bakerloo escalator,' Baxter announced into the radio, only realising that it was Special Agent Chase as she checked for a pulse.

She didn't find one.

At each of the exits, a lone FBI agent faced the impossible task of locating a single face among the army of people advancing towards them. Meanwhile, London Underground staff struggled to hold a swarm of inconvenienced commuters at bay outside the station's entrance.

Out of the hundreds of people hurrying away from her, just one glanced back.

'Keaton's ten metres from Exit 3!' she updated the team. 'Do . . . not . . . let him out!'

She started pushing forwards, relief washing over her when she spotted Rouche beyond the open ticket barriers, making a beeline for Keaton.

'Rouche!' she called after him.

He was too far away to hear her.

Rouche had noticed the man with the scar looking back every few seconds.

The man, however, had failed to notice Rouche.

Following directions to Regent Street, St James's and Eros, he was only a few congested metres behind as they started to pass the threshold into the building storm.

'Keaton!' Rouche tried to yell, pointing towards him, his hoarse whisper almost inaudible. 'It's Keaton!'

The agent hadn't heard him, but Keaton had, looking back to discover just how close his pursuers were.

Rouche caught sight of the black device in his hand as Keaton lowered his head and passed within inches of the FBI agent, breaking into a run the moment he emerged into the freezing night.

Rouche clambered up the stairs to join the mayhem on the street, the metal wings of Anteros silhouetted against the iconic neon signage. The evacuation of the station had spilled out onto the road, bringing the heart of the city to a complete standstill, car headlights stretching as far as the eye could see in every direction.

Beneath the starless sky, the blue snow fell unabated, lit by the flashing lights of emergency-service vehicles. The sudden drop in temperature burned his lungs. A stabbing, short, sharp coughing fit deposited watery blood into his hand as he spotted Keaton running south-east along Regent Street.

Rouche took off after him along the busy pavement, weaving between the oversized jackets and armfuls of shopping bags, the warm blood trickling down his sleeve painting a meandering trail for Baxter to follow.

Baxter waited for a break in the frantic transmissions.

It sounded as though every siren in the city was wailing, her earpiece crackling with harried updates from SO15 as they closed in on another of the bombers:

'Requesting air support,' she panted into the radio. 'DCI Baxter in pursuit of . . . Lucas Keaton . . . along Regent Street . . . towards the park.'

Nearly twenty metres behind, she reached the crossroads with Pall Mall, almost colliding with a scooter that was darting in

and out of the stationary traffic. She continued along Waterloo
Place, the bronze figures that reside there emerging ominously
out of the blizzard.

Baxter sprinted between them, her radio buzzing in her ear,
fighting to make itself heard over the howling wind as she reached
the steps that descended towards the dark void that was St James's
Park.

'Lost sight of suspect,' one of the assorted voices announced in
her ear as she eavesdropped in on their operation. 'Does anyone
have eyes? Does anybody have eyes on suspect?'

'Confirmed: north-east corner of the square. . . No clear shot.'

Rouche couldn't breathe and he was losing ground, Keaton's
spectral silhouette flickering on the far borders of his vision.

Suddenly, the roar of helicopter rotor blades sliced through the
night air, a searchlight blinding him before sweeping towards the
entrance of the park, illuminating the monument standing guard
– a dark angel, rendered in blackened bronze. Azazel.

And then it was gone, the circle of light chasing blindly after
Keaton as Rouche stamped dark footprints across the pristine
frozen scene. Ahead of him, the snow-laden weeping willows were
bent double over the icy water, as if the lake had lured them in,
only to freeze while they drunk greedily from it.

The city had disappeared, nothing but the storm existed beyond
the borders of the park. As they reached an open space, Rouche
released the magazine from his gun and reloaded.

He ceased his pursuit and took aim, the frozen lake reflecting
the spotlight back up at the heavens.

Keaton was no more than a shadow, growing smaller with
every passing second.

Trying to suppress the pain in his chest, Rouche extended
his arm, lining the sight dead centre on the figure's back. He
embraced the wind against his face, judging its speed and direction, adjusting accordingly, waiting until the beam bathed his
target in light.

He exhaled to steady his limbs and then very, very gently squeezed the trigger.

'Take the shot!'

'Civilian down! Target wounded . . . No visual. Repeat: I no longer have a visual.'

Baxter had been distracted both by SO15's transmissions as they hunted their prey and by the trail of bright red blood staining the ground when the crack of the gunshot cut through the snowstorm. She could see that Rouche had stopped up ahead, but Keaton had been engulfed by the whiteout.

Her throat burning, she caught her breath and continued after them.

Keaton had dropped to the ground instantly, framed in the unsteady circle of light.

Rouche walked over to the injured man, who was reaching desperately for the device a few feet away; long, gasping breaths rose up from his prone form like clouds of smoke.

'Rouche!' Baxter shouted in the distance, her voice barely audible.

He looked up to see her running towards them.

As Keaton dragged himself over to the small black box, Rouche stooped down to pick it up, discovering that it was a mobile phone.

A little disconcerted, he flipped it over to look at the screen. A moment later, he tossed it away from him and turned to Keaton with a murderous expression.

Six feet away, the uploaded video, destined to be viewed by tens of millions of people across the world, entertained itself as flake by flake it was claimed by the snow.

During the forty-six-second film, a tearful but unremorseful Keaton claimed responsibility for everything, all the while holding up photographs of his family crudely annotated with their names

and the dates on which they died . . . Not once did he make any
mention of Alexei Green or his beloved lost fiancée.

'Rouche! We need him! We need him!' yelled Baxter as she
watched her partner press his gun into their prisoner's temple.

A spotlit performance on a dark stage.

'Where is it?' she heard him shout over the noise of the helicopter somewhere overhead, suggesting that the recovered device
had not been what they had hoped.

She had almost reached them.

'Shots fired! Shots fired!' her earpiece buzzed. 'Suspect down.'

Rouche struck Keaton viciously with the heavy weapon, but
the man simply smiled up at him through bloodied teeth as the
snow turned crimson beneath him.

'Rouche!' Baxter shouted, sliding up to them.

She dropped to her knees, sinking into the powder, then pulled
at Keaton's clothing as she searched desperately for the source of
the blood loss. Her fingers found the gaping exit wound beneath
his shoulder before her eyes did. Sliding the sleeve of her jacket
up over her hand, she pushed it deep into the wound.

'What's the target?!' Rouche demanded.

Baxter could see the utter desperation on her colleague's face,
the realisation that his one chance to redeem himself was slipping
away from him:

'He can't tell us if he's dead, Rouche! Help me.'

Sat on the wet floor of the filthy underground toilets, Green's
last remaining Puppet began to weep to the relentless hum of the
helicopter circling overhead.

He had never felt so alone.

He could hear them above him, scurrying around the
entrance as they repositioned themselves, their overladen foot-
falls like the padding feet of a hound whose quarry had gone to
ground.

He cried out in frustration and pulled at the chunky vest that he had been entrusted with, the wires and components pressing uncomfortably into his back.

Despite all that Dr Green had told him, had taught him, he had allowed himself to be herded into a deserted street and, like a timid animal, had taken the only refuge available to him . . . had taken their bait.

'Aiden Fallon!' an amplified voice boomed, all distortion and malice. 'You are completely surrounded.'

Aiden put his hands over his ears, but he couldn't block out the voice:

'Remove the vest and come out slowly or we *will* have no choice but to force detonation. You have thirty seconds.'

Aiden looked around the rancid room that would serve as his tomb, an appropriate memorial for someone who had failed as utterly as he. He only wished that he could see Dr Green one last time, to tell him that he was the greatest friend he'd ever had and that he was so sorry for letting him down.

'Fifteen seconds!'

Aiden slowly got to his feet, wiping his hands on the fabric of his trousers.

'Ten seconds!'

He caught sight of himself in the dirty mirror. He really was the most pathetic excuse for a man. Maintaining eye contact with his reflected twin, a smile formed on his face as he tugged on the short cord dangling from his chest . . . and felt the fire engulf him.

'Rouche, help me here!' winced Baxter, shoving more of her jacket sleeve into the life-threatening wound.

There was an explosion somewhere in the distance.

Rouche staggered away from Baxter and their dying prisoner to stare out over the trees, the spotlight abandoning them as the helicopter was rerouted towards an orange glow in the sky. He wore an expression of confusion and disbelief, unable to comprehend that they had failed, that he'd never had any greater purpose . . . that there really was no plan.

All any of them could do was watch the sky fall and catch snowflakes.

'Rouche!' Baxter called as she struggled to stem the bleed beneath her hands. Her earpiece distorted with overlapping transmissions. 'Rouche! We don't know what's happened yet.'

'What more could we have possibly done?' he asked, his back still to her.

She couldn't be sure whether he was talking to her or to *somebody* else.

Anxiously, she watched him raise and lower the gun in his hand.

'Rouche,' said Baxter as calmly as she could over the confusion crackling in her ear, her sleeve sodden and cold with Keaton's blood. 'I need you to leave . . . for me . . . *please*.'

He turned back to her with tearful eyes.

'Just go, Rouche . . . Walk away,' she pleaded.

She glanced nervously at the weapon in his hand.

She couldn't lose him, couldn't lose another friend to the undeniable allure of a glorious and violent retribution.

'Are you going to kill me, *Rouche*?' Keaton wheezed weakly, having heard Baxter use his name.

'Keep quiet!' Baxter hissed. She needed to call in for an ambulance but couldn't move her hands any more than she could interrupt the urgent radio traffic.

'Do you *honestly* think I care?' Keaton continued, slurring a little from the blood loss. 'I've achieved what I needed to in this world. There is nothing left for me here.'

'I said, shut up!' Baxter snapped, but Rouche was already making his way back over to them.

'My family are with God, and wherever I'm heading, it can only be better than here,' Keaton told them. He looked up at Rouche expectantly as he kneeled down beside him.

Sensing the situation rapidly deteriorating, Baxter risked removing a hand from Keaton's chest to push the transmit button on her radio:

'DCI Baxter requesting an emergency ambulance to St James's Park. Over.'

She looked across at Rouche with imploring eyes as she returned her hand to the wounded man's chest.

'I wonder if He's here . . .' Keaton spluttered on noticing the silver cross dangling round Rouche's neck, '. . . right now . . . listening to us,' he said, watching the night sky for any sign. 'I wonder if He's *finally* paying some *fucking* attention!'

Rouche couldn't help but recall the literal translation of Azazel's name: *Strength over God*.

He forced it from his thoughts.

'A year and a half . . .' coughed Keaton, half laughing, half crying. He adjusted position in the snow to make himself more comfortable. 'A year and a half I visited that hospital room to sit at my son's side, much as you are now. A year and a half I quietly prayed for help . . . but it never came. You see, He doesn't hear you when you whisper, but He can hear me now.'

Rouche watched the man beneath him dispassionately.

They were alone, the park silent bar the tinny buzzing of Baxter's earpiece, Keaton's laboured breathing and the wind.

'Rouche?' Baxter whispered, unable to decipher the look in his eyes.

Slowly, he reached round and unclipped the metal crucifix from round his neck, the silver cross spinning on its chain as he held it out.

'Rouche?' she repeated. 'Rouche!'

He looked at her.

'We still don't know what's happened, but whatever it was, *none* of this is your fault. You *do* know that, don't you?' she asked.

To her surprise, he smiled as if a crippling weight had been lifted from his shoulders:

'I know.'

He let the necklace slip through his fingers and fall into the discoloured snow.

'Are we OK here?' she asked him, her eyes flicking back down to Keaton.

Rouche nodded.

'Call it in,' she told him with a relieved sigh, her friend proving, yet again, just how strong he really was.

Looking down at the man one final time, he removed his phone from his pocket and struggled to his feet.

As he began to walk away, snippets of MI5's transmissions filled Baxter's ears.

'Rouche, I think it's OK!' she called after him excitedly, the bleed between her fingers slowing. 'They're saying they got him! They're saying it was contained! . . . One fatality . . . the bomber!'

Unable to help herself, Baxter smiled down at Keaton triumphantly:

'Did you hear that, you *fucker*?' she whispered. 'They got him. He's dead.'

Keaton rested his head back and closed his eyes in defeat, habit prompting him to recite the words bestowed to him on too many occasions during his cursed time on this earth: 'I guess God just needed another angel.'

Rouche froze mid-stride.

Baxter hadn't even realised that she'd removed her bloody hands from his chest, her eyes blurring with tears – Curtis's beautiful face all she could think of.

She never heard the crunch of snow underfoot.

She didn't feel the warm blood spray across her face in time to the muffled gunshot, didn't understand why the body should shake so violently . . . as three more bullets tore through it.

Rouche was standing over Keaton, tears streaming down his face.

She looked up at him blankly as he pulled the trigger again . . . and again . . . and again . . . until he'd reduced the corpse to no more than a fleshy mess in the dirty snow, into non-existence, until the weapon clicked with empty rounds.

'There is no God,' he whispered.

Baxter just sat there, staring open-mouthed at her friend, who took a few unsteady steps and then collapsed to the ground.

A sigh of relief escaped Rouche's broken lungs.

He could hear Baxter calling his name as she scrambled over to him.

But he just smiled sadly, raised his head to the falling heavens . . .

. . . and stuck out his tongue.

EPILOGUE

Wednesday 6 January 2016

9.56 a.m.

'. . . is . . . no . . . God.'

Agent Sinclair stormed past the mirrored window on his way out of the interview room.

'Nice job. Thank you for your *co-operation*, Detective Chief Inspector. Now, we're done,' Atkins sighed, dabbing at his sweaty forehead while he collected up his things.

Baxter waved him off sarcastically as he hurried out after the enraged FBI agent, an hour of shameless arse-kissing no doubt ahead of him.

'Boss as diplomatic as ever,' scoffed Saunders, grinning back at Vanita and the man in the corner as an important-looking American saw himself out of the cramped viewing room.

Vanita groaned:

'Why can't she just be civil? Just for twenty *bloody* minutes? Am I really asking *that* much?'

'Apparently so,' shrugged Saunders.

The man in the corner nodded in agreement.

'Don't *you* start. You shouldn't even be in here,' she told him, massaging the building headache in her forehead.

Baxter brusquely dismissed the consultant psychiatrist, assuring her that she was absolutely fine and had no interest in 'talking anything through'.

Apparently forgetting that there might be, and indeed were, people still watching, she placed her head in her hands and slumped down onto the table.

'And where do you think you're going?' Saunders asked the man in the corner, who was no longer in the corner but making his way out of the room.

'I want to see her,' he replied simply.

'I'm not sure you're *totally* grasping this whole "under arrest" thing,' said Saunders.

The man looked to Vanita, who appeared almost as tired and resigned as Baxter did.

'We had an agreement,' he reminded her.

'Fine,' she said with a dismissive wave of her hand. 'It's not like this mess could get any worse.'

The man smiled cheerfully, turned and stepped out into the corridor.

'We're all gettin' fired for this,' said Saunders, watching him leave.

Vanita nodded: 'Yes. Yes, we are.'

Baxter heard footsteps approaching, neither the regimented march of the American nor the lazy shuffle of Atkins.

She groaned into her hands.

A metal chair scraped across the floor, and then she felt the flimsy table rock as this latest annoyance took a seat opposite her. She let out an exasperated sigh and lifted her head, her breath escaping her as violently as if she had been kicked in the gut.

The imposing man smiled awkwardly at her, deliberately leaning back in his chair a little, just in case she decided to take a swing at him, his dark, wavy hair longer than she had ever seen it, but the bright blue eyes unchanged – able to look right through her, just as they had when he'd walked out of her life.

Baxter could only stare blankly at him, incapable of even processing another devastating assault on her emotions.

'So . . . hey!' he tried casually, as though they'd only seen each other the previous day. He placed his handcuffed hands on the table between them as he attempted to come up with something profound to say, something to render the year and a half of silence trivial, something to restore her faith in him.

In the end, Wolf settled on:

'Surprise!'

ACKNOWLEDGEMENTS

I'm still not entirely sure what I'm doing but I am lucky enough to have a long list of very nice and supportive people looking after me. They are . . .

My family – Ma, Ossie, Melo, B, Bob, KP, Sarah and Belles.

From C+W – My wonderful agent Susan Armstrong, Emma, Jake, Alexander, Dorcas, Tracy and the much missed Alexandra.

From Orion – My editor Sam Eades for putting up with me, the cloud of vapey smoke that is Ben Willis, the best copy editor in the business Laura Collins, Claire Keep, Katie Espiner, Sarah Benton, Laura Swainbank, Lauren Woosey and the rest of the Hachette team in the UK and around the world.

Last but not least, a sincere thank you to all of the readers for keeping me in a job and for your endless enthusiasm for these characters and their messed up lives that I take so much pleasure in destroying. I don't really do social media and certainly don't do reviews but apparently you're out there, so thank you!

AUTHOR Q&A

1. Baxter takes centre stage in this novel. How has she changed since the events in _Ragdoll_?

Hangman picks up the story almost eighteen months after the Ragdoll murders. In that time, Baxter has made valiant efforts to get on with both her personal life and her career; although, it becomes apparent that these attempts to forget about Wolf are in fact driven by him and the void that he has left in her life. She's as irritable and blunt as ever and yet, her friendship with Edmunds has somehow blossomed into something special.

2. Tell us about Rouche. Was it hard introducing a new lead character? How did his character develop?

Writing Hangman, I realised that these are actually Baxter's books. She's the real lead. Ragdoll was Wolf's story and Hangman may be driven by Rouche and his secrets, but Baxter is the constant. She's the one getting swept up in these characters' imploding lives.

Rouche himself is a very different protagonist to Wolf. He is affable and relaxed, spiritual and selfless . . . and perhaps just a little bit odd.

3. Much of the action is set in New York, with those dramatic set pieces. How much research did you do? Did you visit?

I have been to New York in the past but it was important to me to make it feel as though Baxter was a tourist in an unfamiliar place. Truth be told, when I first started thinking about writing a sequel to Ragdoll, I decided from the outset to make life as hard for myself as possible: I wanted to know whether I could drop my main character, do a cringe-worthy relocation to New York City, and still write a book that was better than the first.

4. How hard was it to write a story that connected to *Ragdoll* but also entertained new readers too?

Very hard. I am writing these (first?) three Ragdoll books as a trilogy. They are all interconnected and overlap and reference each other. There's no way to get round the fact that people will get far more out of the book if they've read Ragdoll but it does work as a self-contained story as well. It's a difficult balance to bring new readers up to speed, remind casual readers of Ragdoll of certain things, while not alienating the fans who already know these characters inside out. That is, of course, the dilemma faced by every sequel, of any medium, ever made.

5. Humour plays a large part in *Ragdoll*. How do you weave this humour into *Hangman*?

In exactly the same way. I'd say there's even more humour in Hangman, but I suppose there would have to be to balance out the darkness and despair. I really put these characters through the wringer in this book but that just makes those sparks of genuine warmth and camaraderie and affection all the brighter.

6. You write cinematically. Are you inspired by film and TV?

I am and I don't think that these books would work otherwise. I don't like to get too bogged down by the constraints of reality and I feel that although gruesome, those are moments of 'movie gore'. The entire point of these books is to entertain not to upset or disturb anybody.

7. How has life changed for you since *Ragdoll*? What are the highlights of being a successful author? Any drawbacks?

Life's been great, thank you. Cliché answer – but I've met so many really great people ever since this all started, and I mean that – like genuinely only one person who I thought was a bit of a nob . . . Well, maybe two. Definitely no more than three. But that's pretty good going for a year and a half of being a writer. I get to travel, which is fantastic. The downside being that after getting flown out, put up in a hotel, fed and watered, people tend to expect me to do some form of public speaking at the end of it, which never ceases to strike me as unreasonable.

8. Have you started book 3? Do you know how the series will end?

I have started book three. As mentioned earlier, I've planned these books as a trilogy so do actually have a pretty good idea of how I want it to end. Beyond the trilogy, who knows?